Andrew Liddle is a writer and politic
Political Correspondent for *The Press*
for *The Courier*. His first book, *Ruth Davidson and the Resurgence of the Scottish Tories*, was published in 2018. He lives in Edinburgh.

Praise for *Churchill: The Scottish Years*

'Well-researched, well-written and genuinely groundbreaking . . . forces us to look anew at Winston Churchill's relationship with Scotland'
Andrew Roberts, author of *Churchill: Walking with Destiny*

'A rich and well-written history of stirring times, as well as a vital insight into the early career of a politician who . . . was not always the dogged old reactionary of modern political legend'
Joyce McMillan, *The Scotsman*

'A brilliant book'
Andrew Adonis, *Prospect Magazine*

'Genuinely new and useful . . . fills [the] gap in the historical record admirably and with no small measure of panache too'
Alex Massie, Scotland editor, *The Spectator*

'A fascinating story'
Times Radio

'In a carefully researched and lively account, Andrew Liddle finally sets the record straight on Winston Churchill's attitude to Scotland'
The House Magazine

'A triumph of fact over the ubiquitous myths about Winston Churchill's hatred towards Scotland'
Alastair Stewart, former journalist and newscaster

CHURCHILL
THE SCOTTISH YEARS

ANDREW LIDDLE

BIRLINN

This edition first published in 2024 by
Birlinn Limited
West Newington House
10 Newington Road
Edinburgh
EH9 1QS

www.birlinn.co.uk

ISBN 978 1 78027 859 9

British Library Cataloguing-in-Publication Data

A catalogue record of this book is available on request from the British Library

Typeset by Hewer Text UK Ltd, Edinburgh

Papers used by Birlinn are from well-managed forests and other responsible sources

MIX
Paper | Supporting
responsible forestry
FSC® C018072

Printed and bound by Clays Ltd, Elcograf S.p.A.

Contents

Preface

Scotland had a profound impact on Churchill – practically, politically and personally. Practically, it provided him with a constituency for almost 15 years, five election victories and a platform from which he could launch his cabinet career. Crucially, the voters of Dundee backed Churchill during some of his most difficult moments. Without victory in Dundee in 1908, Churchill's political career would have been in serious jeopardy. Equally when voters in Dundee chose to endorse Churchill in 1917, they helped cast off the aspersion that he was a political liability in the wake of the failure of the Allied Dardanelles campaign in 1915. These were two crucial endorsements, but the strength of his support was clearly apparent at every election he contested in Dundee until 1922. Even then, as the city voted him out, he received more than 20,000 votes.

Politically, and perhaps most importantly, serving in Scotland changed Churchill's Liberal perspective from one concerned solely with economics to one that also embraced progressive social reform. Churchill had left the Conservative Party for the Liberal Party in 1904 because of his belief in free trade, and his alignment with the Liberal Party until 1908 was fundamentally due to economic policy. It was support for free trade that won Churchill the Manchester North West constituency in 1906, and it was international affairs that dominated his ministerial career between then and 1908. It was only once he became MP for Dundee – and came to more fully understand poverty, slums and ill health – that his political priorities evolved and he became a champion of social, as well as economic, progress.

Personally, and most prosaically, Scotland also had a profound social and private influence on Churchill's life. His wife, Clementine, hailed from Angus, and Churchill retained many lifelong friends from Dundee and wider Scotland. His holidays in places such as Aberdeenshire and East Lothian provided much-needed respite from the trials and tribulations of high office. Most importantly, it was a Scottish regiment that helped Churchill recover when, in 1916, his career was at its lowest ebb to date. With his mental health under strain, Churchill took command of the 6th Battalion, Royal Scots Fusiliers, and it was in the trenches, among the Scottish accents and Glengarries, that he began his recovery.

Despite the significance of Scotland to Churchill, it is a subject that is curiously missing from the vast mass of work on his life. Only one full-length book on the topic, published more than 30 years ago, has ever been attempted. Even then, the focus of that volume is primarily on telling the chronological narrative of Churchill's life between 1908 and 1922, rather than also exploring his relationship with Scotland in depth. Equally, given the vast scope of Churchill's life and achievements, more recent biographers understandably pay little attention to his time as an MP in Scotland, which is generally referred to in passing. While several useful academic articles on Churchill's time in Dundee do exist, they tend to focus on placing Churchill's defeat in 1922 in the context of broader political or socio-economic trends. The International Churchill Society, which seeks to promote the life and work of its namesake, dedicated a 2020 issue of its quarterly magazine *Finest Hour* to the topic of Churchill and Scotland, which received considerable press interest. But a void undoubtedly still remains on this important aspect of Churchill's political and social life.

There are several explanations for this absence. Even the most persuasive writer could hardly claim Churchill's political life from 1908 to 1922 – while not without its considerable achievements – was more significant than the role he played in British and world history in the 1940s. It is therefore completely natural that this is where the interests of the public and most historians and writers lie. At the same time, the emergence of the Black Lives Matter movement and a broader awareness of racial injustice has sparked a greater interest in Churchill's views on race and empire, the study of which tends largely to ignore his earlier life and period in the Liberal Party.

In this void, misinterpretations, misunderstandings and even outright falsehoods about Churchill's association with Scotland have gained increasing traction among historians and the public. Many of Churchill's main biographers give the impression that he had a difficult relationship with Dundee and Scotland more widely. He is often described as a 'carpetbagger' with little interest in the affairs of the city, while many also assume Churchill opposed devolution or was dismissive of Scottish national identity and culture. Much of this is based solely on Churchill's defeat in what he thought was a 'life seat' and that, in 1943, he tersely rejected an offer of the Freedom of the City of Dundee. Churchill's amusing outbursts about unsophisticated Dundee hospitality add to this impression, despite making up a tiny proportion of his private writing on the city. In a similar vein, it is taken as a given that Churchill loathed his arch-adversary, the prohibitionist Edwin Scrymgeour, because the pair were the political and personal antithesis of each other. Churchill's relationship with Edmund Dene (E.D.) Morel, the Labour candidate in 1922, is similarly dismissed because of the latter's socialism and pacificism.

As well as such assumptions, genuine falsehoods abound, most infamously that Churchill ordered tanks into Glasgow's George Square to suppress strikers in 1919. This myth is now so pervasive in Scottish society that it has been put on school syllabuses and been included as a correct answer on exam marking keys. Some of this is a result of contemporary political debates in Scotland overshadowing Churchill's life. The legacy of the man voted the Greatest Briton by BBC viewers in 2002 is often held up by both pro- and anti-Scottish independence activists to support one point of view or another. Scotland's rejection of Churchill is, for example, often cited as Scotland rejecting Britishness, a metaphor that is strengthened by the fact that Dundee had the strongest pro-independence vote in the 2014 independence referendum. Scotland is far from unique in this phenomenon. For example, Churchill's legacy was invoked by both Leave and Remain campaigners in the 2016 EU referendum. Nevertheless, there is clearly an absence of understanding about Churchill in Scotland that needs to be addressed.

Churchill: The Scottish Years is primarily a narrative history of Churchill's time in Scotland and his political battles with Scrymgeour and Morel. It tells the compelling story of how and why Churchill won elections in Dundee, his rhetorical clashes with Scrymgeour, his real clashes on the Western Front and his eventual defeat at the hands of a teetotaller. It explains how Scrymgeour – and, indeed, Morel – rose from almost nothing to defeat one of the most prominent politicians of the era. And it highlights how women – Churchill's wife Clementine, but also suffragettes – played an outsized role in his victories and defeat in Dundee. The aim has been to make the account open and engaging, and so that – as much as possible without excessive divergence – readers need little background knowledge of the period or Scotland in order to understand and enjoy it.

But this book also seeks to challenge the key assumptions made about Churchill's time in Scotland, as well as his relationship with Dundee. This has been possible by returning to and re-evaluating the wide-ranging source material from the time. Not only did Churchill himself leave extensive correspondence, notes and reflections on the period from 1908 to 1922, but those of his staff and parliamentary colleagues are equally voluminous and accessible. Both Scrymgeour and Morel also left substantial personal papers, many of which pertain to Churchill's time in Scotland and their political battles with him in Dundee. Newspaper reports, as well as photographs and even early film, add significant metaphorical if not physical colour and help develop understanding of the period even further.

By revisiting this material, a more nuanced picture of Churchill in Scotland emerges. While he could hardly be described as a good constituency MP – apart from anything else, such a term, pre-welfare state, is anachronistic – Churchill was not dismissive of Dundee or its constituents. Much of the progressive legislation he introduced, particularly before the First World War, helped improve the lives of his constituents, including raising wages in Dundee's dominant jute industry. He also genuinely cared about issues in the city and was responsive to even minor requests from individuals, such as helping secure artillery pieces for the city's Boys' Brigade. If he visited the city less frequently than his critics would have liked, this was common practice among his contemporaries – including his fellow Dundee Labour MP, Alexander Wilkie, and his successor, Morel – who felt they were sent to represent their constituents in Westminster, not *vice versa*.

Cheers, Mr Churchill! also reveals for the first time the close relationship that existed between Churchill and his Prohibitionist adversary, Scrymgeour. While Churchill undoubtedly had a trying relationship with Scrymgeour, he retained a begrudging respect for his keenest adversary. This respect extended to hosting Scrymgeour as his guest at the 1919 Paris Peace Conference, with Churchill even lending him his car and driver. Likewise, this book also sheds light on the early relationship between Churchill and Morel. Contrary to popular belief, the pair were on good terms in the early 1900s, with Churchill being the first MP to contribute to Morel's *West African Mail*, a journal that helped expose the horrors taking place in the Belgian Congo. Even Churchill's rejection of the Freedom of the City of Dundee is more complex than first assumed: Churchill was in fact acting on the advice of his Scottish Secretary, the Labour MP and former Dundee representative Tom Johnston, who had urged him against accepting because of divisions among city councillors over the offer.

Churchill: The Scottish Years also fully explores for the first time Churchill's attitude to Scottish nationhood and political autonomy. It reveals how he advocated for a system of devolution as early as 1901 and continued to be open to a form of Home Rule for Scotland throughout his time as an MP in Dundee. In a speech in 1913, he described a federal United Kingdom as inevitable. Much of this thinking was brought on by the question of Irish Home Rule, but Churchill – with both cruel logic and sincerely held belief – applied the same questions and principles to Scotland as well.

None of this is an attempt to recast Churchill as a Scottish hero, or to suggest that Dundonians were wrong to reject him in 1922. Churchill made many mistakes during his time as an MP for Dundee, both on a local and national level, which are deservedly highlighted in this account. Rather, *Churchill: The Scottish Years* is an attempt to better understand what Churchill actually thought of Scotland, and what Scotland thought of him, particularly during the period he was an MP in Dundee. A century on from Churchill's defeat, it is more important than ever to understand his place in Scottish history.

Author's Note

For currency conversions, I have used the National Archive's *Currency Converter: 1270–2017* to give an indication of the modern purchasing power of the sums described. The converter offers input on a five-year basis (i.e., 1900, 1905, 1910, 1915 and 1920) and, where the dates are not exact, I have rounded up to the nearest year. If multiple figures are quoted in succession, a conversion of only the first figure is included.

All individuals are referred to initially by their full name, and from then onwards by their surname. The exception to this is members of Churchill, Asquith and Scrymgeour's family who, to avoid confusion, are referred to initially by their full name, but from then onwards by their first name.

The book follows a chronological timeline as much as possible. However, in some of the more thematic chapters it has been necessary, for both readability and argument, to include material from elsewhere in the timeline. Where this has occurred, it has been clearly marked. As a guideline to help readers, each chapter also contains an approximate date range for the events being discussed.

I have included references as endnotes and a select bibliography of materials I have consulted. Any and all mistakes, however, remain my own.

Acknowledgements

I am grateful to the staff at the Churchill Archives Centre, Dundee Local History Centre, LSE Archive and British Newspaper Archive for all their help and assistance with the research for this project. I am also grateful to Murray Thomson for his early help and advice, as well as to David Powell, the D.C. Thomson Archive manager, for his assistance.

This project never would have happened without the support and enthusiasm of Hugh Andrew at Birlinn. He saw its potential from the start and has fought for it ever since, providing crucial feedback along the way. I am also extremely grateful to Andrew Simmons for his insightful editorial suggestions and to all the other staff at Birlinn who have helped produce this book. Craig Hillsley, in particular, has my enduring thanks for his judicious and thoughtful editing of the manuscript.

The study of Churchill in Scotland is far from my exclusive remit and many others have undertaken extremely valuable and important research on the topic. I am particularly grateful to Gordon Barclay, whose work on Churchill and the events of George Square in 1919 is ground-breaking and invaluable, and Alastair Stewart, who has almost single-handedly fought to ⊠raise the profile of Churchill and his Scottish links. He has been generous with his time and knowledge from the off, and I am extremely grateful for his help and support. I am also indebted to the vast field of historians and writers who have contributed to the wider study of not just Churchill – but also Scrymgeour, Morel, Dundee and the period as a whole – whose work has been an influence on this book. It is obviously not possible to thank them all individually, but I have included a selection of the materials consulted in the bibliography section.

A number of close friends have read early drafts of the manuscript and provided helpful feedback. My thanks, in particular, to Gordon McKee, David Torrance and Christopher Smith for their insightful and useful comments. Tony Halmos has been a consistent and extremely generous supporter of my literary efforts, for which I am enormously grateful. Freddie Burgess, Hatty Hubbard and The Disco also deserve thanks for, at one point, lugging my collection of books across the country.

My parents, Caroline and Roger, have been an enduring support not just with this project but throughout the last 33 years of my life. Their encouragement and advice have been key, and I am particularly grateful to Roger, who kindly lent me much of the secondary material for this book from his own library. Thank you both so much, for this and everything.

Shonagh has had to live with ups and downs of *Churchill: The Scottish Years* more than anyone. It has accompanied us throughout our engagement, new house, marriage and honeymoon. At one point, I even disappeared for four whole weeks to finish the first draft. Not only has she never complained, but she has been a constant source of inspiration, support, encouragement and love. I could not do this – or anything worthwhile – without you.

This book, however, is dedicated to my grandfather, George Thomson. George was one of Churchill's successors as MP for Dundee and provided the introduction, more than 30 years ago, to the only other dedicated book on this subject. But, much more than that, he inspired me to love history and politics, and his influence is one of the main reasons I am able to write this book today. I hope he would have enjoyed it.

Facing Oblivion

1922

Winston Churchill sat alone in a corridor in Dundee's newly completed Caird Hall on 16 November 1922. Despite being dressed in a thick wool three-piece suit, he occasionally shivered. It was winter in Scotland, and cold. Earlier, he had briefly chatted to the bemedalled porter who had carried his solitary seat into the corridor. Churchill had inquired into his war record, but otherwise had spoken to no one for more than an hour. He was pensive and valued the peace. In his right hand he held a large cigar, which he puffed at reflectively, indifferent to the ash falling on the recently polished marble floor. He looked and felt tired. His usually cherubic face was gaunt and emaciated, his suit hung off his body. Not only had it been a tense and trying election campaign, but the wound from his recent surgery was still fresh. If you were to run a hand along his waistcoat, you would feel the raised stitching along the five-inch incision across his abdomen.

Occasionally, Churchill stood up and strode determinedly towards the open window at the end of the corridor, from where he could see the Tay River, Dundee's most dramatic feature, shimmering in the crisp winter sun. Commercial ships dotted the estuary, travelling to and from the city's docks and out into the stormy North Sea. Further in the distance was the Tay Rail Bridge, which had been one of Churchill's main conduits to the city over the last 15 years. But his vista was dominated by the vast monuments to the city's main industry – jute. Smoking chimney stacks towered over the city's sandstone tenements, factories sat on street corners, vast warehouses overlooked neighbourhoods. This titanic array of industry was connected by arteries of cobbled streets where carters, manning horse and wagons, moved raw jute or finished fabrics around the city and down to the docks for export.

It was a scene Churchill knew well, but today it was of little interest. Instead, he looked immediately down on the city's Shore Terrace, where a vast crowd of voters had gathered. What could he divine from the thousands of dirty, hungry, upturned faces? What did they have in store for him this time? They certainly shared his anxiety. Excited murmurs intermittently rippled through the crowd. Predictions and anecdotes from polling day were exchanged. Jokes were made, breaking the tension, and nervous laughter could be heard, only to quickly die down again. From time to time a shout went out in support of one candidate or another and, as Churchill strained to look more closely, he could see the faces of his supporters, many of whom had backed him at every election since 1908. Had things really changed so much since then, he wondered.

Dundee had saved Churchill's political career. When he was invited to stand as the Liberal Party candidate in the city, his future was in the balance. Churchill had just been defeated in the Manchester North West by-election and his first cabinet role, as President of the Board of Trade, was under threat. If he had been defeated in Dundee, his career – not to mention the Liberal government itself – would have been in jeopardy. One by-election defeat looks like bad luck, but two in a row looks like incompetence. Instead, Dundee resoundingly returned Churchill as their MP, and continued to do so over the next four elections. He won the seat at both 1910 general elections. In 1917 – even after Churchill's prominent role in the Dardanelles debacle – Dundee kept its faith in him, re-electing him and endorsing his return to the cabinet as Minister of Munitions. In the 1918 general election, he received one of the biggest majorities in the country. Far from hubris, Churchill's prediction to his mother that Dundee was a 'life seat' and 'cheap and easy beyond all experience' was so far proving notably accurate.

This was largely because, despite these private displays of confidence, he did not take the Dundee electorate for granted. After his election in 1908, he threw himself into delivering the progressive, reforming agenda his constituents demanded. He and Lloyd George soon established a reputation among Conservatives as the 'terrible twins' of the Liberal Party, introducing measures such as old-age pensions, minimum wages and labour exchanges, which helped form the foundations of the welfare state. Further afield, he won the support of his immigrant Irish constituents by being an active supporter of Home Rule – willingly extending the concept to Scotland, as well.

But as Churchill stood at the window in the Caird Hall staring down into the crowds on 16 November 1922, he knew that despite these efforts, all was not well. Many of the personalities who had helped him in Dundee were now gone. His erstwhile running mate, the moderate Labour MP Alexander Wilkie, had stood down, deciding the 1918 general election would be his last. Wilkie had sat alongside Churchill in the two-member Dundee seat for his entire period representing the constituency, and they had developed an excellent working relationship. His absence was a bitter blow. So, too, was the loss of Sir George Ritchie, the chairman of the Dundee Liberal Association. Ritchie had been influential in securing the Dundee nomination for Churchill, and it was Ritchie's wise advice and shrewd political counsel that he was most grateful for – and which, today of all days, he missed the most. Worse still, Churchill had also made prominent enemies. David Couper Thomson, mogul of the eponymous Dundee media empire, had always distrusted Churchill, but in recent months their relationship had soured, descending into public acrimony. Churchill had accused Thomson of bias against him. Thomson, in turn, had accused Churchill of trying to bribe him, with the entire tit for tat exchange published prominently in his newspapers.

Then there were his two main political opponents, who Churchill knew all too well. As far back as 1903, he had supported the Labour candidate, Edmund Dene Morel, in his early work to expose the horrors of King Leopold II's rule in the Congo. But since then, the pair's paths had significantly diverged. Morel had been a prominent opponent of the First World War, even being imprisoned because of his pacificist campaigning. That experience, which had drawn him towards the Labour Party and eventually the constituency of Dundee, held little truck with Churchill.

But it was his second opponent, Edwin 'Neddy' Scrymgeour, who was his most implacable and remarkable foe. Scrymgeour had challenged Churchill at every election he had ever fought in Dundee. In his first, in 1908, Scrymgeour barely secured more than 600 votes and lost his deposit. But he did not give up, and each time he fought a campaign, his level of support slowly rose. By the 1922 general election, Scrymgeour hoped he might finally be on the cusp of the great victory that had so far eluded him. His commitment to defeating

Churchill is in itself notable – few other politicians could weather constant defeat and still keep going. But it is all the more remarkable because of Scrymgeour's unique ideological platform. He was leader of the Scottish Prohibition Party and viewed it as his divine mission to ban the sale and consumption of alcohol, which he argued was the root of all evil. It would be hard to find a political candidate that Churchill, at face value, had less in common with.

Yet, over the course of their 15-year rivalry, Churchill had developed a begrudging respect for his erstwhile political opponent. He admired Scrymgeour's resilience in the face of adversity, and his determination to succeed despite seemingly insurmountable odds. While he disagreed with him on practically every issue, he also respected his authenticity and sincerely held beliefs. The two were never friends, but Churchill did not hold him in contempt. In 1919, Churchill even helped Scrymgeour with a journalistic assignment at the Paris Peace Conference. Yet Churchill still found it difficult to view Scrymgeour as a credible political threat going into the 1922 general election.

The campaign itself had been difficult to read. Apart from anything else, Churchill had only been able to get to the city four days before polling day as a result of his emergency surgery. In his absence, his wife, Clementine – whose family came from nearby Kirriemuir in Angus – had ably campaigned in his stead, but it remained unclear how well Churchill's support was holding up. Recent events – particularly the Russian Revolution and the Anglo-Irish War – had certainly put his electoral base under strain. Many workers in Dundee resented Churchill's bellicose attitude to the Bolsheviks, while his standing with Irish voters had been damaged by his support for the Black-and-Tan paramilitaries in Ireland. His record as a reforming cabinet minister, Irish conciliator and Home Rule supporter was being increasingly forgotten by voters more concerned with recent events. As the votes were counted in the Caird Hall that day, Churchill's future in Dundee once again hung in the balance.

After a few minutes looking down at the crowd, Churchill turned away from the window to walk back to his solitary seat. As his footsteps echoed across the marble, a returning officer entered the corridor carrying a single sheet of paper. Churchill had been to enough election counts to know it contained the result of the vote. Without hesitating, he took the piece of paper firmly in his hand and looked down to learn his fate.

Chapter 1

'What's the Use of a W.C. without a Seat?'
1908

On 8 April 1908, Churchill was formally invited to join the cabinet for the very first time. The Prime Minister, Herbert Henry Asquith, offered him the presidency of the Board of Trade – roughly akin to Secretary of State for International Trade today – which Churchill readily accepted. At 33 years old, he would be the youngest member of the cabinet since Spencer Cavendish, the 8th Duke of Devonshire, in 1866. He would be one of only a handful of political prodigies – such as Pitt, Palmerston and Peel – to secure such a role in their early thirties. But the appointment was not unexpected. Churchill had already performed admirably – if not quietly – as Under-Secretary of State in the Colonial Office, a junior ministerial position, and, as a rising star in the Liberal Party, he was ready for promotion. But there was one significant problem. In order to be promoted to the cabinet for the first time, Churchill had to submit to a by-election in his constituency of Manchester North West. If he was defeated, it could throw his entire political future into jeopardy.

Churchill had first won his constituency of Manchester North West two years earlier, at the general election of 1906. It was a significant step on what had already been a remarkable political journey from Conservative whippersnapper to Liberal leading light. Yet, little about Churchill's life or career to date had been conventional.

Born on 30 November 1874, at Blenheim Palace – his family seat – he was the son of Lord Randolph Churchill and his wife, Jennie. Lord Randolph, the third son of the 7th Duke of Marlborough, had just embarked on his career in politics when Churchill was born. As Conservative MP for Woodstock, Lord Randolph quickly made a name for himself as an impressive parliamentary performer, but he also established a reputation as a political opportunist with a penchant for self-promotion. He was particularly good at fashioning memorable and cutting quips, the most famous of which came in relation to his support for Ulster unionism: 'Ulster will fight, and Ulster will be right.' Lord Randolph's career culminated in his brief appointment as Chancellor of the Exchequer, at the age of 37 in 1886, in Lord Salisbury's second administration. After just five months in the role, Lord Randolph resigned in a dispute with his cabinet colleagues over his plans for the budget. The move was probably meant to be a feint, but Lord Salisbury – fed up with Lord Randolph's erratic behaviour – readily accepted it, effectively ending his political career. He died just eight years later, in 1895 – possibly as a result of a syphilis infection, which may also have contributed to his fitful behaviour. Churchill was barely 20 years old, and the death of his unfulfilled and embittered father affected him deeply.

Churchill enjoyed marginally closer relations with his mother, Jennie. The daughter of a wealthy New York businessman, Leonard Jerome, Jennie had married Lord Randolph in April 1874. The marriage, however, was not a happy one and both partners engaged in extramarital affairs, leading to questions over the paternity of Churchill's younger brother, Jack, born in 1880. Churchill retained a great admiration for Jennie, however, and regularly wrote to her from boarding school and, later, when serving in the military overseas.

Churchill enjoyed a fairly typical education, despite the turbulent public and domestic life of his parents. He attended Harrow, a public school in the north-west suburbs of London, but did not excel academically and, rather than attend university, applied to the Royal Military Academy at Sandhurst, gaining entry on his third attempt in 1893. Commissioned as a second lieutenant in the 4th Queen's Own Hussars – a cavalry regiment – he was initially posted to India. But, eager for action, he used his mother's influence in high society to get posted on several military campaigns, including in Cuba, modern-day Afghanistan and Sudan. These campaigns were extremely dangerous, and Churchill often saw combat. But he also combined his role as a soldier with that of a journalist, writing lucid accounts of the wars he witnessed. Newspapers were soon paying him for articles, and he also published full-length books recounting his experiences, such as The

River War, a best-selling account of the war against the Dervishes in modern-day Sudan. These books and articles marked Churchill's first foray into professional writing, which proved a lucrative hinterland for him for the rest of his life.

Churchill's most famous military escapade came in modern-day South Africa when he was nominally working as a foreign correspondent covering the outbreak of the Second Boer War in 1899. Churchill was captured by Boer commandos and held prisoner in Pretoria before plotting a daring escape across the country and eventually to safety in modern-day Mozambique. The incident made Churchill, who already enjoyed a famous name, a national celebrity in Britain and across much of the Empire, and he embarked on a profitable speaking tour recounting his experience.

But Churchill's ambitions were not limited to military glory and journalistic scoops. In 1899, before his departure for South Africa, he contested and narrowly lost a by-election in Oldham, where he stood as a Conservative Party candidate. In the general election the following year, however, he won the seat, eventually taking his place as the Conservative MP for Oldham in the House of Commons in early 1901. While many would have wanted to toe the party line in their opening period as an MP, this was not Churchill's style, and he increasingly spoke out against aspects of government policy he disagreed with. Over the ensuing months, Churchill became gradually more critical of his government and moved politically closer to the Liberal Party.

Churchill's decision to finally shift allegiance from the Conservative Party to the Liberal Party came over the former's support for economic protectionism, often referred to as 'tariff reform'. As a convinced supporter for free trade, he could not support Joseph Chamberlain's proposal to place tariffs on goods imported from outside the Empire. On 31 May 1904, he crossed the floor – to use the parliamentary parlance – and joined the Liberal Party. This was an ideological move, but it was also politically prudent. In 1906, the Liberal Party won a landslide election victory, and Churchill was resoundingly elected as the MP for his new constituency of Manchester North West. He had made tariff reform and his commitment to free trade a key component of his campaign. His slogan during the campaign was: 'Vote for Winston Churchill and Free Trade.'[1] With a majority of 1,241,

Churchill was ready to begin his career in the Liberal government, and he was delighted to be appointed Under-Secretary of State for the Colonies, which suited his interest in international affairs. Soon, he hoped, he would follow in his father's footsteps as a cabinet minister and beyond.

The Manchester North West by-election took place on 24 April 1908, and it was brought about by Churchill's ascension to the position of President of the Board of Trade. The fact a by-election had to take place was the result of a rule that had been in place since 1705 which decreed that whenever a new member was appointed to the cabinet they had to seek re-election in their constituency. Initially designed as an anti-corruption measure, it continued in varying degrees until 1926, and Churchill would become increasingly familiar with it as he moved in and out of cabinet in the coming years.

By the early 20th century, it was generally considered bad form to contest a ministerial by-election, and they were often unopposed. But Churchill was not so lucky. The Conservative Party announced that William Joynson-Hicks would contest the by-election in a bid to unseat Churchill. His problems were further compounded by confirmation that a Socialist candidate, Dan Irving, would also run, potentially pulling much-needed votes from the left away from Churchill.

Joynson-Hicks' decision to run against Churchill despite convention can be explained by two key factors. First, many in the Conservative Party establishment remained resentful of Churchill, who they viewed as a traitor for his decision to join the Liberal Party in defence of free trade. Many remembered the self-promotion and unreliability of Lord Randolph and, believing Churchill was very much cut from the same cloth, wanted to trim him down to size. This is an early example of how Churchill's family, personality and zest for self-publicity could incite resentment as well as awe. Here, he had so antagonised his former colleagues in the Conservative Party that they were determined to see him fail. In the coming years, it was these same traits that would see powerful men, such as the media mogul David Coupar Thomson, take against Churchill in Dundee. Secondly, despite his victory in the general election of 1906, Manchester North West was far from a safe Liberal seat. In fact, apart from Churchill's recent victory, it had returned a Conservative at every election since its creation in 1885. With the issue of tariff reform on the wane, the Conservative Party therefore saw an opportunity to deliver a blow to a Liberal government still riding high after its landslide election victory two years before. For Joynson-Hicks, who Churchill had defeated at that 1906 election, this was also an early opportunity to regain the seat.

As is the case in most by-elections, a handful of niche issues – almost all of which hurt Churchill – came to dominate the short but intense campaign. The Liberal government's Education Bill threatened protections for denominational schools and so was particularly controversial among the constituency's Roman Catholic and Anglican populations. Churchill was also criticised by the constituency's significant Jewish population, who pointed out he had failed – despite his promise – to reform the Aliens Act, which imposed large naturalisation fees on Jewish arrivals, many of whom were fleeing pogroms in eastern and central Europe. But while Churchill suffered grief on this issue, it is questionable how much it impacted the election. Joynson-Hicks, an inveterate anti-Semite, certainly failed to make any political capital out of it, idiotically declaring: '[I am] not going to pander for the Jewish vote.'[2] Another issue Churchill had to face down was the Liberal government's proposed Licensing Bill, which sought to curb the damaging effects of alcoholism and drunkenness by limiting the opening hours of pubs, but was stringently opposed by Manchester's big brewers.

Despite these challenges, Churchill remained upbeat about his chances of retaining the seat. On his arrival in Manchester at the start of the campaign, Churchill claimed (using language he would later echo in reference to Dundee): 'I am looking out for a safe seat and I think I have found one here in North West Manchester.'[3] He also sought and secured permission from Asquith to confirm that the Irish Home Rule issue would be definitively addressed in the Liberal government's second term. In the event, this appears to have had little truck with the constituency's Irish voters, who may have been unmovable due to the pulpit pleading to oppose Churchill and the Education Bill. But it was an issue that Churchill felt particularly passionate about and – despite its failure to carry the day in this case – one that he would frequently return to.

Churchill therefore greeted polling day with a mixture of excitement and trepidation. The drive to get out the vote started early, with campaigners encouraged by the clear spring day. In a not-so-subtle campaign ploy, Churchill's campaign hired a van emblazoned with posters showing a 'large Free Trade loaf' of bread alongside 'the small loaf' of Protectionism.[4] This suggests that Churchill, at this point, put Liberal economic, rather than social, policies front and centre of his campaign. Churchill's van was one of scores of vehicles that were draped in party colours, with many used to ferry voters to polling stations. Turnout looked to be high and, as polls closed, both campaigns knew the vote would be tight.

Churchill was the last candidate to arrive at Manchester Town Hall for the count. He was accompanied by his mother – then known by her married name, Jennie Cornwallis-West – and his younger brother, Jack. Jennie had been in Manchester for several days to try to drum up support for her son. Addressing one crowd on the eve of poll, she said: 'I hear a good deal about dear coal, and dear beer. But what I say is: "Vote for dear Winston".'[5] Campaigning was not a novel experience for her. Jennie had practically run her sickly husband's 1885 ministerial by-election in his constituency of Woodstock, earning a strong reputation both as a canvasser and as a platform speaker. Indeed, strong campaigning would be a common theme among the Churchill family women, with Clementine performing a very similar role for Churchill in Dundee.

As the trio entered the count in the famous Gothic building just after 9 p.m., Churchill was outwardly confident. The 33-year-old greeted the other candidates warmly and exchanged brief comments with the officials present. But despite this bonhomie, he was tense. Not only was his constituency on the line, but so too was his first cabinet job. When his agent, who had been monitoring the ballots as they were stacked on the tables, approached him, he knew the news was not good. Churchill had narrowly lost, and his political future was now very much an open question.

Despite what was clearly a devastating blow, Churchill's reaction was one of magnanimity. Before the final result was even official, he approached Joynson-Hicks to concede defeat and offer his congratulations. 'I must say, you are a real brick to say what you have done,' a clearly taken aback Joyson-Hicks remarked after Churchill's salutation.[6] But Churchill's generosity in defeat is not surprising. He had tasted defeat before – in Oldham in 1899 – although now, of course, the stakes were significantly higher. Yet, as a democrat, he always respected the verdict of the people, even if he often disagreed with it. As he explained some 24 years later: 'I have nearly always had agreeable relations with my opponents ... after [the election] is over, whatever has happened, one can afford to be good-tempered.'[7] It is also the case that he had only been the MP for Manchester North West for two years. He had few ties there and, given his slim majority and the Conservative tendency in the seat, had – despite his public declarations of considering it a 'safe seat' – not expected to hold it indefinitely. He may therefore have already mentally adjusted himself to finding an alternative parliamentary seat in the future.

The Conservative hierarchy, however, was not as magnanimous in celebrating its victory. The Conservative-supporting *Sheffield Daily Telegraph* effervesced: 'Churchill out – language fails us when it is most needed. We have all been yearning for this to happen with a yearning beyond utterance. Figures – oh! Yes, there are figures – but who cares for figures today? Winston Churchill is *out*, OUT, *OUT!* [original emphasis].'[8] More cruelly still, a joke circulated of a stock exchange telegram supposedly sent to Churchill after his defeat: 'To Winston, Manchester: What is the use of a W.C. without a seat?'[9] While Churchill would surely have disagreed with the tone, he could not have disagreed with the sentiment.

After the result was confirmed, Churchill and his familial entourage made the short walk to the Manchester Reform Club to thank and console his supporters. Many of Lancashire's Liberal elite would be there, licking their wounds, including the wealthy mill-owner, Gordon Harvey, MP for Rochdale, and Sir William Bailey, the engineer responsible for the Manchester Ship Canal. The Venetian-Gothic building – opened by Earl Grey, Gladstone's Foreign Secretary, almost 40 years earlier and adorned with carvings of winged beasts – would have well matched Churchill's dark mood. Yet, as he strode through the entrance, Churchill was handed an urgent telegram. It was sent from one George Ritchie and transmitted from Dundee.

Churchill later recollected that this telegram 'contained the unanimous invitation of the Liberals of [Dundee] that I should be their candidate in succession to the sitting member'.[10] He continued: 'It is no exaggeration to say that only seven minutes at the outside passed between my defeat at Manchester and my invitation to Dundee ...'

This is a nice and distinctly Churchillian anecdote, but it only tells part of the story. In fact, the decision of the Dundee Liberal Association was far from 'unanimous', as the membership was bitterly divided. Many were strongly opposed to Churchill taking the seat and were desperate to find a local candidate instead. But, in Ritchie, Churchill had by far the most able political mind in Dundee on his side – and he was determined to get the Dundee nomination for Churchill.

Chapter 2

The Road to Scotland
1908

Dundee was an attractive offer for Churchill, but it was not his only option. The constituency, which encompassed the entire metropolis on the banks of the Tay River in north-east Scotland, was a rare two-member constituency. This meant that, unlike most constituencies, voters in Dundee had two votes and elected two MPs to represent them. This form of representation had existed since 1868* and, given it was a particularly strong Liberal area, both seats had been occupied almost continuously by Liberal MPs since then. The only exception came at the most recent general election, in 1906, when a member of the forerunner to the modern-day Labour Party was elected for the first time. Nevertheless, Dundee remained an extremely appealing prospect for any prospective Liberal.

The vacancy in Dundee had arisen after the sitting Liberal MP, Edmund Robertson, who had been elected with a majority of more than 5,000 in 1906, was somewhat unexpectedly elevated to the House of Lords. Rumours quickly circulated that Robertson – who was charming and effective, but relatively undistinguished and sickly – had been given a peerage to create a vacancy for Churchill. There may be some truth in this – Robertson was certainly sad to give up his role as MP for the city – and the *Morning Post* noted there was 'considerable surprise' at the decision. But it would have been a high-risk strategy for the Liberal Party, particularly given the result in Manchester North West was not even known when Robertson was

---

* Dundee was represented by two MPs until the General election of 1950, when it was divided into two constituencies – Dundee East and Dundee West – each electing one MP.

offered a peerage, nor was victory in a potential contest in Dundee certain. Indeed, Churchill's own correspondence suggests that, if the Liberal Party had indeed arranged a by-election in Dundee, it was only one of several they had arranged on his behalf. He wrote on 27 April, three days after his defeat in Manchester and with only a whiff of exaggeration: 'The Liberal Party is, I must say, a good party to fight with. Such loyalty and kindness in misfortune I never saw. I might have won them a great victory from the way they treat me. Eight or nine safe seats have been placed at my disposal already.'[1] Certainly, had the Liberal Party really been determined to parachute Churchill into a safe seat, there were safer and more straightforward landing grounds elsewhere in the country.

Nevertheless, some in the local Liberal Party resented even the notion of receiving 'second-hand goods from Manchester', as *The Courier*, already proving itself a sceptic of Churchill's commitment to the city, frequently described his rumoured candidacy.[2] Many were still suffering from the trauma of the 1906 general election, when they had chosen – alongside the recently elevated Robertson – a London stockbroker, Henry Robson, to run as their second candidate. Robson, whose political experience to date had been as mayor of the Royal Borough of Kensington, was hopelessly out of his depth in the cauldron of Dundee politics, enduring a torrid campaign before slumping to defeat to Labour, despite a Liberal landslide across the country.

Yet in Ritchie – the Dundee Liberal Association chairman who sent a telegram to Churchill in the immediate aftermath of his defeat in Manchester North West – Churchill had both a skilful and determined advocate. The silver-haired 59-year-old was born in Kingsmuir, a small village to the north-east of the city, before moving to Dundee as an apprentice grocer in 1869. Ambitious and a hard worker, Ritchie began his own business 10 years later, eventually establishing a network of successful wholesalers in the city. But Ritchie's primary interest was politics rather than money. A lifelong Liberal, he was first elected to the city's council in 1889 and later won plaudits as treasurer, using his financial acumen to bring Dundee's public finances into order. This was particularly notable because, in the words of one historian of the period, Dundee's councillors were generally 'seen as incompetent, sometimes corrupt and usually profligate with the public purse'.[3] With a reputation as a successful businessman and competent administrator, Ritchie had quietly come to dominate the city's Liberal caucus. Now he was determined to deliver Churchill the Dundee nomination.

There is little extant evidence available as to why Ritchie so favoured Churchill's candidacy at this stage. The two went on to become extremely close – 'one of the best friends I ever had', according to Churchill[4] – but there is nothing to suggest they had met or knew each other well before the 1908 by-election. A cynic might point to personal gain as a motive for Ritchie, particularly given he received a knighthood in 1910.* But this does not fit with his character or career to date, which had been marked by a commitment to public service and diligent business. What seems most likely is that Ritchie – a keen advocate for the city of Dundee – merely desired to secure a well-known and well-regarded politician as the city's Liberal MP. As future events would show, Ritchie retained excellent political judgement and therefore probably anticipated that Churchill would go on to be a figure of major national and historical significance. To have Dundee associated with such a figure, he may well have thought, could only be a good thing.

Ritchie, therefore, got to work before Churchill had even fought the Manchester North West by-election, seeking to gain as much control of the nomination process as possible in case Churchill was defeated and could be tempted to Dundee. Here he had a problem: the standing orders of the Dundee Liberal Association called for the membership as a whole to shortlist and select candidates. An added difficulty was that the nominating process had to begin before Churchill was even available as a candidate. To make matters even worse, the anti-Churchill faction in the city was well aware of this fact and was therefore determined to speed up the process as much as possible. Ritchie, in turn, needed to ensure it went forward as slowly as possible to give Churchill a chance to become available for selection.

Unperturbed by these challenges, Ritchie used the imminent and unexpected by-election as a pretext to change the rules in his favour.

---

* As a result of the death of Edward VII, Ritchie's investiture was unable to take place on 7 July 1910 as planned and he only received his knighthood from King George V on 23 February 1911. It was, however, backdated to take effect from the 1910 date.

Instead of all members having input into shortlisting, a six-member sub-committee would be formed to draw up a list of suitable candidates, which the membership could then vote on. While Ritchie superficially presented this as a drive to ensure efficiency, the more politically astute members sensed a sinister motive. Their ire was particularly focused on Ritchie himself, who had not only proposed the new sub-committee but promptly placed himself in charge of it as well. Negative but fundamentally correct briefings began to swirl in the Liberal Association – occasionally finding their way into the local newspapers – that Ritchie was attempting to keep the candidate vacancy open as long as possible in the hope of enticing Churchill to Tayside, should he face defeat in Manchester.

The membership's resentment at their sudden and unexpected exclusion quickly evolved into outright dissension as it emerged this secretive sub-committee was, as they suspected, procrastinating in its only task – to find a suitable candidate. In the sort of timeless briefing that will be familiar to anyone involved in local party politics, one anonymous Liberal member launched a thinly veiled attack on Ritchie, telling *The Courier* that the failure to find a candidate was 'just what might be expected from the caucus who attempt to rule the Association according to their own peculiar ideas'.[5]

Amid such hostile briefing, Ritchie was shrewd enough to know he could not just sit and do nothing, but at least needed to go through the motions of finding an alternative candidate. He first approached Charles Barrie, who from 1902 to 1905 had served as the Lord Provost – the ceremonial head of the local government – of Dundee. Barrie, a 68-year-old native of the city, was a self-made man, having served around the world as a commercial seaman before establishing his own shipping business in the 1880s back in Dundee. With money and a prominent local name, Barrie was a sensible – if unimaginative – choice. But Ritchie also knew that, as a man approaching 70, Barrie was unlikely to want to accept the stress of a tough by-election, or the arduous travel between Dundee and London that being an MP would entail. Indeed, Ritchie had approached Barrie to be the Dundee candidate in 1906, before the Robson debacle – but Barrie had declined then, citing old age. Clearly, Ritchie knew that Barrie, now two years older, was unlikely to feel any more inclined to take up the candidacy.

The next potential candidate sought out by Ritchie was John Fleming, who had been born in Dundee and was known to harbour political ambitions. He had already served as Lord Provost of Aberdeen between 1898 and 1902, while his brother, Robert, had made a fortune as an early pioneer of investment trusts in Dundee before going on to found the eponymous merchant bank, Robert Fleming & Co.* But, as Ritchie most likely anticipated, Fleming's business and political connections now centred on Aberdeen, and he also declined to put his name forward. With the by-election growing ever closer, Ritchie continued to approach potential candidates. One was 40-year-old John Leng Sturrock, the son of Sir John Leng, who had himself been a Liberal MP for Dundee until 1906. Another was Liberal Association stalwart James Nairn, who may well have been aware of Ritchie's manoeuvrings. Both declined.

Ritchie's final approach was to yet another prominent local business-man, William Low. In 1870, Low had joined the management of the family's grocers' firm, which had been founded two years earlier by his brother, James, and William Rettie. The company, somewhat confusingly also named William Low – a fusion of the names of the two founders – had since expanded across Dundee.† With a private source of wealth – essential at this time, as MPs were unsalaried – and a local name, Low would have been another fine, if unimaginative, choice. And, unlike the others, he did not immediately rule out running. Instead, he said he would take some time to consider his options. As gossip spread that he was considering putting himself forward for the nomination – and confounding Ritchie's best-laid plans – the anti-Ritchie faction rallied around Low. Responding to rumours that 'a certain well-known local gentleman had undertaken to favourably consider' seeking the nomination, a Liberal Association member told *The Courier*: 'I only wish that he would, for it would take us out of a hole.'[6]

But just as it seemed his plans may have been thwarted, Ritchie received the news of Churchill's defeat in Manchester North West – and his ready availability as a candidate. That night, without waiting

---

* Despite their considerable individual achievements, John and Robert are now best remembered as the great-uncle and grandfather respectively of Ian Fleming, author of the James Bond books.

† William Low was, almost 100 years later in 1994, sold to Tesco for £257 million.

for the approval of his fellow members, Ritchie rushed to send the telegram inviting Churchill to stand in Dundee. Now all he needed was for Churchill to accept.

But Churchill – much to the consternation of Ritchie – demurred on the offer. Ritchie's telegram, perhaps revealing a twinge of self-doubt at his own machinations, had urged Churchill to 'wire if possible tonight' with his intention to accept the offer. Instead, Churchill waited until the next day to respond and, even then, was lukewarm and non-committal. Arriving in London St Pancras by train just after 2 p.m., he told waiting reporters: 'Nothing is yet settled with to my standing for Dundee or any other constituency.'[7]

It is easy to view Churchill's failure to jump at the offer of the Dundee candidacy as a snub, or that he was somehow hesitant about being an MP in Scotland, but that would be a misreading. Ritchie was, given his own manoeuvrings, keen for Churchill to accept the offer immediately, but it was unrealistic to expect such a major decision to be made on the hoof and without time for proper consideration, particularly so soon after the defeat in Manchester North West. Indeed, far from being an insult, the delay arguably shows the gravity with which Churchill treated the offer.

The reality was also that – as a rising star in the Liberal Party, and as he had indicated in his letter of 27 April – Churchill had several attractive suitors aside from Dundee. The Merionethshire Liberal Association in north Wales wanted to offer him the candidacy in place of Osmond Williams, and this would have been extremely attractive to Churchill given the Merioneth constituency was effectively a rotten borough for the Liberals. It had been held by the party without interruption since 1868 and, for the last three elections, Williams had stood unopposed. Another potential safe harbour for Churchill was in the offing further south in Wales, with Liberal Party headquarters intimating it was in negotiation with John Philipps, the Liberal MP for Pembrokeshire, about standing down to allow Churchill to take his place. While Philipps enjoyed a majority of more than 3,000 – less than the current Liberal majority in Dundee – the seat had returned a Liberal member at every election since 1880, and the lack of a Labour presence there (unlike Dundee) would have also made it an attractive proposition.

Churchill's indecision was, unsurprisingly, not well received in Dundee. This was largely a question of civic pride, which was justifiably wounded by Churchill's prevarication. Following reports that he had not immediately accepted the Dundee invitation, gossip quickly circulated the city that Churchill was determined to 'look this gift horse in the mouth'.[8]

Churchill finally accepted the Dundee Liberal Association's invitation on 28 April, some 72 hours after it had initially been offered. During the intervening period, he had taken counsel from close friends and Liberal politicians, including Asquith, on the sagacity of taking up Dundee's offer, not all of which was positive. The editor of *The Westminster Gazette* and a regular confidant of Liberal politicians, John Spender – better known by his initials J.A. – strongly advised Churchill against accepting the Dundee nomination. 'Don't go to Dundee unless you are sure of your Scots,' he advised in a letter to Churchill on 25 April, adding ominously: 'They are queer folk.'[9] Churchill, however, would not be put off and, having made the decision to stand, was exuberant at the prospect of having secured such a seemingly safe seat. Writing to his mother the day after he accepted the nomination, he said: 'They all seem to think it is a certainty – and even though a three-cornered fight will end in a majority of 3,000. It is a life seat and cheap and easy beyond all experience.'[10]

Dundee's Liberal Party members gathered on 28 April to accept Churchill's nomination, in what was effectively a Ritchie-engineered *fait accompli*. Having agreed to send a message of condolence following the death of the former Liberal Prime Minister, Sir Henry Campbell-Bannerman, who had died the previous week, Ritchie rose to inform the members of Churchill's response. Cognisant of his own machinations, Ritchie was keen to stress that he had gone to every effort to secure a local champion, speaking to no fewer than six prominent individuals – for good measure, he suggested that he himself had considered running – but without success. Then came the 'unexpected' news from Manchester North West and the opportunity to recruit Churchill, a national figure, as their candidate – an opportunity Ritchie had immediately seized. The decision to approach Churchill was, he recognised with more than a touch of political spin, the 'implied rather than expressed' will of the Liberal Association.[11] Nevertheless, the offer had been made, and Churchill had accepted it.

If Ritchie had hoped this would be enough to satisfy the more restive association members, he was mistaken. Party member Alex Gow immediately rose to demand Ritchie release the names of the local figures he had approached to run, implicitly suggesting no such conversations had taken place because Ritchie wanted to recruit Churchill all along. Despite attempts among some members to howl Gow down, Ritchie agreed to release the names of those he had approached. In a final *coup de grâce,* Ritchie confirmed that William Low had actively considered standing, until he had discovered earlier that morning that Churchill would also be seeking the nomination.

Yet, despite all Ritchie's efforts on his behalf, Churchill was still unhelpful. On receiving confirmation of his nomination on Tuesday 28 April and an invitation to come to Dundee that Friday – three days later – Churchill responded: 'But why not Monday?'[12] Such a casual response made even Ritchie baulk, and – in the first of several such interventions – he rushed to protect his champion's reputation and persuaded Churchill to agree to arrive on the Friday after all.

After accepting the nomination, Churchill attempted to heal some of the wounds in the Dundee Liberal Association, which he was now desperate to unite behind his campaign. Writing on 30 April with the local party members in mind, he recognised that 'in order to sustain the cause of progress' they had 'set aside personal considerations'.[13] He acknowledged that others, with a 'lifelong knowledge of your industries ... and whose position in public esteem had entitled them to present to you, have sacrificed, unasked and unhesitatingly, their honourable aspirations'.

Before his arrival, Churchill set about introducing himself to Dundee electors via an election address. As a famous man from a famous family, he already enjoyed good name recognition in the city, but Churchill also wanted to set out his political stall to the voters. In recognition of Dundee's radical tradition and in a foreshadowing of his own political development in the coming years, Churchill presented a forthright, progressive message, with an emphasis on social issues such as his desire to improve working conditions and curtail the power of the unelected House of Lords. While the address did mention free trade, Churchill had already recognised the need to lower its prominence compared to his campaign in Manchester North West.

Churchill also revealed to Dundonians, perhaps unwisely, the sort

of constituency MP they would be getting if they voted for him –
namely, not really one at all. With extraordinary – perhaps brazen –
confidence, he wrote: 'It has been your choice to play a direct part in
national affairs rather than seek gratification for local needs, and to
strike a blow in the cause of the common good rather than to gain a
special advantage for Dundee.'[14]

Such forthright honesty naturally prompted criticism, if not
outright consternation, from his opponents. *The Courier* was particularly scathing. In an editorial analysis of the address that dripped with
sarcasm, the paper declared: 'His depreciation of local interests will
doubtless commend itself to those whose livelihood depends on the
prosperity of the staple trades of the city. The electors are requested to
provide a seat for the Right Honourable President of the Board of
Trade. They are not invited to send someone to parliament to represent their interests.'[15] In a separate piece, the same newspaper went
further, suggesting Churchill wanted a seat in Scotland because its
constituents were more likely to acquiesce to his desire to prioritise
his interests over theirs. 'Scotsmen, as [Churchill] well knows, never
dream of imposing conditions [on their MPs] ... they quietly accept
any candidate that may be sent to them,' the paper railed.[16]

Churchill was alive to such criticism and remained concerned
about being perceived as a carpetbagger. There is certainly some truth
to this charge. Churchill would not have been an MP in Scotland had
he won in Manchester North West. His connections to Dundee were
nil and his connections to Scotland at this stage were few and far
between. But Scotland was not a far-away place of which he knew
nothing. He had visited regularly and often holidayed there. More
directly, he maintained political links with Scotland, even before his
defeat in Manchester North West. In March 1908, he accepted an
invitation to stand as the Liberal Party candidate for the rectorship of
Edinburgh University. Many of his closest allies in parliament also
represented Scottish seats. Indeed, Churchill was far from unusual in
being an English MP in Scotland. Many senior figures, particularly in
the Liberal Party, represented Scottish seats despite being born or
raised in England. The Prime Minister, Asquith, for example, had been
the MP for nearby East Fife since 1886. While this does not necessarily prove Churchill was not a carpetbagger, it does show that if he was,
he was one among many. Certainly, contrary to *The Courier's*

assertions, nothing more than crude electoral realities were behind
Scotland's popularity with those seeking a safe seat; the Liberal Party
had been returned as the largest party in Scotland at every election
since 1857, bar one, in 1900. Indeed, Scotland was so popular among
Liberal candidates from across Britain that by 1911 a quarter of Liberal
MPs representing Scottish seats were born in England.

With Churchill's candidacy finally secured and his early introductions
to the voters of Dundee made via his electoral address, there was just
one more piece of administration for the Liberal Party to manage.
Despite Robertson's resignation – 'taking the Chiltern Hundreds', in
political parlance – in mid-April ahead of his elevation to the House
of Lords, no date had yet been set for the by-election. Indeed, despite
the government being able to announce the date for the by-election
on 29 April, it failed to do so. This may have been mere incompetence,
but it sparked allegations of gerrymandering among the Liberal Party's
opponents in Dundee. 'Dundee is suffering from unnecessary procras-
tination,' *The Courier* argued on 30 April, adding: 'The excitement of
the contest – an excitement that is not only costly but also disturbing
to business – is being unduly prolonged.'[17]

But the Liberal Party hierarchy may have had an even greater plan
in mind than merely ensuring Churchill was safely installed as their
Dundee candidate. Asquith was due to deliver the much-anticipated
budget on 7 May.* It would state – for the very first time – the Liberal
government's intention to provide old-age pensions. The Liberal Party
hoped that such a sweet and historic electoral giveaway – particularly
among the working men and women of Dundee – would be the final
push required to help get Churchill over the line.

---

* While Lloyd George was now Chancellor of the Exchequer and traditionally
would have delivered the budget, it was agreed Asquith was best placed to deliver it,
given he had written it before his ascension to Prime Minister just a few weeks
before, on 8 April.

Chapter 3

'I Chose Dundee'

1908

Ritchie arrived at Dundee's Caledonian Railway station early. It was an unusually clear and bright day for the time of year – 1 May 1908 – and the chairman of the Dundee Liberal Association was determined everything should run smoothly. He anxiously paced up and down the station's south platform, pausing intermittently to stroke his silver goatee beard. At 9.15 a.m., Dundee's leading Liberal patriarchs began to join him. Dressed in top hats and morning coats, this distinctly Edwardian group smiled and exchanged platitudes about the weather while they awaited their prized arrival. Among those selected to greet their new nominee were two of the would-be Liberal Party candidates for the upcoming by-election, Charles Barrie and John Leng Sturrock.

Behind them, at the station gates, a crowd of several hundred lesser citizens of the city had also gathered to witness this historic arrival. Others leaned out of nearby open windows, hoping to catch a glimpse of the new Liberal Party candidate. Two policemen, along with Station Superintendent James McNaughton, watched the crowd nervously, wary of potential trouble. Rumours had earlier circulated that suffragettes had infiltrated the well-wishers and intended to disrupt proceedings. Just after 10 a.m., the buzz of an electric bell indicated the London sleeper train – now running twenty minutes behind schedule – was about to arrive. A ripple of excitement gripped the crowd and security men alike: Churchill was coming.

As the train screeched to a halt in a fog of steam, the crowd surged forward onto the platform, engulfing the assembled Liberal dignitaries, whose role quickly evolved from exclusive welcome party to crowd stewards. Amid a cacophony of cheers, a bareheaded and beaming Churchill quickly emerged from a white-panelled first class sleeping compartment, waving to the crowd, which strained and heaved to get a look at the famous politician. Ritchie need not have worried – Churchill was clearly delighted with this reception. After quick greetings on the platform – conversation was practically impossible due to the noise of the crowd – Churchill made his way towards the booking hall, before pausing to respond to calls for a speech.

'Dundee has stepped forward into the fighting line,' he shouted over the crowd, clearly caught off guard by the unexpected reception and without any prepared remarks.[1] 'What has she done it for? She has done it to strike a good blow. Yes, gentlemen, not only a blow but a good blow. And if you are to strike a blow before all the country, before the whole of this island in which we live, let it be a smashing blow.' Churchill – along with his brother Jack and Alexander Murray, MP for Peebles and Selkirk and the Liberal Party's chief whip – then pressed forward behind Ritchie, as he struggled to cut a path through the crowd. Churchill had arrived in Dundee.

The enthusiasm for Churchill among the citizens of Dundee did not diminish as the day went on. The entire city was suddenly gripped in the fervour of a major political campaign. As the city's *Evening Telegraph* noted: 'Now the election fight in Dundee will wax fiercer than ever, more meetings will be held, the flood of oratory will increase and the various parties will redouble their efforts on behalf of their respective candidates.'[2] Having earlier settled into the Queens Hotel, which became a regular residence during his visits to Dundee over the next 15 years, Churchill wasted no time in proving the *Evening Telegraph* right by getting his campaign underway with a speech at the city's Drill Hall.

This was not his first speech in the city. He had visited eight years earlier, in 1900, as part of a lecture tour to share his experiences of the Boer War. But, given Churchill had then been on the cusp of becoming a Conservative MP, as well as Dundee being a hotbed of opposition to the Boer War, it is perhaps unsurprising he chose not to remind voters of this earlier engagement. On this occasion – eight days before polling day – nearly 6,000 people turned up to hear him speak, with many more turned away before proceedings had even begun. Several hundred chose to remain standing outside, while the nearby YMCA building was used as an overflow, after Churchill agreed to give them a brief supplementary address.

The atmosphere in the Drill Hall – 'packed in every corner' – was so stifling that the organisers had to open the building's roof lights in a bid to cool the expectant multitudes down.[3] As Churchill entered at 8.15 p.m., the crowd was ecstatic, with many waving handkerchiefs amid loud applause. Churchill stood on the candidate's platform, surrounded by many of the same Liberal dignitaries that had greeted him earlier that day, and spoke for more than an hour and a quarter. As he finished his remarks, his language took on a distinctly martial tone, invoking his supporters to campaign hard on his behalf: 'It is to come forward at your head in this battle that you have [had] me to come to Dundee. I accept the duty. Tonight, we go on active service. Tonight, we unfurl our standard.'[4]

Such formal rallies – organised in Dundee's biggest auditoriums – would be a mainstay of Churchill's campaigns in the city at this election and in the years to come. In the age before television and radio, inviting crowds to hear your candidate speak was the most effective method of disseminating your message to as wide an audience as possible. Ideally, those remarks would then be reported by local and national newspapers, spreading your message even further. If you did not hold public meetings – and if newspapers did not report them – then there were few alternative mediums to engage the electorate. This helps explain why – in both Manchester and Dundee – Churchill was particularly concerned with local media coverage and why, justifiably or not, he put significant stock into how they reported his speeches and campaign events.

The format and formula of such events were homogeneous between campaigns and would change little over the course of Churchill's time as MP for Dundee. Each morning popular local newspapers such as *The Courier* would advertise when and where a party's candidate was speaking that evening. In Churchill's case, a typical event would usually see him issue a speech for around an hour, before taking questions from the audience. This speech would be given without notes, although it was generally a prepared campaign stump speech, elucidating key themes, but varying only marginally depending on the given audience. Indeed, Churchill had a 'phenomenal' memory and was already well versed in giving extemporaneous remarks by the time he arrived in Dundee.[5] Given the lack of any electronic assistance – and the fact halls were often hazy with a thick fog of tobacco smoke – addressing crowds of several thousand was an arduous task, even in venues with good acoustics. Nevertheless, as an energetic and effective public speaker, Churchill revelled in addressing substantial crowds, arguing it was far more trying to engage 'twenty or thirty extremely stolid-looking persons in a hall which will hold six or seven hundred'.[6] Big-ticket events – inevitably taking place in the evening so those working could attend – were often supplemented by more impromptu addresses around the city during the working day. These normally involved visiting large mills, factories or other businesses during lunch or tea breaks, when a large audience could be more or less guaranteed. While conventional canvassing and the distribution of party literature did take place, it was largely unscientific and disorganised, limiting both its uptake and utility.

There were two major issues with such large rallies. The first was the expense of hiring halls and, if necessary, arranging tickets and stewards. By 1913, receipts show Churchill was spending £54[*] on booking meeting halls in the city – a significant sum for a local party or candidate to be expected to bear. This is particularly the case when we consider 1913 was not an election year, when significantly more rooms would need to be hired. The second, and more problematic issue with large rallies, was disruption from the audience. This was less of a problem when visiting local businesses, where employees were reluctant to become too bellicose for fear of embarrassing their employer – often a friend of the candidate – and potentially losing their job. But it was a constant fear at larger rallies, where the stakes were already significantly higher. To try to ensure meetings ran smoothly, Churchill relied heavily on the local knowledge of Ritchie and his electoral agent, Peter Husband, a local solicitor. Both not only knew the city's Liberal supporters – and could therefore try to pack the hall with as favourable crowd as possible – but also their most implacable opponents. The duo would scan the faces of the crowd looking for troublemakers, but it was simply not possible to filter out every political opponent or constituent with a grievance.

* Approximately £4,250 in 2017.

The problem of heckling was further accentuated by the fact that political meetings in the early 20th century were a form of entertainment for the general public, particularly in cities such as Dundee. There was little other recreation in the city – pubs being an exception – while tenements were overcrowded, dirty and noisy. With little to do outside or at home, political speeches became significant events that broke the monotony of daily life, as evidenced by the substantial crowds that turned up to hear them. For a candidate, that meant people were likely to turn up, but it also meant they expected a show. If the speaker was boring or quiet, then the crowd would be forced to make its own entertainment. Writing more than two decades after the by-election, but with his Dundee experience firmly in mind, Churchill vividly described such rowdy meetings: 'Here you have excited crowds, Green-eyed opponents, their jaws twitching with fury shouting interruptions, holloing, bellowing insults of every kind, anything they can think of that will hurt your feelings, any charge that they can make against your consistency or public record, or sometimes, I am sorry to say, against your personal character.'[7] Particular scorn was reserved for the 'nasty question' from the 'vehement-looking pasty youths' and 'young short-haired women of bull-dog appearance'.

Churchill could generally handle hecklers and disruptors with grace and often a witty put-down – and he suggested he actually preferred such meetings to calmer affairs as they were more interesting. 'Rowdy meetings are a great relief,' he claimed, adding: 'You have not got to make the same old speech.'[8] Indeed, he argued heckling could in fact be beneficial: 'A long sagacious argument makes the audience yawn [but] a good retort at a turbulent meeting makes friends by the dozen, even sometimes of the enemy.'

But despite his later bravado, Churchill privately feared opposition agitators and loathed being interrupted. One letter to Ritchie, sent ahead of a planned rally in the city in 1911, is typical. 'It is important that the meeting should be in every way successful,' he dictated to his secretary.[9] 'Do you think there is any chance of the Socialists trying to disrupt the meeting or make demonstrations against me? This should be carefully inquired into … if there is any danger of the meeting being spoiled special precautions must be taken to deal with the interrupters with the upmost promptitude.' This was not a one-off, but a theme Churchill constantly returned to when discussing potential meetings with Ritchie. In 1919, he said: 'It is so easy for 50 or 60 people to spoil altogether the effect and usefulness of a meeting by simply going and shouting interruptions.'[10] Churchill was inevitably subject to greater heckling because of his high-profile status, but much of it – particularly pre-1918 – was unrelated to constituency issues. Instead, national campaigners would come to Dundee seeking to highlight their grievance. The 1908 by-election was no exception, and here Churchill – as the police had feared – would face the wrath of the suffragettes.

Mary Malony* arrived at the meeting at Dundee's Blackness Foundry early. It was just before 1.40 p.m. on 4 May and many of the nearby workers were gathering outside the factory during their lunch break. Malony, 24, knew they had come to hear Churchill – she had seen the meeting advertised in the newspaper that morning. But the Irish-born suffragette and member of the Women's Freedom League – a breakaway faction from Emmeline Pankhurst's Women's Social and Political Union, founded just eight months before the Dundee by-election – was determined that they would enjoy an entirely different show.

As Churchill's car approached the crowd, Malony stood up in her horse-drawn carriage, brandishing a large dinner bell, and shouted: 'He will not face me.' As Churchill passed, he smiled and doffed his hat, but said nothing. When Churchill made to stand in the car to address the crowd, Malony violently rang her bell – the Liberal candidate simply could not be heard. A comic scene then ensued as Churchill's car attempted to move out of range of the noise of the bell, only to be hotly pursued by Malony, 'balancing herself on the driver's seat [of her carriage] and again ringing the bell with great vehemence'.[11] This game of cat and mouse continued, much to the entertainment of the crowd, who delighted as the two groups stalked each other around the factory. After a brief interlude, Churchill's campaign realised hosting a meeting would be impossible. 'Disgraceful is not the word for this,' an infuriated Ritchie remarked as they beat a hasty retreat.[12] Malony, *The Evening Telegraph* reported, left 'in a state of high triumph'.[13]

---

* Also spelt Molony or Maloney.

Churchill was understandably irritated by the disruption to his meeting and, probably as much if not more, by the embarrassment of the retreat. 'I would call your attention to the methods adopted by these women who are anxious to obtain a vote,' he said, referring to the incident, adding: 'Observe how [the suffragettes] conduct themselves. Observe what regard they have for other people's rights. I won't attempt to compete against a bell.'[14] Such a response is unsurprising, but harsh. Malony herself conducted conventional political campaigning alongside her more disruptive activities, regularly holding rallies and meetings throughout the by-election campaign. After one such rally, Malony was praised in *The Courier* for a speech 'delivered in a fluent and convincing manner' as part of a meeting that was 'most enthusiastic throughout'.[15]

Churchill himself attempted to sidestep the politically contentious issue of votes for women during the by-election. His response to a question on whether he would introduce legislation in support of votes for women – given the day after he was heckled by Malony – was a masterclass of equivocation: 'Such a question should be submitted to the country at a general election, although I agree there is no logical reason against it, and I look forward to the day women will exercise their influence on politics.'[16] He then added, with his recent experience firmly in mind: 'I hope it will be on the gentler side of politics.' Privately, Churchill was not as opposed to the extension of the franchise to women as some of his colleagues, such as Asquith. His objection was political – that an expansion would harm Liberal electoral prospects, as he believed women were more likely to vote Conservative.

While the disruption of the suffragettes garnered significant attention, Churchill had to focus his efforts on defeating his three main opponents. His primary challenger was Sir George Baxter, the candidate for the Conservative Party – referred to as the Unionist Party in Scotland until 1965. The 55-year-old Baxter was the scion of a prominent Dundee family. His father, William, had been MP for nearby Montrose and had held several minor ministerial positions in Gladstone's first administration, while George Baxter's great-aunt, Mary Ann Baxter, co-founded the city's University College, now the University of Dundee. Sir George Baxter himself enjoyed a fine, if unremarkable, political pedigree. He had been chairman of the Dundee Liberal Unionist Association since its foundation in the latter part of the 19th century. The Liberal Unionists had broken away from the Liberal Party in 1886 over the question of Irish Home Rule, and they worked in concert with the Conservative Party. It was on this platform that Baxter had contested his father's former seat of Montrose in the 1895 general election. While he was defeated in that contest, he did achieve the Unionists' highest ever vote share in the seat, coming within 1,100 votes of unseating the Liberal incumbent. While Dundee enjoyed a reputation as a bastion of the Liberal Party, there was a significant Unionist element within the city. Churchill himself warned that Dundee Unionists were 'full of combative spirit' and a real threat.[17] At the 1906 general election, the Unionists had even convinced a young Ernest Shackleton – at that point still to find fame as an explorer – to stand. While he was defeated, the collective Conservative/Unionist vote was significant despite a poor performance nationally.

As well a conventional threat from the centre-right, Churchill also faced – in his view, a more dangerous – insurgent candidate on the left, which threatened to draw support away from the Liberal Party's traditional base in the city. The 38-year-old George Harold Stuart was, like Churchill, a stranger to Dundee. He had been born in Oldham – coincidentally, the first seat Churchill held – before becoming a postal worker, union activist and, at the 1906 general election, the unsuccessful candidate for the fledgling Labour Party in York.

Yet, while he clearly enjoyed a convincing Labour pedigree, Stuart's candidacy was controversial. Despite being selected by the local Dundee Labour Party as their candidate on 21 April, his candidature was not officially endorsed by the National Executive Committee of the Labour Party, leading to frantic rumours that he might withdraw, willingly or otherwise. It was even suggested that the national Labour Party was actively seeking Stuart's withdrawal because they wanted Churchill to win, fearing a consecutive by-election defeat would irreparably damage the Liberal government. The internal debate over Stuart's candidacy was eagerly highlighted by Churchill's supporters, who had a great deal to gain if they could convince Dundee's working-class voters that even the Labour Party leadership wanted Churchill to win. As Stuart himself joked to his supporters during a speech in Dundee's Gilfillan Hall: 'If [the Labour Party National Executive Committee] really do favour Mr Churchill and are to withdraw, it will not be the first time in the history of these kingdoms that the House of Churchill has gained an advantage . . . at the expense of the House of Stuart.'[18]

It took the Labour Party 10 days to finally contradict the rumours, by which point much of the damage had already been done to Stuart's campaign. Ramsay Macdonald, then the Labour Party's General Secretary, telegrammed to deride the story as 'absolutely untrue'.[19] But despite the categorical – if delayed – denial, support from the central party remained circumspect. In another telegram sent to James Urquhart, Stuart's agent, the party suggested he 'negotiate' with the Labour MP George Roberts to see if any supportive speakers could be arranged to join the campaign trail.[20] While the situation will have understandably infuriated Stuart – and did undoubtedly help Churchill – the Labour Party's prevarication was understandable. Apart from the national political implications of another defeat for the Liberal government, the Labour Party already had one MP in situ in Dundee and having a second candidate in place would risk splitting the Labour vote at the next general election. Equally, the Labour leadership at this time preferred to cooperate rather than compete with the Liberal Party, effectively creating an electoral pact in two-member constituencies such as Dundee.

Nevertheless, Churchill still feared Stuart and focused his most vitriolic – and effective – rhetoric of the campaign against the Labour candidate. His main salvo came during a speech at Dundee's Kinnaird Hall – then the biggest auditorium in the city – on 4 May, just five days before the city went to the polls. He began with the sort of rhetorical olive branch necessary during a by-election, suggesting he had the 'greatest respect' for a 'great many Socialists'. But he continued: 'These delightful, rosy views of a great and brilliant future to the world are so remote from hard facts of daily life and of ordinary politics that I am not very sure that they will bring any useful or effective influence to bear upon the immediate course of events.' Having defined his opponent as a deluded idealist, he then went on to outline what he viewed as the 'great gulf' between liberalism and socialism. It is an illuminating passage and worth quoting at length:

Liberalism has its own history and its own tradition. Socialism has its own formulas and its own aims. Socialism seeks to pull down wealth; Liberalism seeks to raise up poverty. Socialism would destroy private interests; Liberalism would preserve private interests in the only way in which they can be safely and justly preserved, namely, by reconciling them with public right. Socialism would kill enterprise; Liberalism would rescue enterprise from the trammels of privilege and preference. Socialism assails the pre-eminence of the individual; Liberalism seeks, and shall seek more in the future, to build up a minimum standard for the mass. Socialism exalts the rule; Liberalism exalts the man. Socialism attacks capital; Liberalism attacks monopoly.[21]

Amid cheers from the audience, he concluded: 'These are the great distinctions which I draw, and which, I think, you will think I am right in drawing at the election between our philosophies and our ideals.' Churchill was delighted with the speech and even more ecstatic about its reception. 'I think this was upon the whole the most success-ful election speech I have ever made,' he wrote in 1932.[22] 'The entire audience, over 2,000 persons, escorted me, cheering and singing, through the streets of Dundee to my hotel. Thereafter, we never looked back.'

But beyond its immediate impact on the campaign, Churchill's speech at the Kinnaird Hall was notable for two further reasons. Firstly, the speech reflected his growing adherence to, and understanding of, liberalism, which would be his political home for the next 15 years. His suggestion that the Liberal government 'seeks [and] shall seek more in the future' to 'build up a minimum standard for the mass' was indica-tive of his growing recognition – since his arrival in Dundee – of the need for progressive social, as well as economic, reform. Just days into the campaign, Dundee was already helping to influence and shape Churchill's political thinking, and it continued to do so in the coming years. Secondly, the Kinnaird Hall speech began a pattern of Churchill making significant set-piece speeches to a Dundee audience, often on matters of national and international significance. While, as he admit-ted in his election address, he had little understanding or interest in local issues, he often still chose his Scottish constituency as the crucible in which to express his views on the issues of the day.

As well as grand speeches, Churchill also addressed practical issues during the campaign. The first was a national shipbuilding strike, which had begun earlier that year after workers refused to accept a downgrade in pay following a downturn in orders. As President of the Board of Trade – albeit without a seat – Churchill had taken on responsibility for trying to resolve the dispute amicably. The precedent was not good: Lloyd George, his predecessor in the role, was widely recognised as a master conciliator, but had failed to reach an agreement. Dundee, as a shipbuilding centre, was directly affected; more than 1,000 people immediately found themselves without work. As the situation escalated, *The Courier* suggested that, without urgent action, thousands more could find themselves destitute. Despite being in the midst of the by-election campaign, Churchill sprang into action and travelled to London overnight to join in talks to settle the dispute. The 24-hour dash proved fruitless – Churchill would successfully negotiate a settlement in September that year – but his efforts on behalf of Dundee workers did not go unnoticed. 'If Mr Churchill can show he is as good a conciliator as Mr Lloyd George, and, moreover, can lay claim to have settled one of the biggest labour disputes of the last twelve months, this will help him in his candidature,' *The Courier*'s London correspondent noted.[23] Churchill's action was, in part, cynical electioneering, but – despite his protestations in his election address – it was the first of several interventions at a cabinet level in aid of his constituents. Indeed, Churchill recognised that maintaining a base of support among Dundee's vast working class would be essential if he were to win the seat at the by-election and retain it in the coming years.

As well as attempting to resolve the shipbuilding dispute, Churchill also set about courting Dundee's sizeable immigrant Irish population. Irish immigration to Dundee had begun in earnest almost a century before, with workers lured by the prospect of jobs in the city's linen and jute trade. By 1908, a considerable Irish population had settled in the city, particularly around the Lochee area – James Connolly, a well-known Irish republican and future leader of the Easter Rising, is thought to have resided there in 1898 – and around 1,500 voters were thought to identify as Irish. As in Manchester North West, this was generally thought to be a single-issue block, willing to support whichever candidate they felt would most likely progress the cause of Irish

Home Rule. Here, Churchill – an avid Home Ruler – was on solid ground. O'Donnel Derrick, Secretary of the Irish League in Scotland, urged his members to 'go to the polling booths and make the sign of the cross opposite the name of Winston Churchill', while the *Dundee Catholic Herald* was also supportive.[24] Together with Dundee's workers, the city's Irish population would make up Churchill's electoral base in the city over the coming years.

The night before polls opened on 9 May, Churchill issued a last-ditch appeal for voters to back him. Carefully ignoring both the machinations of the Dundee Liberal Association and his own prevarication, Churchill told a packed Kinnaird Hall:

> When you asked me to come to Dundee you knew perfectly well you were plunging into the storm . . . You did not hesitate to give me a unanimous invitation – to a great industrial centre – a great manufacturing and labouring city, and I accepted that invitation. Other seats – safe seats, seats where there would have been no contest at all – were placed at my disposal by patriotic Liberals who were willing to make sacrifices of their personal position in order to carry the cause forward.[25]

Amid cheers from his jubilant supporters, he closed: 'I chose Dundee. Now it is for Dundee to choose.'

Chapter 4

A Seat for Life?

1908

Churchill stood alone in the corner of Dundee's sheriff court. Dressed in a dark suit with a wing-collar shirt, his face betrayed his anxiety. It had been a good campaign, but the disappointment of Manchester North West had convinced him to take nothing for granted. The mood among some in the Liberal camp was also one of concern, if not abject defeatism. 'It was said I was out again,' Churchill later recalled, 'and that this would be final.'[1] Having arrived at the count just after 9 p.m., he watched warily as the ballots were tipped onto the counting tables, ready to be sorted by eager volunteers. All the proceedings were carefully watched over by Sheriff Ferguson, the returning officer. Churchill's experience – this was his fifth election as a candidate – told him that it would take at least two hours of counting before a decent estimate of the result could be formed. His greatest fear was a tight contest where 'the last few scraps of paper hold their secret till the end'.[2] As the count slowly got underway, Churchill picked up a small packet of rubber bands and began wrapping them round his fingers with great concentration. When the tension became too great and the band snapped, he dismissively tossed it away, ready to begin again.

Churchill's day of reckoning had begun brightly, and Dundee was bathed in sunshine as the city's 19,000 registered voters – at this stage just the male rate payers – headed to the polls on 9 May. Aided by the good weather, turnout was unusually high, with more than 1,500 – 8 per cent of electors – having voted by 9 a.m. Groups of children filled the streets, many waving ribbons in party colours or rosettes, which were a new innovation in Dundee electioneering. Churchill's

Liberals were adorned in red and yellow, his rival Conservative/ Unionists in red, white and blue, and Labour supporters in red or tartan. Thousands of these emblems were sold to voters and campaigners, in what *The Courier* described as 'the cult of the badge'.[3]

As the effort to encourage voters to the polls began in earnest, Churchill was ushered into a motorcar, where he spent most of the day, being driven between polling stations. While every candidate did this, as Churchill himself later pointed out, it was of dubious effectiveness. 'You watch the electors coming up, getting their ballot papers and going off into their little pen to put their fateful cross the in the right – or wrong – place,' he reflected, almost 24 years later.[4] 'You do not need to be a reader of thought or character to make a shrewd guess at how the bulk of them have voted. An averted look or a friendly wink will usually tell you all you need to know.' Churchill's use of a motorcar was unusual – previous electioneering had largely been conducted in a two-horse landau – and the Liberal Party's near-monopoly on this novel form of transport was mocked, somewhat bitterly, by their opponents. The Labour candidate Stuart, for instance, could only muster a colourfully clad corps of cyclists to circulate the city on his behalf. But that did not matter much to his supporters who, according to *The Courier*, 'did not hesitate to make themselves comfortable amongst the sinking cushions of motorcars bearing placards such as "Vote Churchill"'.[5]

Churchill and the other candidates were not the only campaigning presence at polling stations. Despite not being on the ballot paper, the suffragettes stationed themselves strategically to greet voters as they arrived, urging them – in a final push to defeat Churchill – to 'keep the Liberal out, Sir'. Most of this was good-natured, but opponents of female suffrage occasionally engaged in puerile attacks, which were met in kind. In one incident, a local minister loudly proclaimed that the suffragette campaign was 'the funniest thing' he had ever seen, to which one of the campaigners responded: 'Well, you evidently don't dress yourself before a mirror.'[6]

As the day wore on, a sense of foreboding began to infect the Liberal Association. Not enough of Churchill's supporters were turning out, while the Conservative/Unionists appeared increasingly bullish about their chances. Churchill attributed this 'wave of panic' to his friends and Liberal Party staff from London, who had been drafted in to help get out the vote on polling day.[7] But the mood among the Dundee Liberals was more upbeat. Ritchie, no stranger to Dundee election counts, confidently predicted a majority of around 3,000.[8]

By the close of the polls, an unprecedented crowd of more than 30,000 – 'a great expanse of humanity', according to *The Courier*[9] – began to gather outside the city's sheriff court to hear the result. The fact that such a large number had gathered was 'typical of the extraordinary interest in this election'. The *Evening Telegraph* suggested, with just a touch of hyperbole: 'There was not one house in the city that did not have at least one representative at the great finale.'[10] Indeed, the atmosphere was more akin to a carnival than a by-election. The city's Lord Provost had earlier opened the Drill Hall where a 'Cinematograph Display' was put on for those awaiting the result, while a military band was also drafted in to entertain the revellers.

But despite the city's enthusiasm, the crowd was not entirely peaceful. At 11 p.m., the 'human tide' broke through the interlocked arms of the Dundee policemen deployed to keep them a safe distance from the courthouse, filling the square directly beneath the balcony where the result would be declared, before settling down once again. Further trouble was sparked by the arrival of a group of suffragettes – including Churchill's bell-ringing tormenter, Malony – who had obtained tickets to observe the count. The group were jeered by some in the excitable crowd and, when they left the court after the result was declared, had to be given a police escort and bundled into a cab back to their hotel. Despite the quick exit, a gang caught up with several members of the group and accosted them outside the Lamb's Hotel, ripping Malony's jacket in a brief but traumatic scuffle. As the night wore on, the 'intense pressure of the mob' was so great that dozens of people began to faint and had to be carried to the edge of the crowd or into the nearby police station to receive medical attention. *The Courier's* correspondent attributed this 'mild hysteria' to the 'unprecedented' number of women present.[11]

Just after midnight, a ripple of excitement broke through the crowd as the courthouse door opened and the returning officer stepped out onto the balcony to announce the result. With such a substantial crowd, he initially struggled to make himself heard. But the sudden appearance of Churchill by his side told the crowd all they needed to know. The Liberal Party candidate – those 'second-hand goods from Manchester' – had been elected the MP for Dundee.

Churchill received 7,079 votes, a majority of 2,709, almost exactly as Ritchie had predicted. Despite representing the governing party in a mid-term contest, he had secured 43.9 per cent of the vote – no mean feat given the vagaries of by-elections, albeit three points lower than his vote share at Manchester the previous month. Pound for pound, Churchill had also enjoyed the best returns, despite spending more than he did in Manchester – the total Liberal expenses for the Dundee by-election were £1,021* compared to £842 in Manchester. Put another way, in Dundee, Churchill only spent approximately two shillings a vote. That compared favourably to the Conservative/Unionist's Baxter, who spent a total of £934 or more than four shillings a vote, and Labour's Stuart, who spent the most of any candidate – £1,076 – and paid more than five shillings a vote.

Equally cheering was Labour's failure to make significant inroads into the Liberal vote. Stuart's return of just over 4,000 votes was viewed as a disappointment and many in the local Labour Party blamed the National Executive for failing to fully support the campaign. In a vote of thanks to Stuart for standing in Dundee, the local Labour Party sought to shift blame for the defeat onto others: 'When we ... first invited you to contest Dundee ... we certainly never anticipated that your chief opponent would be a cabinet minister, from what is known as the strongest government of modern times, nor did we ever anticipate anything but the heartiest support from every true friend of the great Labour movement. Why that support was not extended can best be explained by those who were responsible for withholding it.'[12]

But, despite defeat and ensuing recriminations, Stuart had done enough to ensure the Liberal Party could not be complacent, and Churchill himself quickly recognised he would have to work to retain the city's progressive vote in the Liberal column. Privately, he conceded that the prospect of old-age pensions, announced as part of the conveniently timed budget, had been a crucial factor in ensuring

---

* Approximately £80,000 in 2017. Of this, Churchill himself contributed around half.

more voters did not peel away to the Labour candidate. This recognition – that voters wanted action, as well as warm words on social justice – would help encourage Churchill's embrace of progressive politics over the coming years.

The Conservative/Unionist candidate Baxter received 4,370 votes – 505 more than his 1906 predecessor, Shackleton – increasing his share of the vote by 3 per cent. However, given strong – and, as it turned out, inaccurate – canvass returns, some optimists in the Conservative/Unionist camp had hoped for a better showing and the most romantic, a shock victory. With the vote as it was, Baxter found himself in a philosophical mood, telling his supporters: 'It might have been better, and it might have been worse. I am not ashamed of the result.'[13]

While not explicitly on the ballot paper, the suffragettes had played an active part in the campaign and had hoped voters in Dundee would reject Churchill, as they had in Manchester. Understandably they were therefore disappointed with their result. Malony, who had pursued Churchill with occasionally devastating effect, was particularly melancholy. 'The result came as a shock to me, and I could not quite realise it,' she said.[14] Somewhat wistfully, she added: 'I see I do not understand the Scottish character. I thought Sir George Baxter, being a local man, and he and Lady Baxter being so popular, the electors would have preferred him. You see the Scottish are very conservative.' But, despite her disappointment with the result, she was upbeat about her own performance: 'We thought we had made a certain amount of impression – there is no doubt we have done good propaganda work.' She was particularly pleased to see that women in Dundee had become more engaged with politics – including many turning up to hear the result – predicting, presciently, that 'this will bear fruit in the future'.

Dundee was exuberant following the announcement of Churchill's victory. While his supporters naturally led the celebrations, even some of his opponents were swept up in the moment. Rather than disperse, the majority of the crowd stayed, chanting 'He's a jolly good fellow' and hoping to catch another glimpse of their new MP.

On police advice, the Liberal Association arranged for a car to quietly whisk Churchill back to his hotel. But word of his travel plans leaked out and quickly spread among the crowd who – despite the best efforts, once again, of the Dundee constabulary – surrounded the waiting car. Never one to miss an opportunity for self-promotion, a jubilant Churchill clambered up onto the back seats of the open landau and – cigar in one hand, hat in the other – waved to the ecstatic crowd. Ritchie, seated next to him, allowed himself a wry smile as he watched the celebrations. The scene was caught by waiting photographers and used on the front page of several national newspapers. If Churchill hoped his show of affection would encourage the throng to disperse, it was ineffective. Instead, after a brief conference, 20 police officers clung to the side of the vehicle – another sat astride the bonnet – ushering the crowd out of the way as the car made its agonising half-mile journey to the city's Nethergate. By the time this comic motorcade reached the Queen's Hotel, the crowd was so thick and rowdy that Churchill had to be physically dragged by police officers into the lobby. Breathless from the ordeal, he had to sit for several minutes while he recovered.

In a final flourish – and perhaps with one eye on ensuring he could get a decent night's sleep – Churchill bowed to public pressure and agreed to make one valedictory appearance on the hotel's balcony. After several appeals for silence, he addressed the crowd in a halting voice, gripped by the emotion of the occasion. The result, he said, was a 'thunderbolt from the north' and a 'triumph for the people's cause . . . and for the grand old Liberal Party.'[15] He added: 'Let us follow the main road. Let us march straight forward . . . upon the road of progress to peace, justice and to truth. Dundee forever, Scotland to the fore – I bid you all goodnight.' Amid cheers from the crowd below, Churchill took out a bone-white handkerchief and waved it vigorously towards his supporters, before turning back to the hotel and disappearing behind the balcony curtains.

As news of Churchill's victory spread across the country, he was inundated with messages of congratulation. More than 15 Liberal Associations sent their warm wishes in the hours following the declaration, including Churchill's former colleagues in Manchester, while representatives of Dundee's Irish community also noted their pleasure at his triumph. As well as political groups, family and close friends hastened to write. Victor Spencer, Churchill's uncle and a Conservative Party supporter, graciously wrote to say that while 'politically I would like to have seen you beaten ... personally I am very glad you have got it.'[16] Another telegram came from Churchill's former Boer adversary turned friend, Louis Botha, who suggested, somewhat extravagantly, that 'all South Africans rejoice and heartily congratulate you'.[17] More bizarre entreaties also arrived, including one, dispatched from the pier at Limehouse, conveying the best wishes of a crew on a steamship named *London*. Perhaps most unusual and embarrassing – not only politically, but also because Churchill was an Old Harrovian – was a telegram that appeared verbatim on the front page of the city's *Evening Telegraph*, reading: 'All Etonians congratulate you on a brilliant victory.'[18]

The following day, a large crowd gathered at Dundee's Tay Bridge station to bid their new MP farewell. After back-to-back by-election campaigns, a noticeably weary Churchill was finally returning to London. But he still managed to exchange pleasantries with many of the well-wishers, including Ritchie, who had gathered to see him off. He once again thanked them for organising a successful campaign and assured them that he would return to his new constituency within the month. Entering the carriage, Churchill paused briefly, raising his hat one final time to his supporters, just as he had when he arrived in Dundee nine days earlier. As the train pulled away from the station, Churchill looked back with satisfaction on the city that had returned him to elected office. The battle had been hard fought and the result far from certain. But, after the ups and downs of the campaign, it had ultimately been a success. He had, he was confident, finally secured his coveted 'life seat'.

Of all the potential threats that could disrupt his tenure in Dundee, Churchill would have given little thought to the last-placed party at the election. The Scottish Prohibition Party had, in fact, barely registered either with Churchill or the voting public throughout the campaign. It garnered only occasional press coverage during the election – it was a fringe outfit, almost too irrelevant to even ridicule. Its unique selling point – such as it was – was the total prohibition on the sale and consumption of alcohol, while its broader policy platform was a cocktail of socialist economics and evangelical Christian militancy. Perhaps unsurprisingly, the fledgling party secured a paltry 655 votes in the election and suffered the humiliation of losing its deposit.

But despite the drubbing, its candidate, founder and leader – one Edwin Scrymgeour – was surprisingly upbeat.

'I feel deeply thankful to almighty God that he has enabled the Prohibition Party to put me forward as the first British Prohibition candidate,' he told his supporters following his defeat.[19] He added: 'I look forward to another day when success will attend our efforts.' For Scrymgeour, this was just one more setback in what had already been an arduous personal and political struggle. He was used to defeat, but he believed – with God's help – one day he would win. This was not the end but merely the beginning.

Chapter 5

Vote as You Pray
1866–1908

Edwin Scrymgeour watched the three policemen approach. He had recognised Superintendent Gordon, Sergeant Brown and Sergeant Davidson immediately, even amid the thick crowd at Dundee's Kinnaird Hall. He knew what they wanted and had expected them to come. In some ways he was grateful to them, even surprised. They could have disrupted the meeting – they could have tried to cause a scene. Instead, they had politely waited, affording his Scottish Prohibition Party and their guest of honour a courtesy that, he reflected, he would not have accorded them had the situation been reversed. That was the problem with public officials in this town, he thought. Too polite.

Scrymgeour directed the three men to an anteroom behind the stage, careful to avoid the prying eyes of the crowd. The fact more than one had come suggested they expected trouble. Superintendent Gordon and Sergeant Davidson were both dressed for the occasion, the buttons on their uniforms sparkling. Sergeant Brown, perhaps drafted in as a last-minute reinforcement, was in his civvies. It was a Sunday, after all. Even Scrymgeour – a man not renowned for his deference to authority – understood that Sundays were to be respected.

The men did not have to wait long for their subject to arrive. If she was tired after her address to the crowd in the Kinnaird Hall, on 6 December 1908, she did not show it. Indeed, standing at more than six feet, she was taller than most of the men in the room and positively intimidating – and that was before you even knew her reputation. Superintendent Gordon, as the senior officer, spoke first. He told Carrie Amelia Nation, of Washington, District of Columbia, and Councillor Edwin Scrymgeour, of Dundee, that a formal complaint had been made against them for a breach of the peace. The police, he said, were investigating the allegation and could well charge them both. The offence was said to have taken place at four different locations, including at the splendidly named Bodega on Murraygate and the Buffet on High Street. All four locations had one thing in common: they were licensed to sell alcohol. Nation and Scrymgeour both had, Superintendent Gordon suggested, best prepare their defence.

Like Scrymgeour, Carrie Nation had expected the police to turn up. It was, for better or worse, a common occurrence for her. Someone who was both affectionately and fearfully known as 'the Saloon Smasher' was inevitably going to be familiar with the authorities. She had been born in Kentucky in 1846 and was one of the most famous – and radical – members of the American anti-alcohol movement. For the last seven years she had gained national and international fame – or notoriety – for her 'hatchetations', where she would smash up pubs, bars and saloons with a hatchet embossed with the slogan 'Death to Rum'. Before settling on the hatchet as her bludgeon of choice she had used rocks, a billiard ball and even a sledgehammer borrowed from a blacksmith. The method, she thought, was immaterial – it was the result that counted. Scrymgeour described her as 'a woman of determined purpose, firmly believing her God-given call to do vigorous battle with the forces of hell upon earth'.[1] In her own words, she was 'a bulldog running along at the feet of Jesus, barking at what he doesn't like'.

The previous evening – a Saturday night – Nation and Scrymgeour had set out to tour what she called Dundee's 'hell houses'.[2] While on this occasion she refrained from physical violence, their prohibition pub crawl was still designed to cause confrontation and disruption. Guided by Scrymgeour, Nation stormed into pubs and bars, admonishing stunned drinkers and proprietors. At the first establishment they visited, Scrymgeour had to intervene to stop an angry publican physically removing Nation after she verbally assaulted customers. As the pair moved up the street, an increasingly large crowd followed, determined to catch a glimpse of this extraordinary man and woman, and their extraordinary protest. Among those following Nation was a gang of barefooted children, who she paused to pat on the head and warn of the dangers of alcohol. Reaching a 'fashionable bar', Nation turned her ire on the female bar staff pouring drinks for customers. 'It is a shame to womanhood,' she cried in her distinctive Kentucky drawl.[3] 'I call upon you not to remain in such a hellish business,' she added. Nation had time to briefly scold a young mother, who was sitting in the bar with her baby, before Scrymgeour ushered her back to her lodgings.

Even after the events at the Kinnaird Hall, where the police had informed her she might be charged, Nation remained nonchalant and unrepentant. 'I am ready for them,' she told a reporter for the *Evening Telegraph* in the lobby of her hotel the day after her visit from the police.[4] 'If [this] case does come on I'll have no lawyers to defend me. I have no need for lawyers. If they take me to court it will be a great advertisement for prohibition [and], you know, there is nothing like advertisement.' Perhaps heeding Nation's advice, the police in Dundee decided it would be better for everyone – not least the city's publicans – if the matter was quietly dropped. Nation and Scrymgeour were free to go.

Nation's visit shocked and appalled many in Dundee. Scrymgeour himself would describe it as 'never-to-be-forgotten'. Certainly, while the city had an active temperance movement, such direct action against the drink trade was unprecedented – and yet, given recent events, not entirely unexpected. Since his emergence in Dundee politics almost a decade previously, Scrymgeour had become renowned for his outspoken attacks and uncompromising and unique brand of politics. After Nation's visit, many were left wondering – somewhat fearfully – what Scrymgeour and his new Scottish Prohibition Party might do next.

The Scottish Prohibition Party was entirely a creation of the Scrymgeours – but it owed almost as much to his father, James, as it did to Edwin. Born in Kirriemuir, north of Dundee, James had an unlikely upbringing for someone whose future would be spent confronting vice and promoting religious faith. His father – Edwin's grandfather – ran a small business as the town's local greengrocer. But this respectable façade was in fact a mere front to cover his activities supporting smuggling operations around Glen Prosen, north of Kirriemuir. His speciality was providing barley and molasses to traffickers to avoid duties – but the business came to a crashing halt when King George IV dispatched a unit of dragoons to cut off the smuggler's operation. Without his illicit income, Edwin's grandfather struggled to make ends meet and, in 1840, was forced to move with his wife and son James to Dundee, where he took on work in one of the city's many warehouses.

Perhaps still reeling from the effects of being caught on the wrong side of the law, James showed no interest in following his father's criminal footsteps. Instead, he dedicated himself to learning, attending evening classes to make up for his lack of formal education. James soon became a prominent figure among the city's more intellectual inhabitants, helping to found the grandly named Dundee Literary Institute, which met to discuss literature in the city's coffeehouses. Professionally, he found work with the local newspaper publisher John Leng & Co., which was run by Sir John Leng, a Liberal Party MP in Dundee. This role not only introduced him to journalism but brought him and his family into contact with politics and politicians.

James's primary interest, however, was not literature and publishing but temperance. In a pamphlet published after his death in 1887 he was described – in a depiction that could just as easily be of Edwin – as 'an uncompromising champion of total abstinence from intoxicating liquors in every shape or form'.[5] This opposition to alcohol partly stemmed from personal experience. While attending a wedding near Kirriemuir aged nine, James was encouraged by other guests to drink whisky and was soon 'rolling helplessly under the influence'. Admonished by his uncle, he vowed never to drink again, even refusing to drink a glass of wine a day when it was prescribed by his doctor.*

As he grew up amid the poverty of Dundee, James began to see alcohol not just as a personal but also a social vice. These views were strengthened and encouraged by his devout Methodism. James and his wife, Jeanette, were active members of the Wesleyan Church, which championed abolitionism, but he maintained cordial relations with other denominations, including the Church of Scotland and the Free Church of Scotland, which regularly offered him a platform to

---

* As a chronic sufferer of deafness, he did once consent, on his doctor's recommendation, to cleaning his ears with drops of brandy. While initially effective, he found the treatment made his hearing worse over time, further entrenching his opposition to the use of alcohol in all forms.

share his views. His style of faith displayed a dogmatism that would be inherited by Edwin. In one prize-giving for Dundee schoolchildren, he ominously warned them: 'If you ever allow polluted thoughts to dwell on your minds . . . or if you ever do a dirty deed – this . . . bible will testify against you.'[6] 'Be industrious [and] be sober,' he added.

As well as his overtly religious engagements, he became a key figure in the Independent Order of Good Templars (IOGT), a semi-masonic group which worked to encourage abstinence. But his membership was not without its controversies, and he was an aggressive opponent of anything he viewed as likely to encourage alcoholism or other social vices. In one instance – and in a foreshadowing of Edwin's behaviour – James shocked Dundee society by organising a street demonstration against a festival honouring Scotland's national poet, the whisky-soaked Robert Burns. His attacks on a new theatre as place that would attract 'the worthless scum of all classes' also proved deeply controversial.[7]

It was into this potent mix of temperance, religion and firebrand activism that Edwin – affectionately known as Neddy – was born on 28 July 1866. He was the fifth of eight children, and his initial prospects were inauspicious, particularly compared to his more overtly ambitious siblings. He left school at the age of 14 and – despite inheriting both his father's religion and belief in the evils of alcohol – initially decided against committing himself to politics and prohibition. Instead, as often typical for young men then and now, he moved to London to find a profession. A stint with his two older brothers, George and Charles, who had founded a textile firm in the capital, ended abruptly when the business collapsed. Other roles with the Caledonian Railway and as a company clerk were equally short-lived, though he would retain his knowledge of shorthand and use it for personal notes and even postcards throughout his life. Despite being socially conservative and having a penchant for heavy three-piece suits, Scrymgeour found the office environment and tedium of employment difficult. His often abrasive and forthright manner did little to endear him to managers. By 1898, he had little to show for his stop-start career and he was left feeling frustrated and adrift. His marriage to Margaret six years earlier – although it was and would remain childless – had been his only real achievement to date. His passion, determination and stubbornness needed an outlet. Now

32 years old and back in Dundee, he needed to make a success of something.

The fact he found his calling in the temperance movement is, given his background, unsurprising. As James Scrymgeour's son, he was already well-known in abstinence circles and his reassimilation into Dundee Methodism was straightforward. Charismatic, uncompromising and energetic, Scrymgeour quickly became a high-profile anti-alcohol campaigner and, like his father previously, was regularly called on to speak against drink at church and public meetings. Much of this campaigning swung between being paternalistic and overtly judgemental, but Scrymgeour nevertheless was soon well ingratiated in many of Dundee's working-class communities. On one occasion, he made a bargain with a heavy drinker to give up his beloved pipe if the man would give up drinking.*

But Scrymgeour quickly became frustrated with what he perceived as a slow pace of change. He felt the IOGT, which he had joined as a boy and had been a mainstay of his father's career, was not radical enough, and he increasingly came to the view that compromise was almost as great a sin as drinking. He was, in his own words, a 'soul on fire for God and humanity' who had little time for 'damnable patience'.[8] IOGT members advocated and encouraged abstinence, but Scrymgeour now believed only the total prohibition of alcohol would be enough to end the scourge of drunkenness that so afflicted Dundee and other cities across the country. At the same time, Scrymgeour began to adopt socialist rhetoric and policies which were at odds with many of the more conservative members of the IOGT. He had joined the Independent Labour Party in 1895 and, while he found its secularism off-putting, nevertheless retained its socialist ethos even after his departure at the turn of the century. Prohibition, he believed, was not only necessary but the key first step to building a more equitable society.

Such a view would be dismissed by most people in the 21st century as fringe or unworkable – or, more likely, both. Yet, in the 19th and early 20th centuries, debates of increasing restrictions or even total bans on alcohol were part of mainstream political

* Whether the man did stop drinking is not recorded, but Scrymgeour never smoked again.

discourse. The Liberal Party had, for example, long supported offering communities a local referendum on whether to allow alcohol sales – often referred to as 'the local option'. After the Temperance Act in 1913, more than 35 local boroughs in Scotland chose to ban the sale of alcohol. Many of those communities that opposed the sale of alcohol took inspiration from the United States where, in 1920, total prohibition would famously be introduced. Scrymgeour himself maintained close relations with prohibitionists in the US. As well as Nation, he was in regular correspondence with Americans such as William Ferguson, the editor of the pro-Prohibition *Vindicator*, who in 1912 praised the 'virility' of Scrymgeour's anti-alcohol campaign.

Dundee as a city also had a particularly severe problem with alcoholism. In the early 20th century, Dundee had an estimated 30 per cent more deaths from alcohol abuse than the Scottish average. This was the result of a longstanding affinity with heavy drinking in the city. In the 1860s, the city had 'more pubs than bakers . . . more licensed victuallers [alcohol vendors] than clothing shops, and had more offences ascribed to drunkenness than all other crimes combined'.[9] Saturday evenings – pay day – were particularly bad for excessive drinking: 'Workers fought and brawled the length of the Overgate, the jostling heart of the medieval part of the city, and the police were kept busy with their specially constructed wheelbarrows carting away the casualties after the battles had subsided.'[10] Shrewd publicans also plied their customers with complementary salt fish to maintain their thirst. Amid such a severe situation – even Churchill observed that he had never seen such 'bestial drunkenness' as in Dundee[11] – Scrymgeour became tired of the delay and middle-class platitudes of the IOGT. In 1901, he finally led a breakaway movement, calling itself the Scottish Prohibition Party.

By breaking from the IOGT, Scrymgeour was rejecting the more moderate approach of his father, who had sought to help people abstain from alcohol and generally improve their own position, instead embarking on a more radical course that came to embrace 'eschatological fantasy, combined with a social and political critique'.[12] He rallied people, in his own words, around 'the inspirational manifesto of that Prime Minister whose love never dies'. Central to his appeal was his millennialism, which attracted working-class supporters from among the city's jute mills with a Christian-socialist faith that a new, better world was coming.

From the off, Scrymgeour exerted an almost messianic control over the burgeoning party and, by 1904, had cemented himself as its undisputed leader. He would remain such for the entire life of the party, which quickly took on an almost cult-like aura. Members were required to commit themselves to total abstinence from alcohol and support nothing short of total prohibition – they even had to wear 'purity badges' to symbolise their rejection of alcoholic sin. Party meetings took place on Sundays and opened with Scrymgeour or a guest reading from the Bible. Hymns were sung, and party members referred to each other as 'brother' and 'sister'. Dissent was not an option and, while chapters of the party sprung up in other Scottish cities – and efforts were made to expand the party even beyond Scotland's borders – it was always centred and headquartered in Dundee and around the charismatic personage of Scrymgeour. As leader, he immediately adopted a fire-and-brimstone message more absolute and extreme than anything Dundee – or Scotland – had previously seen. His rhetorical style was a natural inheritance from his father – but the language was a powerful mix of prohibition, socialism and evangelical millennialism. Given the Scottish Prohibition Party was the offspring of a schism with the IOGT, Scrymgeour came to value loyalty and ideological purity above all else.

As is the case with any political rupture, Scrymgeour's decision to reject the IOGT and temperance led to significant bad blood between the former anti-alcohol comrades. This was partly a result of ideological differences, which could not be reconciled, but Scrymgeour also held personal responsibility. In the years following the split, he proceeded to attack his former colleagues with a vitriol and venom that he rarely used even against his most implacable opponents. The attacks were so strong that many supporters of temperance or prohibition felt compelled to respond in kind. One letter from the prohibitionist Edward Tennyson Smith, leader of the Christian Crusade Against Liquor Traffic, is typical of the exchanges between Scrymgeour and his former fellow travellers. Tennyson Smith accused Scrymgeour of 'gross misrepresentation and wicked falsehood combined with blushing impudence and brazen egoism and bombast', dismissing his treatment of others in the temperance movement as 'ludicrous'.[13]

Scrymgeour, however, relished such controversy. His view is perhaps best represented by one of his favourite biblical verses, Mark 13:13: 'And ye shall be hated of all men for my name's sake.' Scrymgeour was determined that there should be only one prohibition party – and he was not worried if he was hated for it because he believed he was doing God's work.

In spite – or perhaps because – of his extreme views, the Scottish Prohibition Party initially faced ridicule as a fringe outfit and struggled to be taken seriously, not least by the press. Indeed, Scrymgeour's own eulogy to Nation after her death in 1911 gives an interesting insight into his views on his own nascent political career: 'The British press said Mrs Nation was not taken seriously, which, of course, is one of the best proofs that she was in earnest.'[14] But soon after the founding of his party, Scrymgeour – convinced he was doing God's work – set about silencing his critics.

In 1905, he secured his first electoral success, winning a seat as a councillor, representing Dundee's fifth ward. While this electoral victory was a personal triumph for Scrymgeour, Dundee's voters had already made their concerns about alcohol clear in previous votes; an analysis of Dundee council elections between 1875 and 1910 shows that candidates who were publicans enjoyed only a 43 per cent success rate at the ballot box, compared to an average of 66 per cent for other small business owners.

More local election victories for other Scottish Prohibition Party candidates followed, with the party's anti-alcohol message finding some support among the disaffected working class. In 1906, he utilised his father's other gifts – literature and publishing – and began producing *The Scottish Prohibitionist*, a weekly newspaper. With an accessible style and reputation for impartiality – or, at least, attacking everyone equally – it soon proved popular and provided a useful income for Scrymgeour's fledgling party. On its masthead it carried the slogan, which would be adopted by the Scottish Prohibition Party itself, 'Vote as You Pray' – a perfect summation of Scrymgeour's fusion of righteous religion and uncompromising politics.

If the Dundee establishment or the wider temperance movement had hoped the responsibilities of elected office would cause Scrymgeour to moderate his tone, they were to be sorely mistaken. Nation's visit was just one example of how Scrymgeour terrorised

Dundee's political and social milieu. He was repeatedly ruled out of order or suspended from council meetings, most often for accusing other councillors of being liars and dramatically refusing to withdraw the allegations when asked. On one occasion a fellow member was so enraged with Scrymgeour's comments that he attempted to strangle him mid-session. Bob Stewart, who acted as Scrymgeour's election agent and was elected as a Scottish Prohibition Party councillor in 1908, remembered Scrymgeour's disruption fondly: 'We certainly enlivened the council meetings. The first night I took my seat we were both suspended for being offenders against decorum.'[15] Such was Scrymgeour's reputation for drama and disorder that council meetings became something of a popular spectacle, and by 1908 crowds began to assemble two hours before meetings in the hope of securing a coveted space in the public gallery. While much of his behaviour was about point-scoring, Scrymgeour did not cause trouble purely for trouble's sake and, despite his bombast, he began to develop a reputation as an uncompromising pursuer of corrupt and ineffective office-holders and officials.

For a man of Scrymgeour's fanaticism, however, the council could only deliver so much. If he wanted to change the law and fully deliver prohibition, he needed to represent Dundee in the House of Commons. Now only Churchill stood in his way.

Chapter 6

Enter, Clementine
1908

On the evening of 24 August 1908, Churchill sped north towards
Scotland, comfortably ensconced in the compartment of the sleeper
train from London to Inverness. It was a journey he would become
intimately familiar with over the ensuing 15 years, as by far his most
preferred way to visit Dundee. But on this occasion, it was not, in fact,
his new constituents that he was travelling to see. He had a far more
delicate, personal mission to attend to. It was one that would take him
to the village of Cruden Bay, on the Aberdeenshire coast, and from
there to the remote Slains Castle, set in the cliffs above the North
Sea.* Churchill knew he would need to utilise all his reserves of tact
and resoluteness if he were to be successful. Tomorrow, he had to tell
his closest female friend – his admirer of more than two years – that
he was engaged to another woman, and that they would be married
in three weeks.

When Clementine Hozier first met Churchill, she was far from
impressed. 'He never uttered a word and was very gauche,' Clementine
recollected, long after they were married, of their first meeting in
1904.[1] 'He never asked me for a dance, he never asked me to have
supper with him – he just stood and stared.' Fortunately for Churchill,
however, first impressions were not everything and when they met
again at a dinner party in March 1908 – just before the Manchester
North West by-election – he was 'engrossed' by her, and *vice versa*. 'He

---

* Bram Stoker wrote the last pages of *Dracula* at the village hotel in Cruden Bay, and
Slains Castle is therefore often cited as the inspiration for Count Dracula's lair in
Transylvania.

paid no attention to [his host],' Ruth Lee, a wealthy American and fellow attendee at the dinner reported in her diary, adding: 'He became suddenly and entirely absorbed in Miss Clementine Hozier ... and paid her such marked and exclusive attention the whole evening that everyone was talking about it.'[2] Never one to let an opportunity slip, Churchill persuaded his mother – Jennie – to invite Clementine and her mother, Lady Blanche Hozier, for a weekend to Salisbury Hall, the house where Jennie was currently staying in Hertfordshire. By the end of the weekend, Churchill had decided that Clementine was the woman he wanted to marry.

In Edwardian marriage stakes she was, however, not necessarily an ideal candidate to be wed to someone of Churchill's pedigree and status. Despite an aristocratic lineage, her recent family life had been turbulent and – in a descriptor used by a number of her biographers – 'rackety'.[3] Lady Blanche's marriage to Henry Hozier had not been a happy one, and questions over Clementine's paternity remain unanswered to this day. As Mary Soames bluntly put it of her grandmother: 'There is no doubt that Blanche Hozier was promiscuous ... gossip had it that she had at least nine lovers.'[4] It is not certain how much Churchill knew, or would have cared, about this family soap opera – but it seems likely very little. Churchill, after all, was no stranger to parents having extramarital relationships, which in any case were a relatively common – if unmentioned – occurrence in late Victorian and Edwardian Britain.

The Hoziers' marriage ended in separation in 1891, and Lady Blanche – already not well-off – was left practically penniless and eventually retreated with Clementine, for financial reasons, to live in the town of Dieppe, on the Normandy coast. Their situation was so severely strained financially that Clementine often had to make her own clothes and hats. This is not to suggest she was totally destitute – Clementine's wealthy great aunt, Lady St Helier, helped ingratiate her with 'high society' in London. Indeed, it was at a dinner party held at Lady St Helier's house that Churchill became 'entirely absorbed' with Clementine in 1908. But there was no escaping the fact that, for Churchill, he would be marrying a woman of few financial means and a dubious family life.

But Clementine's positives far outweighed these relatively minor negatives. Then 22 – more than 11 years Churchill's junior – she was regularly cited as a beauty by contemporaries, with a tall and slender physique and fair features. This is attested to by the number of suitors for her hand that she had already rebuffed by the time of the fateful 1908 dinner party. She had broken off three engagements to be married – poor Sidney Peel, grandson of the famous Sir Robert, was twice rebuffed – and pressure was mounting for her to settle down. The engagement to her second suitor, a wealthy civil servant named Lionel Earle, went on long enough for wedding gifts to begin arriving before, fortunately for Churchill, Clementine decided against it.

Far more important than her appearance, Clementine also had a formidable mind and a strong character equal to Churchill's own. Her early education had been disrupted and, as was typical for a woman of her social standing at the end of the 19th century, she went to finishing school rather than university. Despite this, she retained a great interest in the world around her and could boast numerous intellectual achievements, such as fluency in French. Her ability at the language was so strong – presumably aided by her time living in Dieppe – that she was able to earn money as a private tutor. 'What a comfort and pleasure it was to me to meet a girl with so much intellectual quality and such strong reserves of noble sentiment,' Churchill wrote after their weekend at Salisbury House.[5]

Clementine also had strong political views and a mature social conscience. Despite Churchill's evolution in the coming decades, she privately remained an admirer of liberalism and progressive politics throughout her life. This concern for those less fortunate than herself undoubtedly stemmed from her own experience of growing up in strained circumstances. Being so close to luxury and yet being unable to have it must have been particularly agonising as a young woman, but it was an experience Clementine never forgot. Indeed, part of her later success as a campaigner in Dundee was a result of her empathy and ability to relate to those struggling to make ends meet. Clementine was also an impassioned supporter of women's rights, particularly the right to vote. Before she married Churchill, she regularly dressed in the suffragettes' 'uniform' of a shirt and tie and she continued to support the cause even as they disrupted her husband's campaigns in Dundee.[6]

Far from objecting to his wife's differing views, Churchill, it seems, actively welcomed private debate and respected Clementine's intellectual independence – although, in this instance, it did not change his public position. Crucially for Churchill, Clementine married her bright mind and interest in politics with sound judgement. This was proved repeatedly in Dundee, where her ability to read a situation and understand the political implications of a decision far outweighed her husband's. On several occasions, it was Clementine's interventions that helped Churchill understand the political and personal dimensions at play. As Mary Soames wrote after Clementine's death: 'Clementine possessed that most important ingredient in a politician's make up – good political instinct. She was also, on the whole, a better judge of people than [Churchill].'[7]

For Churchill, the newly elected member for Dundee, Clementine also had another, more practical advantage – strong links with Scotland. Lady Blanche was the eldest child of the 10th Earl of Airlie, whose family seat, Airlie Castle, is just outside Kirriemuir and less than 20 miles north of Dundee. The title was created by Charles I and the earls of Airlie fought for the royalists during the Wars of the Three Kingdoms, and later for the Jacobites during the 1715 rising. Later that century, however, the family was pardoned and assimilated into the British establishment proper. While Airlie Castle had been sacked and largely destroyed in 1640, the family later erected a Georgian mansion on the same site, incorporating some of the ruined castle, and it was here that Clementine spent her summers. In the company of the Dowager Countess of Airlie – Lady Blanche's mother – Clementine explored north-east Scotland and became familiar with the land and people in and around Dundee. Clementine also became versed in another Scottish pursuit – golf – which she learnt to play to a good standard.

That Churchill's love interest had such Scottish connections was well known and did not go unnoticed in political circles. Ritchie, as would become a common occurrence in the years ahead, summed up the situation well in his spidery, hand-written note of congratulation to Churchill on their engagement: 'A Scottish constituency showed its wisdom and sound judgement in electing you to represent it in parliament. You have reciprocated their action by wooing and winning an ancestor of one of our noblest and best beloved families in Scotland.'[8] He added: 'The House of Airlie and Dundee have many ties in common [and] your marriage with Miss Hozier will make another.'

Despite these obvious political advantages, it would be wrong to suggest that Clementine's Scottish links – though extremely useful – played any role in Churchill's decision to court her. After all, the fateful dinner party in March 1908 took place before even the Manchester North West by-election. It would have taken enormous prescience – not to mention pessimism – to predict he would lose that contest and need to fight a seat in Scotland. Yet there is no doubt – as Ritchie's letter shows – that Clementine's heritage was a useful advantage to Churchill once he secured his 'life seat' in Dundee. Certainly, as with her 'rackety' family background, he would have been aware of her lineage before their engagement. Clementine gave Churchill a direct family connection to the very area he now represented, nullifying any suggestion he was a carpetbagger. This would have been particularly the case in the early 20th century, when there was significantly more reverence for local grandees than there is today. Her association and familiarity with the area around Dundee may also help explain why, in future years, she was so confident campaigning there on her own – and so determined to ensure Churchill retained the seat.

Churchill proposed to Clementine on 11 August 1908, in an ornamental Greek temple in the grounds of Blenheim Palace, his family seat. While taking shelter from the rain, the new cabinet minister offered her a ring containing two diamonds, centred on a large ruby. Even for a man as self-confident as Churchill, it is likely he was extremely nervous. He had fallen for women before and been knocked back. Indeed, the fact he missed meeting Clementine for a morning walk earlier that day – this almost made her pack up and leave Blenheim – is indicative of his anxious state. Yet, he need not have worried, with Clementine writing to relatives in the aftermath of the proposal that her life was now 'heavenly'.[9]

But all was not quite as it seemed. Churchill knew that there was one woman who would be deeply disappointed by the news of his engagement, and he felt duty-bound to speak to her in person before his marriage on 12 September. That was why, with his wedding day just three weeks away, he set off from London for Aberdeenshire, to join Violet Asquith on her family holiday.

Churchill had first met Violet Asquith, the daughter of the Prime Minister and his political patron, at a dinner party in the summer of

1906, when he was approaching 32 and she just 19. 'I found myself sitting next to this young man who seemed to me quite different from any young man I had ever met,' she recalled after Churchill's death, making clear that she enjoyed a significantly better first impression of him than Clementine had.[10] She added: 'Until the end of dinner I listened to him spellbound. I can remember thinking: *this* is what people mean when they talk of "seeing stars" – that is what I am doing now [original emphasis].'

While elements of this account have been disputed – there is no reference to the dinner party taking place in her otherwise meticulously collated diaries and letters – there is little doubt that Violet very quickly became enamoured, if not actually in love, with Churchill. But while the pair developed a close friendship, Churchill's feelings were purely platonic. This may partly have been a concern on Churchill's part of not wanting to mix politics with pleasure. Becoming romantically involved with the Prime Minister's daughter might have advantages for an aspiring politician, but if the relationship went wrong, it could have equally severe disadvantages. The reality, however, is probably simpler – that Churchill greatly enjoyed Violet's company, but as a good friend and nothing more.

When news of the engagement reached her at Slains Castle before Churchill's arrival, Violet was devastated. She immediately wrote – with real venom – to her friend Venetia Stanley, who was also Clementine's first cousin and bridesmaid:* 'I must say I am much gladder for her sake than I am sorry for his. His wife could never be more to him than an ornamental sideboard as I have often said and she is unexacting enough to mind not being more. Whether he will ultimately mind her being as stupid as an *owl* I don't know – it is a danger no doubt – but for the moment she will have a rest at least from making her own clothes ... [original emphasis]'.[11]

What exactly Churchill said to Violet during his visit to Slains is unrecorded, but he seems to have persuaded her that there was

---

* Venetia also enjoyed a close relationship with Violet's father, the Prime Minister, 35 years her senior. In the coming years, he became increasingly infatuated with her and emotionally dependent on her. They exchanged hundreds of letters, some of which Asquith would pen during cabinet meetings. Despite the intensity of the relationship, historians generally agree the relationship was not physical, although some contemporaries believed it was.

nothing to stop them remaining good friends. They spent several days exploring the rugged Aberdeenshire coastline around the castle, often taking precarious and treacherous routes over boulders and giant rocks. At one point Violet fell and cut her head. After several days, Churchill clearly felt he had done his duty to his young admirer and returned to London to marry Clementine. His departure, however, plunged Violet into despair once again. Not only did she refuse to attend the wedding but, a week afterwards, she vanished along the cliffs and rock formations she had earlier been exploring with Churchill. Her disappearance prompted a huge search, including volunteers from the village and local fishermen, who used their boats to search the treacherous swell beneath the cliffs. Violet was only located after midnight and it soon became apparent that, far from having an accident, her disappearance may well have been a cry for help. Certainly, her mother, Margot, had little sympathy, branding it a 'foolish and dangerous escapade'.[12]

It would take months for Violet to fully recover from the news of Churchill's marriage and in October she had to be talked back from taking a surprise trip to Dundee to join him – unrequested – on the platform at the Scottish Liberal Congress. But Violet did eventually accept Clementine's role in Churchill's life and move on.* Writing of Clementine after Churchill's death, and in stark contrast to her actual feelings at the time, she said: 'His wife was already my friend ... she had come out [into society] a few years before me, and as I gazed upon her finished, flawless beauty and reflected on her wide experience of the world ... I felt awe-struck admiration. Awe vanished, admiration stayed, and with it began a friendship which no vicissitude has ever shaken.'[13]

The wedding between Churchill and Clementine took place on 12 September 1908, at St Margaret's Church, in the shadow of Westminster Abbey. It was, unsurprisingly, a high-society affair, with peers and politicians filling the pews. But Churchill also invited a significant contingent of guests from Dundee. More than a dozen senior political figures from the city were asked to attend, including Ritchie and

---

* In 1916 she married Maurice Bonham Carter, creating a remarkable political and artistic dynasty, including her granddaughter, Helena Bonham Carter.

Dundee's Lord Provost, William Longair. Churchill also offered further invitations to 'rank and file' Dundee residents who had expressed an interest in attending. While the exact total of invitees from his constituency is not given, *The Courier* reported that 'quite a number' attended the service.[14] Dundee's council also agreed to present the happy couple with a silver cup – possibly a traditional Scottish quaich – as a wedding gift. For those unable to make the journey to London, a party was given at the Dundee Liberal Association, with the building decorated with flags and bunting. Once the completion of the nuptials had been confirmed, the delighted revellers despatched their MP a telegram of congratulation. After a successful ceremony – dubbed the 'Wedding of the Year' by the *Daily Mirror* – Churchill and Clementine stayed the night at Blenheim Palace, before taking a quick honeymoon in northern Italy, first at Lake Maggiore and then the enchanting city of Venice. Within a month, Clementine was pregnant with their first child.

Yet, for all his love for Clementine, Churchill could only be briefly distracted by domestic affairs. With a constituency, a companion and a cabinet post, he was now desperate to get to work. He was alive with reforming ideas and was willing to work tirelessly to see them enacted. But his efforts on the national stage would test his relationship with Dundee for the very first time.

Chapter 7

'Not at Home'

1909

Islay Murray arrived at the Board of Trade in the late afternoon. It was a short walk to the Whitehall office from Dover House, where he had earlier met Lord Pentland, the Secretary for Scotland, and the newly appointed Lord Advocate, Alexander Ure. Murray was in an upbeat mood – the meetings had been a success and his companion, the secretary of the Dundee Landlord's and House Factors Association, Andrew Burns Petrie, was impressed. Perhaps, they cheerfully mused, it would be possible after all to amend the House-Letting and Rating (Scotland) Bill, which they – as landlords themselves – would describe diplomatically as well-meaning but misguided. Certainly, they felt it had been worth enlightening parliamentarians on the likely impacts of the bill in Dundee specifically, and Scotland more generally. The pair were not particularly concerned that they had failed to meet Churchill at the Houses of Parliament earlier in the day. The member for Dundee had his cabinet responsibilities to attend to and there would be plenty of time to lobby him at the Board of Trade before their overnight train back to Dundee later that evening.

Murray presented his card to the waiting attendant at the Board of Trade reception. He apologised – they did not have an appointment, but he explained that they only intended to detain the minister for a few minutes to outline their concerns with the bill. As eminent constituents, he expressed his hope that this would not be an imposition – and then sat down to wait. Five minutes turned to 10 and Murray began to pace the waiting room, his earlier jubilance draining steadily with each step. After 30 minutes, he challenged the attendant on whether he had passed Churchill his card. He was reassured that the President of the Board of Trade did indeed know he was waiting.

It was only after an hour that an indignant Murray – conscious not just of his imminent train, but also his wounded pride – stormed out of the Board of Trade. Such affrontery, he told himself as he marched back along Whitehall, would have to be answered for.

Back in Dundee, Murray immediately informed *The Courier* about the snub from Churchill. Under the headline 'Not at Home', the newspaper stated: 'Repeated complaints have been made at the treatment meted out to representatives of the constituency by the President of the Board of Trade.'[1] In a poorly disguised briefing from Murray, it suggested delegations of city patriarchs were either refused a meeting outright or 'wearied of waiting for the summons to appear before him'. It suggested a delegation from the council had been similarly snubbed by Churchill earlier in the year.

The situation was further inflamed by an anonymous follow-up letter, again printed in *The Courier*, which was signed, somewhat over-dramatically, by 'One Who Has Not Found Mr Churchill At Home'.[2] The author suggested Dundonians had been fooled by the 'fine sentimental talk at election times', highlighting 'that public representatives and other gentlemen sent on deputations from Dundee have to wait for hours, and have to leave disgusted at the treatment meted out to them'. The incensed author concluded: '[Churchill] does not even have the ordinary courtesy to reply to letters of local importance.'

The articles sent shockwaves through the Dundee Liberal Association. This was a contemptible attack, implicitly questioning the character not only of their representative but also a senior figure in the Liberal government. For Ritchie, who had invested so much in Churchill's candidature, it was not only outrageous but positively dangerous. This was exactly the sort of issue his internal critics in the Liberal Association had warned of. If it was not addressed quickly, it was not only Churchill's reputation on the line but his own as well. But the problem with the 'Not at Home' briefing, Ritchie immediately recognised, was that – like all the best political attacks – people might very well believe it.

It was certainly true that Churchill rarely visited his Scottish constituency, generally limiting himself to one or two trips a year, plus elections. When he did visit, he complained bitterly about the lack of creature comforts. 'This hotel is a great trial to me,' he wrote to

Clementine, from the Queen's Hotel, on Dundee's Perth Road.[3] 'Yesterday morning I had half eaten a kipper when a huge maggot crept out and flashed his teeth at me. Today I could find nothing nourishing for lunch but pancakes. Such are the trials which great and good men endure in the service of their country.' He added, more than a touch wistfully: 'I hope the Burgundy [wine] has reached you safely and that you are lapping it with judicious determination.'

Yet, while Churchill complained about Dundee hospitality – in the case of the kipper, it would appear, justifiably – he did at least attempt to enjoy himself. One receipt from the Queen's Hotel, during a two-day visit in 1911, is typical.[4] It shows that Churchill spent almost exactly the same amount* on food, wine, spirits and cigars as he did on the hotel room itself. Additional costs were incurred for the luxuries of log fires in his room and hot baths. While cost does not necessarily equate to quality, such extravagance at least suggests a 'judicious determination' to seek it out.

Aside from the culinary privations making visits a hardship, Dundee's location made regular travel in the early 20th century difficult. Its situation, on the banks of the River Tay, on Scotland's east coast, is quite spectacular but relatively inaccessible. Even today, connectivity to and from the city remains a headache for policymakers. But in 1908, the city was accessible from London by overnight train, which took more than 10 hours – and that was when it ran on time – or steamship. As Churchill himself explained to Ritchie – when contemplating a brief visit to Dundee and having by then served more than a decade as MP for the city – 'the effort of travelling two consecutive nights is considerable'.[5]

The situation was further exacerbated by the limitations of early 20th-century communication, which heightened the sense of isolation. As a cabinet minister – and a particularly active and engaged one at that – Churchill loathed being out of the loop and potentially missing crucial political developments. Churchill, as he had honestly outlined in his 1908 election address, always felt constituency interests were subservient to national ones – apart from also being more interesting to him – and behaved as such. Indeed, as one of the government's best and most prominent voices, Churchill's services were

* Approximately £220 in 2017.

much in demand across the country, including during election periods, to make the case for the Liberal government. It simply was not feasible to marry these commitments with regular travel to Dundee. Churchill expressed similar views himself in a letter to his Dundee agent, Peter Husband, in 1911: 'It should be remembered that these last three years have been a time of exceptional and almost unprecedented political strain [and] that I have had, in addition to the burden of great offices, to take one of the most prominent parts in platform work [public speaking] all over the country.'[6]

Later in his time as MP for Dundee – particularly after the end of the First World War – travel for international conferences further limited opportunities for constituency engagements. For example, in the age before commercial air travel, Churchill's attendance at the 1921 Cairo Conference meant he was absent from the country for more than a month and a half, despite the conference itself lasting just nine days. Such long absences were far from unusual; Lloyd George did not chair a single cabinet meeting as Prime Minister in the first half of 1919, as he was staying in Paris to take part in the negotiations that led to the Treaty of Versailles.

Despite his undoubtedly busy schedule, it is also the case that Churchill had little capacity for 'working the constituency'. He simply had no interest in the sort of mundane constituency engagements that involve gladhanding prominent city figures or opening new buildings. One effusive invitation, running to three pages, to open the Dundee Horticultural Society's annual show in 1909, was immediately dismissed with a large 'NO' scribbled across the front page.[7] Instead, Churchill believed his best service to his constituency was reserving his most impactful speeches for his visits, using Dundee as the crucible to express his grandest visions. As he wrote to Husband: 'It is, I imagine, beyond dispute that in the two years and nine months that I have been connected with Dundee I have addressed more public meetings than ever were addressed by any of the former members for Dundee within a similar period.'[8]

Churchill was not unique in his attitude to constituency business or visits. In the early 20th century, there was little of what would now be termed casework to occupy an MP's time – and, in a seat such as Dundee, there were two members, further dividing the workload. Certainly, Churchill's fellow Dundee member – the Labour MP

Alexander Wilkie – was equally chastised by his opponents for rarely visiting the constituency, while a similar attack would be launched against his successor, E.D. Morel. The welfare state was nascent and there were few issues where an individual felt the need to contact an MP. Rather, MPs chose to focus on the big issues facing their constituencies, such as support for major nearby industries, or national questions.

For his part, Churchill did sometimes show himself willing to engage with local issues both large and small when they appeared – and particularly when they appealed to his individual character. For instance, in 1912 Churchill made personal efforts to secure a new range of field guns for the Dundee Boys' Brigade.[9] More typical were his attempts to improve the macro-outlook for Dundee businesses and citizens, such as his efforts to persuade the Postmaster General, Herbert Samuel, to improve Dundee's telegram service.[10] In common with many other MPs at the time, Churchill also personally donated to local charities and other good causes in the constituency in a bid to win favour with electors. The groups supported by Churchill were wide-ranging, from the Dundee Amateur Gymnastics Society to the Dundee Royal Infirmary. Subsidising local organisations was a common feature of early 20th-century electoral politics, allowing a candidate or MP to nurture support without impacting campaign spending limits, which had been introduced in 1883. Indeed, there was no question that such donations were philanthropic – their purpose was expressly political – and this was the case with Churchill's donations as well. In one case, Husband advised against supporting a particular group because he did not believe 'we could count on getting any special support from [them]'.[11]

Churchill's financial dealings with Dundee were not purely him dispensing patronage – he also received significant sums from local benefactors. One particularly generous constituent was Sir James Caird, who had made a fortune in the city's jute industry and was keen to support the causes of free trade and Home Rule.* On

---

* Caird also supported a variety of wider causes, including Ernest Shackleton's doomed *Endurance* expedition to the South Pole. The lifeboat that allowed Shackleton to escape Elephant Island and save the lives of his stranded crew was named the *James Caird* in recognition of his support for the mission.

Churchill's advice he agreed to fund lectures and pamphlets promoting the subjects, and between 1910 and his death in 1916 he donated approximately £33,500* to fund this activity. Such was the strength of his relationship with Churchill that Caird donated the money to him personally, rather than to the Liberal Party itself or the party's chief whip, as might have been expected. The potential for corruption or misappropriation of funds in such an arrangement is clearly substantial, but there is no evidence Churchill did anything improper with the money and that he dispensed it as Caird intended. As one financial historian stated: 'Despite the temptations of handling funds that dwarfed his own means, there is no sign that Churchill conflated any of Caird's money with his own at this stage and his calculations of his net worth during the period scrupulously excluded it.'[12]

In his dealings with the constituency, Churchill relied heavily on the local knowledge of people like Husband and Ritchie, who had a familiarity with the city that he could never hope to attain. But he was also aided by a diligent and efficient office, which under the stewardship of Edward – known as Eddie – Marsh, helped to manage his constituency business effectively. Born in 1872, Marsh had been educated at Westminster School and Cambridge University before entering the civil service, initially in the Colonial Office. He enjoyed an instant rapport with Churchill, who he began working with in late 1905, and worked as his private secretary for many years. Churchill's son, Randolph, described Marsh and his father as 'inseparable'.[13]

Despite Marsh's best efforts, there were occasions with constituency business where – as in national politics – Churchill allowed his passions to overrule his better political judgement. This mostly manifested itself in robust – but sometimes outright offensive – responses to appeals from constituents. A good example of such correspondence can be found in late 1918. A left-wing Christian minister and ally of Scrymgeour's, Richard Lee, wrote to Churchill questioning the government's strategy in concluding the First World War. An incensed Churchill instructed Marsh to respond. 'I am desired by Mr Churchill to say, in answer to your letter, that while taking every allowance for your strong feeling he considers your letter somewhat wanting both in moderation and in charity,' Marsh wrote.[14] 'He desires me to return

---

* Approximately £2.7 million in 2017.

it to you in order that you may re-read it in the light of this observa-
tion, and see how far it conforms to or falls short of those ideals of
"Freedom, Friendship and Truth" which you profess to serve.' Not
satisfied that he had made his point strongly enough, Marsh concluded:
'[Churchill] desires me to put it to you whether your own judgement,
having been proved so wrong on a matter of ascertainable fact, ought
not to lend you to form your views with greater caution as well as
express them with more sobriety.' It is worth noting that the recipient
of this literary onslaught was a close friend of Scrymgeour's and may
well have been known to Churchill's office as a troublemaker.
Certainly, it is very much the exception rather than the rule in his
constituency correspondence, which is otherwise overwhelmingly
professional and civil in tone.

Nevertheless, the perception that Churchill was aloof persisted and
did clearly impact his dealings with constituents. One example is the
1908 case of Private Jim Leishman, who believed he had wrongly
been denied an army pension. But rather than write directly to
Churchill, Leishman instead brought the case to Scrymgeour's attention, because 'it would have a much better chance of consideration
from Mr Churchill than if it came simply from myself'.[15] Scrymgeour
– presumably with some delight – then forwarded the correspondence to Churchill, who promptly actioned it. This deference towards
Churchill will be partly based on the prominent class distinctions at
the time, as well as an awareness that he was a significant government
figure. But they also point to a detachedness from ordinary Dundonians
that, in time, would prove politically dangerous for the city's Liberal
member.

In 1909, knowing that both Churchill and his reputations were on the
line with the 'Not at Home' allegations, Ritchie sprang into action.
He asked his friend, William Smith, a Liberal Party organiser in the
city, to urgently write to Churchill and appraise him of the situation.
'This subject is being used for all it is worth against [you] – with
effect,' Smith wrote.[16] 'I think it would be well if some action was
taken.' He said he had heard the rumours, repeated in *The Courier*, that
a delegation from the council – including the Lord Provost – had 'a
similar experience' to Murray, before closing ominously: 'Undoubtedly
a very unfavourable impression is being created against you.'

While Smith worked to appraise Churchill of the manoeuvres against him, Ritchie organised a concerted push-back against the allegations themselves. He first arranged a counter letter refuting Murray's claims to appear in *The Courier* as quickly as possible. George Smith – described in a letter to Churchill's office as 'an important and influential man in Dundee'[17] – agreed to take on the task. After appealing pointedly to the editor's sense of 'justice and fair play' and emphasising, not entirely truthfully, that he was 'completely unknown' to Churchill, he set about refuting Murray's version of events: 'On Monday – the same day as [Murray's delegation] were there – and having no appointment, I sent in my card to the attendant ... [and 25 minutes later] ... Mr Churchill came in smiling as usual. I told him what I wanted, he listened patiently and gave me the answer I had hoped for.'[18] He then added: 'He was in no hurry or flurry but to me ... he was the ideal gentleman.'

A spectre of doubt had now been successfully cast over Murray's version of events. Indeed, the evidence suggests that even the earlier incident, when the town councillors claimed to have been snubbed, may have been embellished by Churchill's opponents. On 27 February, one of that party, William Don, wrote to Churchill's office asking if he could meet their delegation on Tuesday 2 March at 11.30 a.m., before they attended a conference nearby from midday. On the top of Don's note, an official in Churchill's office wrote: 'I have said you are engaged at 11.30am ... but would like to find an opportunity to see them some time in the morning.'[19] Whether or not this reply was sent, or if a new meeting time could be agreed, is impossible to tell. But this correspondence suggests at the very least Churchill was willing to try to accommodate the delegation, even at short notice.

With holes now emerging in Murray's account, Churchill's allies in Dundee put the screws to him. Ritchie and Smith visited Murray and gently suggested that, given the inconsistencies now emerging around his account, might it be best if it was 'clarified'? Murray readily agreed and on 1 June he published, this time in his own name, the following letter in *The Courier*: 'A paragraph appeared in your paper setting forth an alleged grievance of mine against Mr Churchill as to want of courtesy on his part in not meeting me. In all fairness to Mr Churchill, I have no grievance against that gentleman. Our deputation did not proceed to London to see Mr Churchill.

We made no appointment to see him, nor did the business on hand particularly concern him.'[20]

A cutting of the piece was sent from the Dundee Liberal Association to Churchill, along with a note of political – but also personal – relief. This attack on Churchill's reputation had been successfully repelled, but the letter also contained a warning: 'A nasty feeling has been created in relation to this matter.'[21] Churchill's close lieutenant in London, his cousin Freddie Guest, agreed. Perhaps conscious that Churchill wanted a 'life seat', Guest said it was an 'absolute necessity' that he did not alienate prominent local people. It would be 'wise', Guest added pointedly, for '[Churchill] to go to Dundee'.[22]

Chapter 8

Our Man in Dundee

1909–1913

Churchill's Dundee was known as Juteopolis. The import, refinement and export of jute not only monopolised the city's economy, but its architecture and even its outlook. The city's skyline was dominated by the flumes of the mills, its streets filled with the pungent odours of the industry. Amid the warren of factories were the city's sandstone tenements, built to house the thousands of mill workers who flocked to the city in search of work. At the docks on the River Tay, leading out to the North Sea, ships arrived and departed at all hours of the day and night, the hopes and anxieties of the so-called jute barons floating in their wake. Dundee was rightly renowned, not just in the UK but across the Empire, as the capital of the jute industry. As one historian has pointed out: '[Dundee had] the largest domination by a single industry of any British city.'[1]

The focus of this industry was on the manufacture of products from jute, a relatively cheap but extremely hard-wearing fabric. The raw jute was shipped from Bengal, where it was produced on smallholdings, to Dundee – a distance of more than 9,000 miles, made only marginally less arduous by the opening of the Suez Canal in 1869. Once in Dundee, it was unloaded and traded at the city's Panmure Street market – referred to unassumingly as 'the shed' – before being taken to one of the city's many mills. There it was beaten and spun into a variety of products, such as sacks, bags or rope, before being loaded back onto ships at the city's docks and exported. Much of it was sent to the United States, where it was used as – among other things – an awning over frontier wagons.

Dundee was not as unlikely place as it may first seem for such an industry to develop; it already had a long history of manufacturing products from flax, and its position on the Tay, with easy access to the sea, naturally lent itself to maritime-based import/export industry. The city's harbour also underwent significant investment in the 19th century, with deep-water quays added in the 1880s to accommodate ever larger ships. The first jute mill opened in the city in 1838 and by the mid 19th century this process had become the city's dominant economic activity, aided by the decline in other areas such as ship-building, whaling and fishing.

Initially, the jute industry was highly successful. Fuelled by an expanding global economy and high demand from overseas, workers from across the country – including Ireland – flocked to the city in search of employment in the jute barons' mills. In the final decades of the 19th century, it is estimated the city had around 60 jute mills employing some 50,000 people. Such an industrial monopoly was far from unique at the time. The Clyde, for example, was synonymous with shipbuilding, while Churchill's previous constituency, Manchester, was referred to as Cottonopolis. The concentration of one industry in a specific place made sense, in many ways. It allowed employers and workers to specialise and encouraged not only competition but also collaboration to improve products and raise standards.

The jute boom, however, quickly turned into a bust. The high international demand from emerging nations in North and South America that had fuelled the industry could not be maintained indef-initely. As orders declined, many mills reduced production and cut jobs. By 1900, the jute industry settled into a pattern of expansion and recession largely in line with market forces. As one historian of the period has noted: 'The welfare of Dundonians was far more affected by international economic factors around 1900 than a hundred years later, a consequence of its distinctive economic structure ... a stock market crash in the USA (such as in 1907), or a sharp rise in jute prices (such as in 1901) could seriously reduce activity.'[2]

At the same time as stuttering demand, the jute industry in Dundee was increasingly being priced out of the market by unwelcome competition from India. With cheaper labour and minimal transport costs – not least cutting out the 9,000-mile trip to Scotland – the Empire's entrepreneurs soon realised there was more profit to be had by simply setting up jute factories at source in Bengal. Industry experts from Dundee itself were among those to move to India and get in on the action. Many were attracted by the lifestyle on offer in and around the Bengali capital of Calcutta (Kolkata), which had a significantly lower cost of living and attendant luxuries, such as servants. 'Dundee's expertise in jute spinning and weaving had helped start the Calcutta industry in the 1850s,' as one historian put it, '... but by 1900 the Calcutta industry dwarfed its Dundee counterpart.'[3]

This was just one of the reasons why economic protectionism was not more popular in Dundee in the early 20th century: the proposed tariff reforms would not have protected the Dundee jute industry from Indian competition, as it was also in the Empire. Another primary reason was the fear of retaliatory tariffs on the industry, which almost wholly exported to markets outside the Empire. As Churchill took his seat in the House of Commons as the member for Dundee, the outlook for Juteopolis was not good.

Churchill was already familiar with the concept of a one-industry town after his time as MP for Manchester North West and its close association with Lancashire's cotton mills. He had become friendly with many of the industry's leaders – a number of whom were Liberal MPs themselves – and would also have seen the plight of the industry's less fortunate employees. But that was not enough to prepare him for what he found in Dundee, where the city's economy and workforce was almost entirely dependent on the boom-and-bust industry of jute. In 1901, it was estimated that 37 per cent of people in Dundee over the age of 15 were directly or indirectly employed by the jute industry, with the wider city's economic reliance on the trade greater still. This meant even small fluctuations in demand for jute could have a devastating effect on the Dundee economy, with market forces effectively throwing hundreds or thousands out of work, often with little warning. Such precarious employment helped contribute to the widespread poverty Churchill witnessed in Dundee, with many regularly laid off.

Even in work, however, the situation was little better. The jute industry was famous – or infamous – for its employment of women, who commanded lower wages than men. In 1901, 27,635 women were reported as working in Dundee's textile industry, compared to just 12,117 men. This meant mill owners could keep costs as low as possible and maximise profits during boom periods. Such was the prevalence of female workers in the city that men were derogatorily known as 'kettle boilers' – *kettle bilers*, in local dialect – because they remained at home doing household chores. The situation was so severe that in 1890 the Board of Trade recognised jute as one of the two lowest paid textile industries in the UK – the other being linen. As such, the average annual wage for a jute worker in 1886 ran to just £26,* meaning even those in work struggled to make ends meet. Again, the low level of pay was more severe than what Churchill would have witnessed as an MP in Lancashire – according to the same report, cotton mill workers received an average annual wage of £36 – 38 per cent more.

The impact of the jute industry's low wages was further exacerbated by the high cost of living in Dundee, with its relatively isolated location and lack of economic diversity pushing up prices. Indeed, when rent and prices of goods were combined, Dundee was the most expensive city to live in Scotland, while Lancashire was among the cheapest places to live in the whole of the UK. In Dundee in 1905, the cost of living was almost equal to London, but in Lancashire and Cheshire the cost of living was 16 per cent lower than London. By another measure, in 1912 a typical basket of goods in Dundee cost 10.2 per cent more than the same basket of goods in Manchester. Not only did workers in Dundee earn less, but they also had to pay more to live than Churchill's previous constituents.

This combination of insecure work, low wages, high prices and a predominantly female workforce helped push more and more Dundonians, and particularly children, into poverty and ill health. The rate of Child Infant Mortality (CIM) – a key measure of poverty – in Dundee in 1904 was 174 per 1,000. To put such a figure in context, in 2019 the World Bank estimated the Central African Republic had the highest rate of CIM in the world at 81 per 1,000. While the CIM figure is likely to have been similar in Manchester North West when Churchill was an MP there, by 1911 it had significantly improved. Indeed, much of Manchester North West was 'prosperous' with a 'substantial business vote'.[4] In contrast, in 1912 in Dundee, the Medical Officer of Health's report suggested a CIM rate of 156 per 1,000, only a modest reduction. Most of these deaths were due to lack of

---

* Approximately £2,133 in 2017.

healthcare and malnourishment, but it has also been suggested that desperate parents, unable to feed or care for their newborn children, sometimes engaged in infanticide.

For those that did make it to adulthood, poverty, ill health and disease remained a constant presence. The cocktail of unemployment, low wages and high food costs meant malnutrition was a perpetual problem, while the city's tenement housing further aggravated the situation. Unlike the cottages of Lancashire cotton mill workers, jute mill employees were housed in three-, four- or even five-storey tenement buildings in the city centre, tightly packed together on narrow streets. Many of these would see whole families confined to just two rooms: boys would sleep in one room, while parents and girls would sleep in the other room, which also functioned as the kitchen. Many were even less fortunate: in 1904 in Dundee there were 813 one-room homes that were recorded as having five or more people living in them.

Such accommodation unsurprisingly lacked adequate light or heat, with often only a single gas light to provide both. Rubbish would be piled in open spaces behind the tenement buildings and cleared only intermittently, creating a breeding ground for foul smells and rodents, while one toilet could be shared by more than 200 people. The jute mills were also dotted around the city, in the midst of residential housing. As well as pollution, the mills released a particularly foul smell during production, which discouraged local residents from opening their windows, thus creating stagnant indoor conditions where airborne viruses could more easily spread.

Life inside the jute mills themselves was hardly better. As well as the constant risk of accident or injury from malfunctioning equipment, the fumes and heat of an operating mill could often induce sickness. In fact, illness as a result of work was so prevalent that 'mill fever' became a defined condition in the city. Inhalation of jute dust was also a major contributor to respiratory and heart disease. One historian has described the textile industry as 'the principal source of the woes of the community'.[5]

This profound level of poverty and ill health was not passively accepted by Dundee's inhabitants. In fact, it spurred a number of innovative civic responses. The most important of these, in 1888, was the advent of the Dundee Social Union (DSU), which sought to alleviate the worst of the city's problems through local volunteering and charity. Many of the DSU's early activities were well-meaning, if paternalistic and relatively inconsequential given the extent of the poverty crisis in Dundee. The largely upper-middle-class membership would organise concerts to 'give cheer' to the city's workers and keep them out of pubs[6] (the city's culture of heavy drinking was recognised early as another significant contributor to both poverty and ill health). More substantively, the DSU took on the role of factoring some of Dundee's tenements in a bid to improve conditions, but in 1891 this amounted to just 102 single-room properties. By the 1890s, the DSU was floundering, unable to seriously improve living conditions in the city and rapidly losing volunteers. It would only be saved and reinvigorated by the strength of one woman – Mary Lily Walker.

Walker, who was Dundee born and bred, was anxious to move the DSU away from broad Victorian acts of charity and instead deliver targeted support to workers and their families. To effectively do this, she argued, the DSU needed to take an empirical approach to analysing the causes and effects of poverty in the city. Such a scientific approach from Walker was unsurprising. She had been one of the first students at University College Dundee after its founding in 1883 and had enjoyed a promising career in academia since, including publishing a number of noted papers on zoology. But the suffering she continued to witness in her home city stirred her social conscious and she was determined to use her scientific mind for practical good.

It was 1904 when Walker finally persuaded the DSU to finance her *Report on Housing and Industrial Conditions and Medical Inspection of School Children*. Despite the rather elongated title, Walker's report was nevertheless ground-breaking and should be considered alongside seminal works such as Seebohm Rowntree's *Poverty – A Study of Town Life*. Over several months, Walker painstakingly researched the wages, occupations, rents and food and fuel prices of Dundee residents. This statistical approach clearly showed the cost-of-living crisis in the city, demonstrating beyond doubt why so many families fell below the breadline. In addition, Walker not only compiled statistics on the rates of CIM in the city, but also assessed the health of children, to discern why it was so high. Much of this work was not easy – for example, medically examining children was hampered by the fact many were sewn into their clothes, because lost buttons were too expensive for families to replace. When Walker's report was published in 1905 it deservedly had a substantive impact not just in the city but far beyond and would have been read by many parliamentarians, including Churchill.

But merely identifying the problem was not enough – Walker wanted to act. She identified in her report that a key factor in the ill health of children was that mothers, having given birth, were forced to return to work immediately to earn money to survive, thus – by necessity rather than design – neglecting the needs of their babies. They also suffered from a poor diet and ill health themselves, which in turn impacted the growth and development of their babies. To try to tackle this problem, Walker and the DSU established a 'restaurant' in the city's West Port, to provide heavily subsidised – in some cases free – meals to women who were breastfeeding. The scheme helped ensure that both mother and baby had decent nutrition and was a tremendous success, with the concept expanding across Dundee and to other cities in Scotland over the coming years.

But, despite its accomplishments, the work of Walker and the DSU was not universally appreciated in Dundee. Many felt that whatever its good intentions, the DSU merely identified and helped ameliorate a problem, rather than actually tackling the fundamental causes of poverty and ill health in the city. 'The causes of the evils lie deep down at the root of our social system,' wrote one angry Dundonian about the DSU in a 1906 letter to the *Evening Telegraph*.[7] 'Pottering with effects rather than dealing with root causes, as these dilettante reformers love to do, is like trying to empty the ocean with a sieve.' While many would not use such charged and emotive language, it was clearly the case that civic society alone could not deliver the changes Dundee needed. Major political reform was required to alleviate the plight of Dundee's working people. After his election in 1908, the only question was whether Churchill could – and would – deliver.

Witnessing such levels of poverty and ill heath had a profound effect on Churchill's political life, adding impetus to his development as a Liberal politician. Indeed, what had begun as a political conversion sparked by a commitment to free trade would, during his time as MP for Dundee, develop into a commitment to progressive social change as well. Of course, Churchill's progressive concience had begun to develop some years earlier. As far back as 1904, he had backed a private member's bill to improve trade union rights and to stop unions being liable to damages as a result of strikes. Even before he joined the Liberal Party, he reported that Rowntree's famous study of poverty in York had 'fairly made my hair stand on end'.[8] Yet it was only once he was elected as MP for Dundee and safely ensconced as President of the Board of Trade that he fully embraced these warm feelings and, crucially, acted upon them.

His main aim – and reflecting his experiences of industry in Manchester but particularly Dundee – was to improve the lot of both workers and the unemployed. He did this via two innovative and significant pieces of legislation.

The first was the Trade Boards Bill, which he introduced in 1909. This was designed to tackle so-called sweated labour, which saw people being paid excessively low wages to produce goods – particularly garments – in small, unregulated workshops. Under the legislation, employers, workers and independent representatives formed boards to effectively set a minimum wage across the industry. Introducing the bill to the House of Commons, and perhaps reflecting on the financial struggles of his constituents in Dundee, Churchill said: 'It is a serious national evil that any class of His Majesty's subjects should receive less than a living wage in return for their utmost exertions.'[9] Churchill – recognising how the bill might frighten Conservative MPs – opted for a gradualist approach, initially ensuring it was limited in scope, covering about 200,000 workers and a specific number of trades. This meant that the jute industry, as a larger and comparatively more legitimate employer, was not initially covered by the legislation, but it would be included later as the scope of the act was expanded, as Churchill had intended. Indeed, the legislation proved so effective at raising pay in Dundee that by 1922 the city's jute barons were lobbying Churchill to get it scrapped.

Following the successful passage of the Trade Boards Bill, Churchill introduced his second legislative innovation in May 1909, this time to tackle unemployment. As it stood, those thrown out of work, such as his own constituents, were left destitute unless they could find another job. Churchill's Labour Exchanges Bill sought to, as the name suggests, introduce labour exchanges across the country to help the unemployed find work by connecting jobseekers with vacancies. The first exchanges opened in February 1910 and by April there were 98 across the country, including seven in Scotland and one in Dundee.

Of course, Churchill's reforms did not solve all of Dundee's problems. Indeed, while they did certainly help people in Dundee, they were far wider in scope and impact than just one constituency. It is also the case that poverty in Dundee had been a feature of previous election campaigns in the city and was a matter of concern to previous MPs as much as Churchill. Equally, Churchill did not develop these policies alone – like any cabinet minister, he had a raft of civil servants and advisers supporting him. One such figure was a young William Beveridge, who was hired by Churchill to work at the Board of Trade in 1908. Beveridge's pioneering work would later lay the foundations for the introduction of the welfare state by the 1945–1951 Labour government.

But this cannot diminish the impact of the political and legislative change delivered by Churchill and others. Beveridge himself cited Churchill's period as President of the Board of Trade as a 'striking illustration of how much the personality of the minister in a few critical months may change the course of social legislation'.[10] Progressive measures such as the Trade Boards Act and the Labour Exchanges Act did make a real difference to the lives of working people in Dundee, Scotland and the whole of the UK. Yet, for Churchill and his close political ally Lloyd George, the Chancellor of the Exchequer, these reforms were just the start. There were even greater changes to come.

Chapter 9

The Peers versus the People
1910

Luigi Barzini pulled his coat tightly around his neck. He had expected it to be cold in Dundee, but never this cold. Here the snow was different to the snow he sometimes saw in Milan; crunchy, icy under-foot – not like the dustings from the Alps he had enjoyed as a child. The streets, pitch black and deserted this early in the morning, added to the chill. Barzini, dragging his luggage behind him – it was too early for porters to be working at the station – had to repeatedly pause for breath as he went from hotel to hotel in search of a room. He cursed his editor at the *Corriere Della Sera*, Italy's best-selling newspaper, for arranging this assignment. Barzini was better than this. He had already made a name for himself as a successful war corre-spondent, having covered the Boxer Rebellion in China at the start of the century. In 1907, he had accompanied the famous Italian aris-tocrat Scipione Borghese as he won the Peking to Paris motor race. He could still remember their triumphal entry into Paris on 10 August, exactly two months to the day after they had set off from the French embassy on the other side of the world. What a difference three years makes.

Barzini had been sent the more than 1,100 miles to Dundee to cover what his editor hoped would be 'a lively election'.[1] 'Go to Dundee in Scotland,' the editor had told him from the comfort of the newspaper's office on the Via Solferino, in Milan's Porta Nuova district. 'A Right Honourable Winston Churchill . . . is set to have an unpleasant quarter of an hour.' As Barzini settled down to rest on that chilly January day in 1910, he wondered what he could possibly find that was either 'lively' or 'unpleasant'. He need not have worried.

★   ★   ★

The January 1910 general election is one of the most controversial and politically significant elections in British history. It was called by Asquith in an attempt to resolve a constitutional stand-off brought about by two factors: the radicalism of his Liberal government's agenda and the obstinacy of the House of Lords. Nine months earlier, in April 1909, the Chancellor of the Exchequer, Lloyd George, had brought forward his so-called People's Budget, which would build on and expand the pay and employment reforms brought in by Churchill. Most innovatively, Lloyd George outlined how the Liberal government would introduce an old-age pension for the first time, giving all those over 70 an income of five shillings* a week. To pay for this new measure, however, he proposed the introduction of progressive taxation – that is, the concept that wealthier taxpayers should pay more and subsidise services for the less well off. This was 'politically crucial' for constituents such as Churchill's in Dundee because it showed that 'state welfare could be funded without recourse to tariffs', which would raise living costs for already struggling Dundonians.[2] But it irked the landowning aristocrats in the House of Lords, who were particularly concerned by the proposal to tax unearned income at a higher rate than earned income, to raise death duties and, most controversially, to tax the value of land when it was sold. Such measures seriously threatened the financial position of Britain's aristocrats, who not only derived the vast majority – if not all – their income from their land but would now be taxed when they sold it or when they died as well.

The Lords, however, were far from powerless to oppose the People's Budget. Not only could they speak out and attempt to rally the press and the country against the plans, but the chamber, which had a Conservative majority, could crucially also amend or even veto legislation. This had already happened to nine other Liberal bills since 1906, which had either been blocked entirely – such as the 1908 Licensing Bill – or massively watered down by the House of Lords. By convention, the House of Lords would not veto a finance bill, but as the contents and consequences of Lloyd George's budget became clear, this understanding quickly dissipated. The noble lords – many hailing from the most famous and esteemed families in Britain – were

* Approximately £19 in 2017.

incandescent, indignant and immobile. In late November 1909, they rejected the People's Budget by 350 votes to 75.

For Asquith, rejection of the budget was unacceptable, and the Liberal Party embarked on a course not only to have it passed, but to permanently curtail the power of the House of Lords. To do this, the Prime Minister decided to bring forward a parliamentary bill that would effectively remove the Lords' veto. If the second chamber refused to pass that bill, he would then ask the king, Edward VII, to flood the chamber with hundreds of newly appointed Liberal peers in order to nullify the Conservative majority and guarantee the passage of legislation. In either event, the power of the House of Lords would be permanently neutered. The king – caught between his innate conservatism but also the desire to avoid a potentially revolutionary constitutional crisis – suggested an election could be used to break the deadlock in parliament. The stakes could not have been higher.

Churchill, despite his aristocratic ancestry, became an enthusiastic supporter of the Liberal Party's 'Peers versus the People' platform and Lloyd George's plans, with the Conservative press dubbing the duo the 'terrible twins'.[3] Indeed, while Churchill's cousin, the Duke of Marlborough, retained a relatively silent opposition to the plans, the Duke of Beaufort went so far as to say he would 'like to see Winston Churchill and Lloyd George in the midst of twenty couples of dog hounds'.[4] For his part, Churchill utilised rhetoric that was equally inflammatory. At a rally in Glasgow on 12 January 1910, he described the House of Lords – in language likely to make even the populists of the 21st century blush – as being 'filled with old doddering peers, cute financial magnates, clever wire pullers, big brewers with bulbous noses. All the enemies of progress are there – weaklings, sleek smug, comfortable self-important individuals.'[5] Such provocative oratory was the rule rather than the exception. On a visit to Inverness, Churchill violently accused the Conservative Party of political opportunism: 'Just as they clutched greedily at the last sour unpalatable dregs of the bottle before it was torn away from them at the last election, so now when they see a possible chance of obtaining power and place, they kick over the whole table in an ugly wish to jam their noses in the trough.'[6] This was no flash-in-the-pan moment or flight of fancy on Churchill's behalf, but a position of conviction, further evidence of how his association with Dundee was burnishing his radical credentials. Even after the January 1910 election was over, Churchill would go so far as to advocate the complete abolition of the House of Lords in a cabinet memorandum.

Despite some reservations among the Liberal Party establishment at the strength of his rhetoric, both Churchill's oratorical skill and his belief in the cause quickly made him the darling of the Liberal Party's re-election campaign. Asquith later thanked Churchill for speeches that 'from first to last have reached high-water marks and will live in history'.[7] Alongside Glasgow and Inverness, Churchill spoke in Scottish towns such as Kirkcaldy and Arbroath, while he was also called upon to persuade voters across England, in towns such as Derby and Birmingham. *The Courier*, always eager to accuse Churchill of neglecting his constituency, took his popularity on the national stage as a personal snub. On 14 January, a day before nationwide polling opened* the newspaper ran a front-page cartoon, under the headline 'Winston Back Again', showing a prostrated individual representing 'Dundee Liberalism' bowing at the feet of Churchill as he shows off the route of his national tour. Such criticism was harsh. Churchill was a prominent government minister and was expected to campaign across the country. Indeed, by focusing his efforts on more marginal seats than his own and thereby increasing the likelihood of returning a Liberal majority, Churchill could well argue he was doing more for his constituents than if he had spent the entire campaign on the Tay. Nevertheless, Churchill was anxious not to give the impression he was neglecting his constituents and, on 15 January, arrived in Dundee. But an old enemy was ready and waiting for him.

Barzini noticed the suffragettes almost as soon as he arrived, describing them later in his article for the *Corriere Della Sera* as being 'on the rampage'.[8] 'Platoons of them are outside the polling stations – young, old, beautiful, ugly, insensitive, and tireless,' he wrote. He said there was a suggestion the suffragettes may even be planning violence, seeking to emulate Guy Fawkes and the Gunpowder Plot of 1605. When he met them, however, he noted – in suggestive language typical of the

* Voting took place on different days across the country over a two-week period. Polling day in Dundee was 18 January.

time – that they were 'tame, smiling [and] seductive'. He added: 'Armed with forms and pencils they leap upon the adversaries and present their two things with unheard of courtesy. They are now doing things the legal way. The elector, taken by his weak side, smiles and signs.'

Whatever Barzini's experience, the Dundee Liberal Association doubted whether their candidate would be accorded such courtesy. At every meeting – every speaking engagement – they feared disruption, or worse. This was particularly the case because the Liberal government, of which he was a prominent member, had so far failed to act on votes for women. There would undoubtedly be attempts to confront him about the government's equivocation, just as there had been in his first Dundee election two years earlier. Those fears were soon realised.

The meeting at the Lochee church hall got off to a difficult start. Hundreds of people had begun to pack the venue hours before Churchill was due to speak at 9.30 p.m. Stewards, provided by the Dundee Liberal Association, were already struggling to maintain order when Patrick Finnigan, a local fishmonger, tried to force his way in. He was handed over to the police, kicking and screaming. A magistrate would, 18 days later, convict him of a breach of the peace, sentencing him to either a 15-shilling* fine or 10 days' imprisonment.

Inside the hall, things were going little better. Amid the hundreds of faces in the crowd, a steward spotted Lila Clunas, the notorious suffragette. Clunas was a Glasgow-born primary school teacher and secretary of the Women's Freedom League. She was also a serial interrupter and well-blooded protester on behalf of the suffragette cause. In 1908, she had even served three weeks in the infamous Holloway prison for attempting to assault Asquith while handing him a petition. As the steward looked closer, he also spotted Elsie – Clunas' sister – and several other suffragette infiltrators. They had arrived, and surely meant to cause trouble.

William Smith – the Dundee Liberal Association organiser tasked with managing the meeting, and who had earlier helped Churchill address the 'Not at Home' allegations – knew he had to act quickly.

* Approximately £60 in 2017.

But he also realised that attempting to forcibly remove the women would cause chaos. Instead, Smith approached Clunas directly. He told her that she and her colleagues from the Women's Freedom League could stay at the meeting and ask questions of Churchill – indeed, they would be very welcome – but perhaps it would be better if they joined the other ladies, sitting behind the podium, via a side door at the church hall? Clunas, thrown off balance by Smith's seemingly reasonable demeanour, agreed, not realising he had in fact locked the side door, quickly trapping the suffragettes outside. Whether or not Smith was pleased with his deception is not recorded, but it was a slight Clunas would never forget.

Despite the removal of the suffragettes, however, Churchill was repeatedly interrupted and occasionally heckled throughout the night, first at the Lochee meeting, and then at a later meeting on Scott Street. Much of the interruption came from Scrymgeour's supporters, with one demanding to know, to great laughter, whether Churchill himself was teetotal. Churchill responded, with equal good humour: 'I am quite prepared to be a teetotaller if everyone else will guarantee to be one too.'[9]

While the suffragettes continued to be Churchill's most implacable foe, the January 1910 election also saw him make a new and valuable ally in the city – Alexander Wilkie, the Labour MP. Wilkie had been born in Leven, Fife, just 25 miles across the Tay from Dundee, but his formative years were spent working on the Tyne in the north-east of England. Indeed, despite representing Dundee for 16 years, Wilkie's heart remained very much on Tyneside and he was regularly criticised, particularly by Scrymgeour in language he more often reserved for Churchill, for alleged absenteeism from the city and disinterest in its affairs. A shipbuilder by training, Wilkie became general secretary of the Associated Society of Shipwrights – a trade union – in 1882 at the age of 32, beginning a career in labour activism that would span the next 40 years. In 1900 he stood unsuccessfully to become the MP in Sunderland for the burgeoning Labour Party, securing a more than respectable 8,842 votes (23.6 per cent) and almost beating the Liberal Party into last place.

The Sunderland campaign influenced Wilkie in two key ways. Firstly, it cemented his place in the Labour movement and honed his electoral skills. By the time he came to contest the Dundee seat in 1906, Wilkie was a rising star who could call on an army of more than 400 volunteers, many of them from Tyneside. He was also an innovator on the campaign trail, giving his supporters cards to hand to party volunteers at polling stations, allowing the campaign to focus on contacting those who were yet to vote. Secondly, and more importantly, the Sunderland contest had taught Wilkie the value of Labour-Liberal cooperation, particularly in dual-member constituencies. Sunderland, like Dundee, had two MPs and, by almost wholly pulling votes away from the Liberal Party,* Wilkie's candidacy in 1900 had – albeit inadvertently – allowed the Conservatives to win both seats in the city for the first time. It is therefore unsurprising that Wilkie became a key advocate of cooperation with the Liberal Party after his victory in Dundee in the 1906 general election, where he was among the first Labour MPs elected in Scotland.

After Churchill joined him in the second Dundee seat in 1908, he and Wilkie quickly formed a personal friendship and, where their views aligned, worked closely together on legislation. Indeed, it has been argued that Wilkie, in many respects, was 'less radical than the version of . . . Churchill which was current in 1908'.[10] By the time of the January 1910 election, the pair had agreed not only a non-aggression pact, but effectively ran on a joint ticket, actively encouraging their supporters to give their second vote to the other. This not only shored up the bases of both candidates – allowing them to focus their fire on their Conservative opponents – but it also sought to maintain Scrymgeour's position as an eccentric outsider.

The Churchill/Wilkie pact was not without precedent. In 1903, Herbert Gladstone, the Liberal Party chief whip and son of the famous Prime Minister, and Ramsay Macdonald, the General Secretary of the Labour Party, had agreed an informal pact, which led to 29 Labour MPs being elected at the 1906 general election. Indeed, at the January 1910 election, at least seven dual-member constituencies – including Dundee but also Wilkie's old stomping ground of Sunderland – ran just one Liberal and one Labour candidate. But this did not stop some in the local Dundee Labour Party questioning Wilkie's commitment

---

* The Liberal Party's vote share plummeted by 37 per cent.

to the cause. The Labour MP, for example, faced a difficult meeting in the city on 13 January, where party supporters sharply criticised his 'flirting' with Churchill.[11] Churchill was on easier ground with his local Liberal members, who backed the decision not to run a second candidate against Wilkie by a margin of two to one. As one historian of the period has noted: 'Ideologically Wilkie was not someone who caused pre-[First World War] Liberals to lose much sleep.'[12] Churchill himself even felt comfortable enough to praise the 'steady yet gradual development of Labour representation' across the country in his own election address.[13] Predictably *The Courier* was less sympathetic, implying Wilkie had been duped into coalition with Churchill who 'fights only for [himself]'.[14]

Despite the criticism of some in the local press and the constant haranguing of the suffragettes, Churchill felt confident of being returned in Dundee. As well as the partnership with Wilkie, which ensured Churchill maintained his working-class base, he was also assured of retaining the other plank of his support – the Irish vote. As an avid supporter of Home Rule, Churchill could in any event reasonably rely on a significant portion of this vote, but the circumstances of the January 1910 election made it particularly resilient. The House of Lords had, in 1893, used the same power of veto it was currently using to block the People's Budget to defeat William Gladstone's Second Home Rule Bill. Churchill's platform – not only supporting Home Rule but actively seeking to undermine the constitutional mechanism that had seen it blocked previously – was particularly appealing. It was therefore little surprise when, on 9 January, the Dundee branch of the United Irish League once again enthusiastically endorsed Churchill's candidacy.

Barzini woke to a chilly, crisp and clear winter's morning. It was 18 January, polling day, and as he looked out of the window of his Dundee hotel room, he could already see voters diligently making their way to the polls, occasionally surrounded and cajoled by activists sporting brightly coloured rosettes. Even dogs were draped in party paraphernalia, with one bulldog, Jimmie, being singled out as a 'particularly fine fighting Unionist' by a reporter for *The Courier*.[15] Meanwhile, a man apparently dressed in rags but clutching a sign saying 'For the Lords' struck Barzini as particularly newsworthy.

Further down the Perth Road at his base in the Queen's Hotel, Churchill was preparing to do an early tour of the polling stations. Having seen the weather – clear if cold – he was now almost certain of victory; his only concern had been whether his substantial support in the city would be deterred from turning out by rain or snow. Ritchie, Churchill's Dundee sage, was equally confident. Indeed, such was the buoyant mood in the Liberal camp that there was little protest when Churchill announced at midday that he was going to play a round of golf at Carnoustie, leaving Clementine to continue the campaign in his absence.* This was Clementine's first taste of campaigning in Dundee, but it would not be her last. On her initial outing, under the watchful eye of Ritchie and accompanied by her sister, she made a strong impression. The only small blip in Churchill's day occurred when he returned to Dundee just before 6 p.m. Striding confidently into the polling station – followed swiftly by a pack of reporters – the Liberal Party candidate bumped straight into Scrymgeour. As *The Courier* noted dryly: 'The rival candidates did not hug in one fond embrace.'[16]

After the polls closed and the votes were counted, Churchill was relieved to find his confidence had not been misplaced. He managed to top the poll with 10,747 votes, with his running mate Wilkie not far behind on 10,365. The joint ticket had paid dividends for both candidates and – despite criticism from the left and some in local business and the press – Dundee was clearly satisfied with their record and approach. Their Conservative/Unionist rivals got 4,552 and 4,339 respectively. Scrymgeour once again lost his deposit, managing just 1,512 votes.

After the result was announced, Barzini spotted Churchill smiling broadly, before being enveloped in an escort of policemen. After inquiring as to what was happening, Barzini learned the police feared someone might try to harm the newly re-elected member for Dundee. 'Are there Anarchists around?' the perplexed Italian reporter asked a nearby police Sergeant.[17] 'Worse,' the officer replied, 'there are Suffragettes.'

⋆   ⋆   ⋆

---

* In his copy for the *Corriere Della Sera*, Barzini noted – with no faux admiration – that Churchill was at least as good a golfer as the Conservative leader, Arthur Balfour, himself a renowned player.

If Churchill was satisfied with the result in Dundee, the Liberal Party's performance nationally left much to be desired. The Conservative Party returned 273 MPs – a net gain of 116 – while the Liberal Party returned 275. Asquith was able to remain Prime Minister with the support of 41 Labour Party MPs – adding credence to the Churchill/Wilkie pact – and 71 Irish Nationalists. This crucially meant that, despite the Liberal Party's setback, there was still a majority to pass the People's Budget and on 29 April 1910, the House of Lords acquiesced, allowing Lloyd George's reforms to be brought into law. But, despite this victory, it was far from the end of the confrontation, with the Liberal Party – and its Irish Nationalist powerbrokers – now determined to curtail the power of the House of Lords permanently.

For Churchill, the January 1910 election brought personal as well as political satisfaction. Having played a vital role in the campaign, Asquith promoted him – after some horse-trading – to become the youngest Home Secretary since Sir Robert Peel in 1822. Here, Churchill continued his reforming zeal. He was a driving force behind the Coal Mines Act of 1911, which raised the minimum age for entering the pits and boosted training and qualifications for managers to improve safety. While this did not directly impact his own constituents, it helped many who lived in the environs of Dundee, such as Fife, which had a substantial mining community. Other measures pushed forward by Churchill included the Shops Bill, which, in the face of fierce opposition, introduced statutory mealtimes for employees and early closing on one day a week. Churchill was also instrumental in helping Lloyd George deliver his National Insurance Act, even though it was now outside his portfolio. In explaining his continued interest in the act, he told the House of Commons: 'There is no proposal in the field of politics that I care about more than this great insurance scheme.'[18]

As Home Secretary, Churchill also had to make a number of difficult decisions, not least having the final say on whether to proceed with the death penalty in individual cases.* A more controversial and politically testing issue to contemporaries was Churchill's treatment of the suffragettes. Heavy-handed policing of a pro-female suffrage demonstration in November 1910 led to a backlash, which Churchill

---

* Churchill granted mercy in 21 of the 43 death penalty cases he was asked to confirm during his 20 months as Home Secretary.

further inflamed by personally instructing police to arrest a suffragette protester after a scuffle on the steps of 10 Downing Street, which in 1910 was still a public thoroughfare. More controversial still was his involvement in the force-feeding of imprisoned leaders of the suffragette movement, several of whom began hunger strikes in protest at their treatment as common, rather than political, prisoners. The process of force-feeding was unsurprisingly gruesome – it involved women being held down while a tube was inserted through their nose or mouth before liquidised food was poured in – and was subject to increasing public criticism. While Churchill did not stop the procedure, he quickly sought to defuse the issue by effectively acquiescing to the demand to change the status of the suffragette prisoners.* Despite this, Churchill became closely associated in the public mind with mistreatment of the suffragettes, which further hardened their opposition to him and the Liberal Party. This would have been a concern at the best of times, but it was a particular problem for Churchill in 1910 – because another general election was already fast approaching.

To curtail the power of the House of Lords, Asquith had brought forward the inconsequentially named but nevertheless incendiary Parliament Bill, which would effectively remove the power of the House of Lords to veto legislation from the House of Commons. Unsurprisingly, the peers – still reeling from their failure to stop the People's Budget – were unwilling to support a measure that would massively curtail their power. A second stand-off ensued, which was further complicated by the death of Edward VII in May 1910 and the ascension to the throne of George V. The new king was anxious to avoid a constitutional crisis so early in his reign and privately agreed to Asquith's demand to create a raft of new Liberal peers to nullify the Conservative majority and vote through the Parliament Bill. His only condition – and to confer legitimacy on the process – was a further general election to endorse this constitutional change. Polling day was set for the first two weeks in December – but now there was a question of whether Churchill would want to fight Dundee.

*   *   *

---

* Rule 234A, which Churchill introduced, was also later used to improve the conditions of some conscientious objectors during the First World War.

In the second election of 1910, Churchill was offered the opportunity to return as the candidate for Manchester North West, abandoning what would be a brief Scottish sojourn for a seat in England. The constituency that Churchill had lost more than two years before was now back in Liberal hands and – given the circumstances surrounding this election – was a solid prospect once again. The offer, however, had not come via the Liberal Party hierarchy, but in the form of a challenge by the senior Conservative MP Andrew Bonar Law. As well as Churchill giving up Dundee, the idea was Bonar Law would give up his safe seat of Dulwich, and the two would meet in a kind of head-to-head duel in Manchester North West.

Given the extraordinary nature of this proposal, it is not surprising that Churchill resoundingly rejected it. But this does not take away from the fact that Churchill was increasingly attached to his constituency in Dundee and had no desire – even when it was suggested – to stand elsewhere. Indeed, the bizarre bravado of the proposal would, in fact, have appealed to Churchill's character, adding greater significance to his decision to reject it.

Confirmed as Dundee's Liberal candidate, Churchill arrived at the city's West station on the morning of 23 November with a larger than usual entourage. As well as Clementine and the usual bag carriers, he was accompanied by three Scotland Yard detectives. Further detectives from the city's constabulary were waiting on the platform. Just days earlier, Churchill had been assaulted with an umbrella by a male supporter of the suffragettes, and the police feared another attempt to do the 36-year-old Home Secretary harm.*

Despite the fears of the police, the campaign was largely peaceful. While Churchill was still in demand across the country – at one point the Liberal Party chartered a private train to ensure he could make a speaking arrangement in Grimsby – there was by now a weariness with politics among the electorate, and the campaign was somewhat lethargic. Churchill, however, continued to receive praise for his oratory, which was even given a favourable reception in the usually critical *Courier*.

---

* In the midst of the election campaign, Churchill was called to give evidence against his attacker at Bow Street magistrates' court. Despite Churchill's magnanimous plea for clemency, his attacker was sentenced to six months' imprisonment.

Perhaps in an attempt to inject some life into the campaign, Churchill accepted an invitation from one of his Conservative/ Unionist rivals, Seymour Lloyd, to a public debate in Dundee's Drill Hall. Such a move was not without risk. The debate would take place on the eve of the poll in the city, meaning there would be no time to recover from any missteps, while Churchill, as the incumbent, had more to lose than gain. As it happened, the debate passed in good humour. The only incident of note came when Churchill launched an attack on the latest Tory proposal to break the constitutional deadlock – a referendum. Churchill dismissed the proposal out of hand, telling the audience: 'The referendum means that though a government is defeated through it, it will occupy the degrading position of remaining in office.'[19] The concept of referenda, Churchill added, along with protectionism, should be 'tied up in a bag together like the Kilkenny cats until there is nothing but the tail left.' While Churchill correctly identified the problem with referenda – he also disliked the notion of politicians being indecisive – he was being disingenuous in his criticism. Just weeks earlier, on 11 December, he had written to Asquith urging him to offer a referendum on whether the franchise should be expanded to include women, believing such a proposal would be defeated. Such a strategy, Churchill argued, would make it appear that Asquith was acting on suffragette demands, while in reality not risking enfranchising large numbers of women who were likely to vote for the Liberal Party's opponents. Churchill was therefore not opposed to the concept of referenda as long as the device was used to deliver a preordained and desired outcome.

On 8 December, voters in Dundee headed to the polls for a second time in just 12 months. They once again returned both Churchill and Wilkie, though this time with slightly less enthusiasm. Churchill topped the poll with 9,420 votes, followed by Wilkie with 8,957. The marginally reduced figures were the result of a 'surfeit of stimulation' among voters.[20] Scrymgeour, meanwhile, gained a few hundred fresh supporters and returned 1,825 votes.

Nationally, there was little change from the result in January. The Liberal Party lost two seats, the Conservatives lost one and Asquith was maintained in office by the Irish Nationalists and the Labour Party. Still, the result was once again enough to ensure the House of Lords had to back down and the Parliament Act, significantly curtailing the power of the upper house, was signed into law in 1911. With the constitutional crisis now seemingly resolved, Churchill – along with almost everyone in the country – hoped for a much-needed period of stability. Such hopes, however, would soon prove premature.

Chapter 10

The Strike before Christmas

1911

The first company of Black Watch soldiers arrived in Dundee by train at 8.30 p.m. on 19 December 1911. Dressed in kilts – cut thick in the green and black of the regimental tartan – and with service rifles slung across their backs, they were an imposing sight. Kit-bags were chucked down from the waiting train to the platform, while more soldiers carefully manoeuvred wooden crates, packed with supplies and ammunition, out of the carriages. Outside the station and behind a police cordon, a crowd swayed nervously in the December cold. Over the noise of the steam engine, they heard orders being barked, heels being clicked and, finally, the synchronised crash of boots marching swiftly away from the platform.

Despite the regimental discipline, the arriving soldiers were as uneasy as the crowd waiting to greet them. Their mission was not only dangerous, but delicate. Many knew the city of Dundee – a popular recruiting ground for the Black Watch – and recognised faces staring out in the midst of the waiting throng. Among the soldiers there was also only a smattering of experience. Many – including the company's second in command, fresh from Sandhurst – had never been deployed before. And as first assignments go, this was a particularly difficult one. As they marched through the city, some in the crowd began booing and jeering. Not everyone was pleased to see them, and there was a sense of relief when they reached the city's Drill Hall – their new base – unscathed. There, a handful of orders were given by the most senior officer, Captain Stewart. Most of the men were told to rest for the night ahead – they needed to be fresh for any potential action in the morning. A handful were put on sentry duty at the entrances to the Drill Hall. A final group was sent to guard three particularly special wooden crates, placed in the corner of the hall itself. These were simply marked: 'Government Explosives'.[1]

The crisis that brought the Black Watch to Dundee – complete with rifles and explosives – began a couple of weeks earlier, at the start of December. The city's carters – men who transported goods around the city, particularly from the docks – had demanded an increase in pay to 23 shillings* a week. This, the trade unions argued, was long overdue as Dundee's carters were the lowest paid in Scotland, despite regularly having to work 65 to 80 hours a week. The city's dockworkers had also demanded an increase in wages at the same time, and businesses balked at the potential increase in costs. Negotiations made little headway and a final offer was rejected by trade unions on 15 December. On Monday 18 December, both the dockers and carters went on strike.

The strike, despite not involving workers in the jute industry, nevertheless effectively ground Dundee to a standstill. 'Dundee has never before had an industrial strike of such serious possibilities,' *The Courier* noted.[2] Without functioning docks, raw jute fibre could not be offloaded on arrival from Bengal, while the finished product could not be exported from its warehouses. Coal, the lifeblood of the loom, also ran short after transporters for the mines downed tools in solidarity with the carters. Even if the docks themselves had been functioning, without carters there was no way to move goods around the city. A handful of carters had attempted to defy the trade union and keep working, but they soon had their horses and traps surrounded and brought to a halt. The organisers among the striking carters made a particular effort to emphasise to the media that their draught horses, used to pull their carts around the city, were being well cared for despite the industrial dispute. With no raw material and no fuel, the jute mills simply had no choice but to shut down, leaving more than 20,000 mill workers idle, on top of the thousands of already striking dockers and carters. The situation was so severe it made headlines as far afield as Australia.

With so much of the city's workforce idle, what began as a peaceful dispute over wages quickly escalated into disruption and violence.

---

* Approximately £90 in 2017.

Anyone perceived to be breaking the strike was at risk of harassment or worse. In one incident, a man driving a horse and cart was pelted with stones and glass bottles by an angry mob. Police, sent to the protect the worker, were also hit by missiles before reinforcements arrived to drive the rioters off. Running clashes between crowds and baton-wielding constables were common, with parties on both sides often needing to be taken to the Dundee infirmary with serious injuries, although there were no recorded deaths. In one case, the crowds became so bold that they repeatedly attempted to rescue an arrested comrade being led away by constables, only to be beaten back and eventually repulsed by reinforcing mounted police. Soon, it was only strikers and police officers who dared to leave their homes, day or night. Other incidents often involved vandalism. A common practice was to push strike-breaking carts off the quayside and into the water at the docks. *The Courier*, despite its Conservative sympathies, was keen to stress that the violence was not the result of the striking carters and dockers, but rather 'youths out for fun' and looking to take advantage of the disruption caused by the strike.[3] Nevertheless, it asked its readers ominously: 'if all this were possible in a few hours [of the strike starting], what might ... happen in a few days?' The police, it was feared, had lost control of the city.

It was in this febrile atmosphere that the city magistrates decided to request help from the army. Having consulted the city's Lord Provost, they sent a telegram to the Scottish Office on 19 December requesting urgent assistance: 'Carters' trouble totally beyond control of the police, even with the aid of contingents from other towns [Glasgow and Edinburgh had already sent a combined total of 90 officers to support the Dundee constabulary]. To protect life and the peace of Dundee we respectfully ask that 300 troops be immediately sent to render assistance to the police.'[4] The Scottish Office quickly responded that 'the assistance asked will be forthcoming'. The Black Watch was then dispatched.

The magistrates' decision to request troops, while extreme, was not unprecedented. Industrial unrest at this time was still very much in its infancy in the UK and there was a fear of the unknown among the upper and middle classes, who easily mistook picket-line disruption or rioting as a prelude to violent revolution. This view was reinforced by the presence of syndicalists – a revolutionary minority who believed in overthrowing capitalism via a general strike – among the unionised workers. Equally, throughout 1911 the entire country had been rocked by similar convulsions to what was now occurring in Dundee. That summer, trade in Liverpool had been paralysed by a dockworkers' strike, while rail workers had ground the country to a halt in a two-day show of force in August. In both cases, troops were utilised either to quell rioting and protect property, or to replace striking workers and keep services running.

It is a common misconception that Churchill ordered the Black Watch into Dundee in an attempt to frighten the strikers. This is not the case. The decision was clearly taken by local law officers, who felt the safety of the city was under direct threat, and it was authorised by the Lord Provost. Indeed, while Churchill was no longer Home Secretary at the time of the Dundee strike, the evidence from earlier that year – when he was preparing guidance for responding to industrial disputes elsewhere – indicates he would have been cautious about the deployment of troops in the city. In July 1911, clear and strict rules of engagement were set out for any troops deployed to points of industrial unrest. They advised: 'In order . . . to prevent a direct collision between the military and strikers every body of soldiers will be accompanied by . . . police. It is for the police to take such action as may be necessary, and the military will not act until called upon by the police, and until the officer in command of the military is satisfied that all the resources of the police are exhausted.'[5] Should the situation deteriorate beyond that, it was suggested that the first role of the army should be to guard those the police have arrested, thereby allowing constables to continue to work to maintain order, rather than engage in any confrontation themselves. There is nothing to suggest that these rules of engagement, set out when Churchill was Home Secretary, would not have applied to the Black Watch soldiers deployed to Dundee in December.

The view that Churchill was determined to crush strikers with military force is, however, not confined to the carters' and dockworkers' strike in Dundee. Indeed, it is a common refrain for his entire tenure as Home Secretary, which coincided with this period of significant industrial unrest across the country. There is no doubt the strikes affected Churchill deeply and sparked in him a fear of militant trade

unionism, but this did not alter his belief in Liberal-Labour cooperation, or his desire to enact progressive social and economic reforms. If
anything, they may have encouraged him of the need for quicker and
deeper reform, out of a desire to avoid further unrest. Certainly, his
response as Home Secretary to the industrial unrest of the period was
considered and designed to avoid confrontation as much as possible
while maintaining law and order.

Most famously – or infamously – is the case of Tonypandy, a mining
village in south Wales. Here, in November 1910, approximately 25,000
miners went on strike in a dispute over pay. As matters escalated –
several shop windows were smashed – the local police chief requested
military assistance, which was forthcoming. Churchill, however, was
wary of inflaming the situation and halted the troops *en route*. As a
result, and despite increasing levels of violence in the town, the troops
never directly engaged with the strikers, who instead only clashed
with police, many of whom were armed with nothing but rolled-up
mackintosh coats. In this case – as in a number of others – it is difficult, as one biographer notes, 'to fault Churchill ... for any sin of
aggression or vindictiveness towards labour'.[6]

But the fact that Churchill is and was perceived as hot-headed and
belligerent is more than partly his own fault. At the forefront of
Dundonians' minds as the Black Watch marched into the city would
have been the so-called Siege of Sidney Street. In January 1911, their
MP had dashed from his work at the Home Office to join police
officers in London as they engaged a gang of Latvian would-be bank
robbers in a firefight. The gang had already killed two policemen in
their botched robbery three weeks earlier and shot dead a third during
the siege. Understandably given the scale of the gunfire – particularly
in the era before armed police were a trained specialty – a platoon of
Scots Guards was called to bolster the operation and attempt to bring
the siege to a satisfactory close. Whether or not Churchill gave operational commands during the siege is unclear, but he certainly did
order firefighters to let the property housing the robbers burn down
after it caught fire during the gun battle. Two charred bodies were
later found, leaving one or possibly two of the gang unaccounted for.
Photos of Churchill at the siege, wearing a top hat and astrakhan-
collared overcoat – every bit the cabinet minister, but taking cover
between armed police and soldiers – were published extensively in

the following days, burnishing his reputation as a cavalier, or perhaps foolhardy, politician.

Though there was no suggestion that Churchill intended to commandeer command of the Black Watch in Dundee, the decision to send in troops was nevertheless not popular in the city, most especially and unsurprisingly among the strikers themselves. The National Transport Workers' Federation said the decision was 'calculated to incite disorder' while the Jute and Flax Workers' Union said the presence of the Black Watch would 'tend to incite to riot'.[7] Scrymgeour, who was determined to play a central role in the strike to bolster his labour credentials, was also scathing about the decision.

But Churchill unusually escaped significant criticism over the crisis, which was instead reserved for Wilkie. As a Labour MP and trade unionist himself, his constituents may have hoped Wilkie would take a more active interest in resolving the strike, or at least blocking the deployment of the Black Watch. Meanwhile, Scrymgeour had an obvious incentive in trying to discredit Wilkie as a socialist and peel away some of his supporters. For Wilkie's part, while sympathetic to the workers in the initial dispute, he found rioting and vandalism distasteful and was keen to see order restored in the city. Nevertheless, many strikers genuinely felt Wilkie did not pull his weight – like Churchill, he did not visit the constituency during the dispute – and openly criticised him.

'Lost, a Labour MP', ran the headline in Scrymgeour's *Prohibitionist*.[8] The article continued: '[The] cruel and most insulting treatment inflicted upon the long-suffering workers of Dundee who were jockeyed into voting foolishly, was only made the more disgraceful by ... ridiculous statements that Mr Wilkie was keeping "a keen eye on the situation". This glass eye outlook would not do at election time.' Churchill was inevitably pulled into Scrymgeour's later motion of censure against the two MPs for their apparent failing during the industrial dispute, but again his truly righteous anger was reserved for Wilkie. 'We never expected [Churchill] to take any notice of his constituency, except at election times,' Scrymgeour noted dryly, before adding of Wilkie: 'But never did [we] contemplate the possibility of an alleged Labour MP showing so long sustained gross indifference to his constituents under such depressing circumstances.'

*   *   *

The Dundee carters' and dockers' strike ended at 3 a.m. on Christmas Eve, just a week after it had begun. Under the headline 'A Happy Christmas Message', *The Courier* confirmed that major concessions had been delivered to the workers involved in the strike, including an increase in pay to 22 shillings, rising to the demanded 23 shillings after six months' employment.[9] They would return to work immediately, feeling they had secured a great victory. Leaving the meeting where the terms were agreed, one carter told *The Courier*: 'Man, I'll hae [have] a rare New Year noo [now].' Not to be outdone, the city's jute mills, now resupplied with coal, also restarted production on Christmas Day. A special six-carriage train was requisitioned to allow the 300 Black Watch soldiers to swiftly depart. Passing a crowd on the way to the station, the soldiers – the three crates of 'Government Explosives' clutched among them – broke out into a classic pantomime refrain: 'I wonder if you'll miss me, sometimes.' The relief was palpable, and the city quickly resumed business as usual.

The deal to end the strike was masterminded by Sir George Askwith, who had urgently travelled to Dundee some 72 hours earlier to seek a settlement. Askwith, employed at the Board of Trade, was the Liberal government's leading arbitrator and conciliator in industrial disputes. Sporting a bushy moustache, he was well known to Churchill, who in 1908 had spotted his talent and promoted him within the department. Even after Churchill left the Board of Trade, the two maintained a correspondence, with Askwith advising Churchill on how to handle industrial disputes.[10]

Trained as a barrister, Askwith was renowned as a tough negotiator who could grind down and wear out his opponents. His chief skill as an arbitrator, however, was his ability to find even the smallest areas of common ground between employer and employee from which a compromise could, perhaps after many hours and late nights, be made. But, regardless of how he managed to secure a deal, Dundee was effusive in its praise for Askwith's role in ending the strike. The Lord Provost, James Urquhart, claimed it was Askwith's 'most extraordinary adroitness, tact, courtesy and persistency in the face of insuperable difficulties' that had won out against seemingly 'impossible' odds.[11]

The fact that Dundee survived its first major strike without significant bloodshed – or, at least, death – was primarily the result of Askwith's ability to persuade dock and carting employers to make concessions and reach a deal. In the few days the strike lasted there had already been significant disruption and violence. Had it gone on longer it seems highly likely that there would have been more serious casualties.

To the extent Churchill had a role to play, it was in *not* interfering or demanding the deployment of troops himself, but in letting local lawmakers make the decision themselves when they deemed it necessary. Had the strike continued, or become more violent, his rules of engagement for troops during industrial disputes may have helped avoid unnecessary bloodshed, but this can only be speculated on. Nevertheless, and despite a grim outlook just days earlier, Dundee was able to welcome the new year of 1912 with a sense of optimism. The worst, Churchill's constituents hoped, was behind them. Unfortunately, the same could not be said for another part of the British Isles, which was about to endure a major convulsion of its own.

Chapter 11

Home Rule

1912

Churchill stepped forward towards the podium at the Celtic Football Club, Belfast, at exactly 1.30 p.m. To his right, clutching his arm, was the wife of John Redmond, the leader of the nationalist Irish Parliamentary Party at Westminster. Following closely behind, accompanied by Redmond himself, was Clementine. Just down from the stage stood Churchill's cousin, Freddie Guest, clutching a revolver concealed in his jacket pocket.

Churchill had been warned to expect trouble. A crowd of more than 5,000 had braved the troop-lined streets to hear him speak in favour of Home Rule and, while the Catholic crowd was assumed to be friendly, his visit to Belfast had, so far, been anything but. He had initially planned to speak at Ulster Hall where, 26 years earlier, his father, Lord Randolph, had given an incendiary speech about the need to defend Ulster from nationalist Catholics. But such a provocation by Churchill did not go unnoticed by the Ulster Unionist Council, who were 'astonished' by the 'deliberate challenge' of holding a pro-Home Rule meeting in 'the loyal city of Belfast'.[1] Any suggestion that the loyalist bark might be worse than its bite was quickly dispelled on Churchill's arrival in Belfast. Despite moving the meeting to a friendlier and less provocative part of town – Churchill had reluctantly acquiesced to security concerns – he nevertheless faced a bitterly hostile reception on his arrival in the city. A crowd of more than 10,000 gathered outside the Great Central Hotel, where Churchill had hoped to rest before his speech, shouting abuse and threatening violence. On leaving the hotel his car was surrounded by an angry mob, shaking fists at the windows and screaming more abuse before an escort of police was finally able to clear a path. As they reached the end of the Falls Road and entered Catholic Belfast, the atmosphere immediately changed, but it had been a traumatic experience.* Churchill would not, however, be intimidated. He had come to promote the cause of Home Rule for Ireland, and nothing would stand in his way.

Home Rule for Ireland had been a key verse in the Liberal Party's dogma for more than 50 years. Exactly what it meant varied marginally depending on the political circumstances in which it was being discussed, but in general Home Rule stood for the creation of an Irish parliament and executive in Dublin to manage domestic policies; foreign policy and defence would be reserved to the Westminster parliament. The party's Grand Old Man – William Gladstone – had doggedly pursued the policy as Prime Minister, introducing two bills on Irish Home Rule in 1886 and 1893 respectively. The first split the Liberal Party and failed to pass the House of Commons, while the second was blocked by the House of Lords. For the Liberals therefore, Home Rule for Ireland – and the failure so far to deliver it – was a totemic issue and very much unfinished business for the party. Now, with the Parliament Act curtailing the power of the House of Lords to indefinitely block legislation, there was finally an opportunity to settle the so-called Irish question and succeed where Gladstone had failed. The fact that Asquith's government required the support of the Irish Nationalists in the House of Commons made pursuing Home Rule a practical as well as ideological necessity.

Churchill had embraced Home Rule for Ireland wholeheartedly since he first joined the Liberal Party. Unlike his commitment to socially progressive policies, his support for Home Rule was prominent before he became an MP in Scotland. In 1908, when his government was publicly stating it would not pursue Irish Home Rule during that parliamentary term, Churchill backed a House of Commons motion by Redmond, leader of the Irish Parliamentary Party, calling for Ireland to be given 'legislative and executive control of all purely Irish affairs'[2] – a particularly bold move given that

---

* The only physical violence Churchill actually suffered on the trip was on the return leg. After his ferry landed at Stranraer in south-west Scotland, he was struck over the head with a green banner by a suffragette exclaiming: 'Take that, you cur.'

Churchill was just months away from being offered a cabinet position for the first time. The drama of the People's Budget of 1909 and the 'Peers versus the People' elections of 1910 pushed Home Rule for Ireland down the agenda but, when Asquith decided to bring forward a bill in April 1912, Churchill was a fervent supporter.

Churchill strongly believed a degree of autonomy for Ireland was not only necessary, but would benefit Britain: 'What harm could Irish ideas and Irish sentiments and Irish dreams, if given their free play in the Irish Parliament, do to the strong structure of British power? Would not the arrival of an Irish Parliament upon the brilliantly lighted stage of the modern world be an enrichment and an added glory to the treasures of the British Empire?'[3] This, however, did not extend to support for Irish independence – indeed, by granting a degree of autonomy to Ireland, Churchill, along with many others, hoped to avert that prospect. As he explained in the same speech, to cheers from the Catholic audience in Belfast: 'The separation of Ireland from Great Britain is absolutely impossible. The interests and affairs of the two islands are eternally interwoven. Ireland, separated by thousands of miles of ocean from any Western country, finds at her door across the channel [Irish Sea] the great English market on which she depends for the welfare of her agriculture, as well as the materials for her trades and industries.'[4]

Given the political strength of the Irish diaspora in the United States, Churchill also hoped that granting Home Rule to Ireland would boost support for Britain across the Atlantic. In 1911, he wrote: 'An Irish parliament, loyal to the Crown, and free to make the best of the Emerald Isle, is assuredly the first milestone upon [a road to closer relations with the United States].'[5]

Churchill's commitment to Home Rule may have come as a surprise to many, particularly given his family and social circles. As we have seen, his father, Lord Randolph, had been a diehard opponent of Irish Home Rule, coining the catchy but now infamous phrase: 'Ulster will fight, and Ulster will be right.' Churchill meanwhile continued to socialise with hard-line Ulster supporters, such as F.E. Smith. But Churchill's support for Irish Home Rule stemmed not from an ideological basis, but a practical one: he believed that granting some autonomy to Ireland would be the fairest and most effective way of meeting demands for Irish statehood, while also retaining the

integrity of Great Britain. Indeed, while he supported Irish Home
Rule, he recognised this was not universally the case across the island
of Ireland and was therefore willing to compromise to try to reach a
solution that was agreeable to all parties. He argued in private, for
instance, that the 'characteristically Protestant and Orange Counties'
should have 'a moratorium of several years before acceding to the
Irish parliament'.[6] But, as Asquith's bill for Irish Home Rule progressed
and the argument around it became more toxic, such nuanced arguments became increasingly difficult.

Given Churchill's passionate support for Irish Home Rule and the
fact he represented a Scottish constituency, it is worth considering
what – if any – views he had on Home Rule for Scotland. While
Ireland dominated the debate around Home Rule in the late 19th
and early 20th centuries, Home Rule for Scotland was not a novel
or alien concept. The Scottish Home Rule Association, for example,
had been formed in 1886 to lobby for its eponymous position. In
1889, the Liberal Party supported a resolution by the MP for
Caithness, Dr Gavin Clark, stating that 'it is desirable that arrangements be made for giving to the people of Scotland, by their representatives in a National Parliament, the management and control of
Scottish affairs'.[7] Similarly, as debate about Irish Home Rule raged,
some politicians adopted a commitment to 'Home Rule All Round',
which would have seen power over domestic affairs handed down
to the constituent nations of Great Britain and Ireland. Some advocates of this concept argued it should even be extended to Britain's
colonies overseas as well.

The debate around Home Rule not just for Ireland but also for
Scotland was therefore a prominent political feature in Churchill's
Dundee. Wilkie, along with many in the Labour Party, was an early
and passionate supporter of Home Rule for Ireland and, after his election in Dundee, soon extended this principle to Scotland and, indeed,
the Empire. Speaking in the House of Commons in 1912, he likened
Britain and its empire to a wheel: 'At the outer end of the spokes we
have our self-governing colonies. Then let us have at the inner end of
the spokes self-government for the four countries comprising the
United Kingdom, leaving the hub, the centre of all, to the Imperial
Government for the whole Empire.'[8] As with Churchill on Irish

Home Rule, however, this did not amount to support for Scottish independence, with Wilkie arguing: 'Scotland is by nature's laws designed to be the northern part of this Kingdom.'

Scrymgeour, given his religiosity, was initially on more difficult ground. While he made overtures to Dundee's Catholic – and almost universally Irish – population, he clashed with local priests who sought publicans as benefactors and won little support from the pulpit. He even publicly attacked the city's Catholic newspaper, the *Catholic Herald*, in the pages of *The Scottish Prohibitionist*. But, in a rare example of cold political calculation, Scrymgeour recognised the importance of the Irish block vote in the city and by 1921 was the most effusive supporter of Irish Home Rule among Dundee's politicians. As with Wilkie, Scrymgeour's support for Irish Home Rule extended to support for Scottish Home Rule as well.

Despite his opponents' support for Scottish Home Rule, Churchill was initially more reticent. 'I would not deny Scotland any liberty that you give to Ireland,' he said when asked about the issue on the second day of his campaign in Dundee in 1908, 'but I am not at all sure that Scotland is in a hurry to give up the great influence that she exerts upon the government of England.'[9] At first glance this is the kind of ambiguous response a prudent politician would give when caught off guard by a question. Indeed, given the rushed nature of the 1908 by-election and the fact it was Churchill's first time campaigning in Scotland, it may well be that he had not yet given the question of Scottish Home Rule much thought. Yet the response also reflects Churchill's character and political position at the time. Given his political upbringing, he could not understand why a constituent country of Great Britain – the most formidable nation on earth – would want to give up that power and responsibility. At the same time, Scottish Home Rule, should it come to pass, would damage Churchill's political career – his 'life seat' would not be worth much if it meant he was excluded from all decision-making on domestic issues in the rest of Great Britain.

But as he settled into life as an MP in Scotland, his views became more formed and eventually evolved into a commitment to the devolution of power across Great Britain and Ireland. This evolution took time and was intrinsically linked to support for Irish Home Rule. He first recognised that, if he supported Home Rule for Ireland, he must also support the same for Scotland, should it want it; logically, he could not defend his support for Irish Home Rule if he denied the principle of Home Rule to Scotland. But much more importantly, supporting the principle of Home Rule for Scotland had several political advantages. It was a relatively popular position among his supporters in Dundee and would avoid him being outflanked by his opponents – particularly Scrymgeour – in future constituency elections. More importantly still, Churchill was able to link Home Rule for Ireland with Home Rule for Scotland, thereby making the former more politically palatable to his constituents, many of whom were Ulster supporters.

The culmination of the evolution of Churchill's support for Scottish Home Rule is best evidenced in a speech he gave in Lochee, a district of Dundee dominated by the immigrant Irish community, in October 1913: 'Another great reason for the settlement of the Irish question in the present Parliament and for disposing of the Home Rule controversy now, while we have the full opportunity presented, is that the ground is thereby cleared for the consideration of claims of self-government for other parts of the United Kingdom besides Ireland.'[10] Referring to a speech he made in the city the previous year, Churchill went on to outline his vision for a devolution of power across the United Kingdom:

> I spoke of the establishment of a federal system in the United Kingdom, in which Scotland, Ireland and Wales, and, if necessary, parts of England, could have separate legislative and parliamentary institutions, enabling them to develop, in their own way, their own life according to their own ideas and needs in the same way as the great and prosperous States of the American Union and the great kingdoms and principalities and States of the German Empire.[11]

He finished the speech with a bold prediction: 'I prophesy that the day will most certainly come – many of you will live to see it – when a federal system will be established in these islands which will give Wales and Scotland control, within proper limits, of their own affairs.'[12]

Churchill's interest in federalism undoubtedly stemmed in part from his predisposition to the United States, but it was also a necessity to tackle the Gordian knot of Irish Home Rule if it came to pass

– namely, whether Ireland would continue to send MPs to Westminster and, if so, whether they would be able to vote on domestic matters affecting the rest of Great Britain but, as a result of Home Rule, no longer Ireland. This was, in effect, the same conundrum that gained renown as the West Lothian Question after the Labour grandee Tam Dalyell raised it in the House of Commons in 1977. One proposed solution was the creation of a separate English parliament to handle domestic questions, alongside those that would also be created in Scotland, Wales and Ireland, with each elected on its own national franchise. Alongside these four domestic assemblies, the existing parliament at Westminster would become a separate 'imperial parliament', elected on a UK-wide franchise, handling only foreign and defence policy. But privately Churchill was vehemently opposed to this proposition, suggesting it was unworkable. As he argued in a cabinet paper in February 1911, it would be 'absolutely impossible' for an English parliament and an imperial parliament to co-exist in any effective way, particularly because it was likely the English parliament would elect a Conservative majority and the imperial parliament a Liberal majority, causing political deadlock.[13]

Instead, Churchill proposed to tackle the Gordian knot with a more substantive form of devolution that would hand significant powers not just to national parliaments in Scotland, Ireland and Wales, but also to groups of English regions.[14] This was not federalism in an American sense – it went beyond recognised 'states' and there was no suggestion of a written constitution – but Churchill believed it would be more effective for that. Under Churchill's scheme, which he proposed 'for discussion' in a cabinet memorandum in March 1911, the United Kingdom would be 'divided into ten areas' with a 'legislative and administrative body, separately elected, to be created for each area'. 'In Ireland, Scotland and Wales,' he continued, 'these bodies [are] to be clothed in Parliamentary form so far as may be desirable in each case.' These 10 new bodies would be given all the power of existing county councils, plus power over areas such as education, policing, housing and roads. Women, Churchill added in his proposal, would be free to vote in the elections for these bodies. Churchill argued such a system would satisfy the demands of national movements, particularly in Ireland but also in Scotland; allow domestic decisions to be taken locally while avoiding the creation of a competing English parliament;

and allow the imperial parliament to focus purely on foreign policy, defence and other specific areas of major importance.[15]

Churchill's scheme would have represented a most radical redrawing of the constitutional arrangement of Great Britain and Ireland, going far beyond the devolution of powers that finally occurred almost 100 years later in 1999. Yet, while it did provide a practical solution to the Gordian knot, it was not Churchill merely coming up with a solution to a crisis at hand. Churchill's proposals for devolution had in fact been percolating almost since he first entered parliament. In 1901, he proposed devolution to local government as a way of improving the efficiency of the House of Commons, which he found 'choked by its often-trivial business'.[16] 'If [the Commons] were relieved of local and personal interest as well as of public legislation which is not controversial it would have time to deal more fully and ably with executive matters, imperial and national, and with legislative proposals of the first importance,' he said. While he acknowledged his scheme would 'further [the] object' of 'meeting local and national prejudices and sentiments', he emphasised that that was not its primary objective.[17] Nevertheless, Churchill was not an opportunistic supporter of devolution, but rather a considered one, who had supported the concept even before he joined the Liberal Party.

As Churchill stepped down from the podium in Belfast to the ecstatic cheers of the crowd, he may have hoped that the Irish question that had dominated British politics for so long would now, finally, be resolved. Indeed, Asquith introduced his Home Rule Bill – the third that the Liberal Party had tried to pass – in April 1912 and, with the support of Redmond's Irish Parliamentary Party, it passed the House of Commons. But fierce opposition from the Conservative Party delayed its passage, and it was not until January 1913 that the bill was passed to the House of Lords where, unsurprisingly, it was resoundingly rejected. But thanks to the Parliament Act of 1911, the rejection by the House of Lords did not kill the bill this time, but only delayed it.

However, despite it being passed by a democratically elected chamber, it remained hugely controversial and there were even fears attempting to implement it could spark a civil war. Ulster unionists, under their firebrand leader Sir Edward Carson, began arming themselves, while Irish nationalists did the same in response. A compromise was clearly necessary, and Asquith tried to find one by amending the Home Rule Bill so that Ulster would not be included. This arrangement was accepted by both sides in principle but wrangling over exactly which counties would be excluded continued until July 1914. Then, with war fast approaching on the continent and a compromise seemingly unlikely, the progress of Home Rule was once again stalled. The failure to reach a deal would have far-reaching consequences for Irish and British politics, and for Churchill in Dundee.

Chapter 12

An Activist Victorious
1900–1913

On the evening of 4 June 1910, London's Adelphi Theatre was filled to capacity. It was the opening night of a new adaption of the Sherlock Holmes adventure, *The Speckled Band*. The crowd that evening was particularly eager – London's thespians had been deprived of theatre for almost a month after venues closed in mourning for the death of King Edward VII on 10 May. Black armbands were still sported by some guests as they headed to their seats.

There were many notable guests at the packed theatre, but three in particular stood out among the crowd. The first, the creator of Sherlock Holmes, Arthur Conan Doyle, would have been well known to many in the audience. Although outwardly calm, the Edinburgh-born author was particularly anxious that evening. He had initially hired the Adelphi to stage an adaption of his lesser-known 1896 novel *Rodney Stone*, but the king's sudden death had scuppered his plans, leaving him with a costly theatre he could not fill and facing a significant financial setback. In desperation, Conan Doyle used the period of mourning to swiftly adapt *The Speckled Band* for the stage, in the hope that the broader appeal of Holmes would help him recoup his losses in the little time he had left at the Adelphi. This was the first test of whether the gamble had paid off.

Conan Doyle's two guests were less familiar to the crowd, but no less distinguished. On one side sat Sir Roger Casement. Good-looking, with a thick beard and flowing black hair, it was his dark tan that betrayed his career in the British consular service in West Africa. Born in Dublin, Casement's association with the African continent began in 1883, when he journeyed to the Congo as a 19-year-old novice trader. By 1892, he had begun his career as a British colonial administrator in Nigeria. Posts in southern Africa followed before, in 1900, Casement was ordered to establish a British consulate in the so-called Congo Free State, which had been the private property of King Leopold II of Belgium for the previous 15 years. It was three years later, in 1903, that the Foreign Office ordered Casement to investigate rumours of abuses by the Congo Free State authorities. 'Go into the interior,' the order read, 'and send reports as soon as possible.'[1]

While Conan Doyle's other guest had never set foot in the Congo, his career was at least as intimately associated with it. Edmund Dene Morel – universally known as E.D. Morel – was born in Paris to a French father and an English mother in 1873. After his father's premature death, Morel left school at 15, scraping a living in France before taking up a position as a clerk with the Liverpool-based shipping firm Elder Dempster in 1891. With a bushy handlebar moustache and eager mind, the bilingual Morel was tasked with acting as a liaison on one of Elder Dempster's most lucrative contracts, the carrying of all cargo between the Congo Free State and Belgium. Initially, he was enthusiastic about the work, finally having found secure and decent employment. But, as he spent more time in Belgium and engaged with Congo Free State officials there, he became not only uncomfortable but increasingly suspicious. Morel noticed that the Elder Dempster ships bound for the Congo Free State were packed with arms, ammunition and other apparatus of terror. Morel calculated that 80 per cent of imports going into the Congo Free State were 'remote from trade purposes'.[2] Yet, as Morel knew from the Elder Dempster records, the returning ships were coming back loaded with valuable ivory and rubber. This discrepancy alone was troubling enough, but it was particularly concerning given that the native peoples of the Congo Free State were banned from using money, meaning they had to be paid in goods. '[But] nothing,' Morel wrote, 'was going in to pay for what was coming out.'[3]

It was this shared interest in the Congo Free State – particularly its rubber trade and, ultimately and most importantly, the fate of its native people – that brought these men together that evening. For almost a decade, both Morel and Casement had led the campaign against Belgian abuses in the Congo. Conan Doyle had joined their cause later, but no less passionately, as one of several famous patrons. The trip to see *The Speckled Band* that June evening was a rare break for three men who had dedicated years to exposing King Leopold's klepto-cratic rule. Their campaign, however, still had several years left to run.

Both Morel and Casement had become convinced of the horror of the Congo Free State independently, but the campaign to stop it only began in earnest after they met on 10 December 1903. Casement had earlier returned to Britain to prepare and publish the report of his investigation into abuses in the Congo, which had been ordered by the Foreign Office earlier that year. It made grim reading, highlight-ing how the Congo Free State authorities used terror and violence to systematically pillage the area of valuable goods. Casement docu-mented the suffering of local people in stark detail, including accounts of hands and penises being chopped off as punishment by European 'traders', and entire villages being held hostage for failing to meet their quota for extracting rubber, the Congo Free State's most valu-able 'export'. Such extreme exploitation had been going on since 1885, when Leopold II persuaded other European powers to allow him to personally annex – the Belgian government refused to partic-ipate in the scheme – much of the Congo basin, an area similar in scope to the modern-day Democratic Republic of Congo. He had promised fellow governments his efforts were purely philanthropic but, once his claim was confirmed at Otto von Bismarck's Berlin Conference, the systematic theft of the area's resources began in earnest.

The devastation – but particularly the frankness – of Casement's account of Leopold's treatment of the Congo shocked Foreign Office officials, who worked to soften its tone in a bid to avoid a diplomatic rift with Belgium. For Morel, however, Casement's unadulterated report was anything but unwelcome. Finally, he had evidence – and not just any evidence, but evidence acquired by a respected British diplomat – of the abuses he had first deduced from the ledgers of Elder Dempster and the docks of Antwerp. Armed with Casement's report, Morel felt he could finally spur the public – and particularly the British government – into action.

When Morel and Casement finally met, they immediately estab-lished a rapport, talking until 2 a.m. Over the coming weeks, the two quickly developed a strong bond, and they remained close, lifelong friends. Morel later described how he was transfixed as Casement read him passages from his as-yet unpublished – and, crucially, unedited – report. 'I [Morel] was mostly a silent listener, clutching hard upon the arms of my chair,' he wrote.[4] 'As the monologue of horror proceeded, I verily believe I saw those hunted women clutching their children and flying panic stricken to the bush: the blood flowing from those quivering black bodies as the hippopotamus hide whip struck and struck again; the savage soldiery rushing hither and tither amid burning villages; the ghastly tally of severed hands ...' Following further meetings between the pair – including a stay at Hawarden in Wales, Morel's then home – they established the Congo Reform Association (CRA), which became the key campaigning group against the Congo Free State.

Much of the work of the CRA involved lobbying the government of Belgium, but also Britain and the United States, to change their behaviour in relation to the Congo and clamp down on abuses. As Casement remained a government employee, all the public-facing work was undertaken by Morel, who resigned his role with Elder Dempster to pursue justice for the Congo full-time. Government ministers, MPs, journalists, diplomats, businessmen – every relevant professional group received voluminous correspondence from Morel. He was relentless in this pursuit, regularly working 18-hour days on behalf of the CRA. In the first six months of 1906, for example, he wrote 3,700 letters, an average of more than 20 a day.

This lobbying effort was coupled with a public relations offensive centred, like a political campaign, on large-scale rallies and set-piece speeches. These took place across the country, including in Scotland, where cries of 'shame' echoed around the crowd as Morel outlined the abuses being perpetrated in the West African territory. On the platform, he was regularly joined by MPs from across the political spectrum, as well as religious leaders and other key figures. As training for a future career in politics, one could ask for little better, and Morel revelled in the limelight, writing: '[I experienced] exhilaration when I had driven home some good thrust, or when that something or other which it is difficult to name gripped me on the platform and I felt I had a great audience in the hollow of my hand.'[5]

At this stage in his life, however, Morel primarily viewed himself as a journalist – one historian has described him as 'the greatest British

investigative journalist of his time'[6] – and it was in this field that he
produced his most devastating attacks on the abuses of the Congo
Free State. He provided numerous freelance contributions to a wide
array of publications outlining the abuses of the Congo Free State, but
Morel's relationship with newspapers was not limited to writing articles – he once gleefully reported that he engineered the sacking of
The Times' Belgian correspondent, who Morel viewed as being too
close to King Leopold. But to avoid censorship and the interference
of the many vested interests who profited from the exploitation of the
Belgian regime, Morel decided he also needed his own organ, of
which he alone would have editorial control. Therefore, in 1903, and
with funding from private philanthropists, he founded the *West African
Mail*.

Establishing a newspaper is never easy, even in the early 20th
century, when print retained a prominence that proprietors today
can only dream of. Morel correctly understood that to be both
commercially viable and politically impactful, the *West African Mail*
would have to be more than a campaigning pamphlet. It would need
commercial, shipping and even meteorological articles to build a
broad readership, who would then also be introduced – via Morel's
investigative journalism – to the horrors of the Congo Free State. To
do this, Morel got the British Cotton Growing Association – a
nascent industry body, with an interest in cotton growing in West
Africa – to partner on the newspaper, as well as lining up distribu-
tors not only in the UK, but throughout Europe and Africa. But,
despite his own prodigious output, he still lacked writers and articles, and quickly set about soliciting as many pieces as possible. His
first port of call was the young Conservative MP for Oldham, who
was already making a name for himself on the backbenches –
Winston Churchill.

Churchill's eagerness to write a piece for the *West African Mail*
came not from his interest in foreign policy – as might be expected
– but rather from his interest in his constituency. Like Manchester
and particularly Dundee, Oldham was a single-industry town, rely-
ing heavily on the cotton mills for its economic prosperity. As in
other constituencies Churchill later represented, the raw material
for this industry was imported from abroad – India, but also the
United States – and manufactured into a finished product in local

mills. The perennial problem was the price of the raw material, which could fluctuate massively, potentially putting mills out of business and cotton spinners out of work. But Churchill saw an opportunity to increase the cotton supply – and thereby limit these negative fluctuations – by growing it in West Africa, which was thought to have a suitable climate for cultivation of the crop. As he explained in the article he wrote for Morel, which was published in the first ever edition of the *West African Mail* on 3 April 1903: 'The fact that the present supply of cotton not infrequently falls short of the demand constitutes a very serious disadvantage and even danger to Lancashire, for the raw material upon which her industries depend becomes not only the sport of speculators but is also inter-cepted in increasing quantities by the mills in the United States of America.'[7]

This is undoubtedly sensible – a detractor might say basic – economics, but it is also an early example of Churchill's desire to marry his interest in international affairs with the interests of his constituency. He continued: 'Anything that can increase the area of cotton cultivation within the British Empire or outside it, preferably of course within it, must be a real advantage to Lancashire.' Morel's newspaper, Churchill added, would deliver 'a real service' by provid-ing a 'sustained public interest' in the region.

Morel was delighted with Churchill's piece, which appeared prom-inently on page five of the new publication, including a substantial photograph of the youthful-looking MP. In fact, Churchill was so enamoured with the photograph that he only reluctantly lent it to Morel for inclusion after a specific promise was given that it would be returned in pristine condition. On his part, Morel went on to frequently drop Churchill's name into letters to other potential contributors to the *West African Mail*.[8]

The work of the CRA and the *West African Mail* over the next decade was crucial in shifting public opinion against the Congo Free State and driving reform. As well as Conan Doyle, other writers such as Joseph Conrad – who based his famous short story *Heart of Darkness* on travels in the Congo Free State – became prominent supporters of the CRA and Morel's work. Like Scrymgeour, Morel also developed close ties with similarly minded activists in the United States. Mark

Twain and the civil rights activist Booker T. Washington were some of the prominent supporters across the Atlantic.

Morel – with the assistance of Casement and his ground-breaking investigation – was the driving force in this campaign. Yet his motives for undertaking it are difficult to discern. He had – as yet – never been a member of a political party and, while nominally a member of the Church of England, he was not religious. Equally, having worked so hard to gain his position at Elder Dempster, and after the hardships of his youth, it was an act of extreme self-sacrifice – even foolhardiness – to trade it in for the uncertainty of journalism and humanitarian activism. Yet, despite his lack of politics or religious grounding, Morel nevertheless seems to have possessed a ferocious indignation and a clear sense of right and wrong. This, coupled with his restless energy, continued to drive his views and actions long after his work with the CRA was completed.

By the time of King Leopold II's death in 1908, the outcry against the atrocities in the Congo basin had become significant and was a major embarrassment to the Belgian government, who took the territory into administration themselves. Keen to press home their advantage, the CRA kept campaigning for a further five years, pressuring the Belgian government to stamp out the system of forced labour and extreme violence that characterised Leopold's reign. This pressure yielded positive results: reports of abuse against rubber collectors, as well as violence against villagers, decreased, while the severing of hands was also officially banned. While exploitation unquestionably continued in what was now named the Belgian Congo, it was of a different and less violent form.

The final meeting of the CRA was held on 16 June 1913 at the Westminster Palace Hotel on London's Victoria Street. The meeting received widespread coverage, with *The Courier* noting the CRA proved 'British public opinion is a force to be reckoned with in European politics'.[9] As well as Morel, many other supporters of the CRA – including Casement – were present. Amid the lavish praise and thanks, Morel declared that the CRA had 'struck a blow for justice that cannot and will not pass away'.[10]

But at just 39 years old, Morel was far from ready for retirement. Not only had he gained invaluable experience as a writer, public speaker and campaigner, but he had tasted victory – and he liked it.

Indeed, as he walked down the steps of the Westminster Palace Hotel, the only question in his mind was what his new challenge should be. Little did he know then that he was about to embark on a path that would lead him not only to prison and near-death, but into a brutal battle with one of his earliest supporters – Churchill.

Chapter 13

The Policeman, the Pilot
and the Prohibitionist
1913–1914

George Webster stopped playing football the moment he saw the policeman. Normally he would not have been afraid of such a figure – the school term had just finished, and he was excited by the prospects of play afforded by the holidays and long June nights. But there was something in Sergeant James Thornton's movements that made the 13-year-old apprehensive. The policeman was not walking normally but staggering. He was struggling to keep to a straight line. When he finally reached the boys he paused, before slumping against a wall. When he composed himself, George noticed he was swaying gently, backwards and forwards, like a metronome. 'Clear out, boys,' Sergeant Thornton suddenly growled, 'and don't get me in trouble.'[1] George and his friends, in a mixture of awe, surprise and terror, quickly fled.

Scrymgeour was working late at the offices of *The Scottish Prohibitionist* when he heard about Sergeant Thornton's strange behaviour. Despite his warning, the boys had quickly spread the word about the policeman and his curious condition. By the time he resumed his erratic journey across town, a small gaggle of fascinated schoolboys were following from a distance. Most of the older residents also kept their distance, following Sergeant Thornton's progress from shop fronts and tenement windows – but Scrymgeour had to see it for himself.

He finally caught up with the sergeant at 8.15 p.m. He found him leaning precariously against a streetlight, staring vacantly ahead. Scrymgeour approached the policeman cautiously, edging his way deliberately to within just a few yards of him. The sergeant's gaze continued to be transfixed on some invisible spot in the distance. Slowly, Scrymgeour circled Sergeant Thornton, like an animal vigilantly surveying its wounded prey, before turning on his heels and marching decisively back towards the office of *The Scottish Prohibitionist*. Scrymgeour was both satisfied and appalled with what he had found: a Dundee policeman drunk on duty.

Scrymgeour wasted no time in unleashing his righteous anger. At the Sunday meeting of the Scottish Prohibition Party, which took place in the open-air in Dundee's Albert Square, Scrymgeour accused Thornton of being drunk on duty and lambasted what he claimed was the moral degeneracy of the Dundee constabulary. Then, in the next edition of *The Scottish Prohibitionist*, published a week to the day after he had first spotted Thornton, Scrymgeour suggested it was his 'painful duty' to report that he had seen the East End police sergeant staggering and drunk on St Andrew's Street.[2] He also mistakenly asserted that Thornton had recently been demoted from a sergeant to a constable.

The article caused a sensation and was followed by a wider attack on the entire force, with Scrymgeour suggesting Thornton's inebriation on duty was not an isolated incident. Another police officer – this time based in the city's West End – had also been recently spotted 'mad with drink ... striking out at the citizens and even one of his own colleagues'. Scrymgeour claimed this epidemic of police drunkenness was the result of a bizarre and incredible conspiracy, where Dundee's police officers were being assisted to drink in public toilets by local government officials. 'We are now, spontaneously and credibly, informed that systemic drinking on the part of policemen takes place in public lavatories, in which practice they are assisted by other public servants,' he wrote in *The Scottish Prohibitionist*.[3] The only solution, Scrymgeour argued, was for the entire police force to commit to total abstinence from alcohol.

Not for the first time, however, Scrymgeour had gone too far. Not only had he erroneously suggested Thornton had been demoted, but he was now trying to tarnish the whole Dundee police force as well. On 6 November 1912, it was confirmed that Thornton was suing Scrymgeour for libel and seeking a mammoth £750 – approximately £60,000 in 2017 – in damages. Naturally, Scrymgeour – confident in not just the strength of his case but also the righteousness of his cause – would fight the charge. The trial would begin on 26 December.

Despite Scrymgeour's bullish confidence, his lawyers were more reticent. They could produce many witnesses who would attest to seeing Sergeant Thornton in what appeared to be an intoxicated state on the night in question. In fact, more than 10 Dundonians – as well as Scrymgeour – said as much under oath to the jury and judge, Lord Guthrie, during the trial, which took place in Edinburgh. While under cross-examination, it emerged several of Scrymgeour's witnesses were paid-up members of the Scottish Prohibition Party, but this appears to have had little impact on the weight given to their evidence. Indeed, the witnesses produced by Sergeant Thornton's lawyers were almost wholly his friends or fellow police officers. Yet it was not enough for Scrymgeour to persuade the jury that Thornton had appeared drunk – he actually had to prove that Thornton *was* drunk and this, to Scrymgeour's understandable consternation, proved impossible. After a two-day hearing, the jury unanimously found Scrymgeour and the printer of *The Scottish Prohibitionist*, John Pellow, had libelled Thornton.

Scrymgeour's defeat – confirmed in February 1913 after an appeal failed – left him facing not just financial but also political ruin. The court had not acquiesced to the £750 of damages Thornton had sought, instead fixing compensation at £185 plus expenses. While this was some relief, it was only nominal: Thornton's expenses amounted to more than £242, while Scrymgeour's own legal bills for his failed defence were more than £284. In total, Scrymgeour still owed more than £712 to various parties, approximately £55,000 in 2017. That was more money than Scrymgeour had had – or ever would have – in his life. He had no wealthy relatives or benefactors to turn to, and sales of *The Scottish Prohibitionist*, while respectable, would hardly come close to covering such an astronomical sum. Yet if he did not find the money, the only alternative was to declare himself bankrupt. This would be a personal humiliation, but it would also end his political career: bankrupts were barred from holding public office. His seat as a councillor would be forfeited and his hopes of defeating Churchill and finally gaining a place in the House of Commons – where he could bring about real change – finished. Such an outcome was totally unacceptable to Scrymgeour. He would just have to find the money, and fast.

Within a week of his defeat, he established the unimaginatively named Scrymgeour Defence Fund. Promoted mostly through the pages of *The Scottish Prohibitionist*, the fund sought donations from party members and wider supporters of Scrymgeour. Many of his appeals were written in such a guilt-inducing manner they almost amounted to emotional blackmail. The following example is typical: 'Many are doubtless thinking that we shall get the money all right. That altogether depends on the necessary responses being made promptly to our renewed appeals. Indeed, we may yet have to go under ... So long as such appeals are to be ignored, so long will the workers deserve the treatment of a football [i.e., to be kicked].'[4]

Such appeals yielded immediate results. Apart from a raft of local donations, Dundonians and others living abroad also sent funds, most accepting his narrative that Scrymgeour was an underdog who had been unfairly slighted by the establishment. A group in Titaghur, India, contributed £12 to the Scrymgeour Defence Fund, for example, while anti-alcohol groups in America also picked up the cause. The editor of the Pennsylvania-based *Vindicator* – William Ferguson, whom Scrymgeour regularly corresponded with – was particularly supportive. In one article, Ferguson shared a theory – propagated by Scrymgeour himself – that Thornton's lawsuit had been encouraged by establishment figures in Dundee to try to bankrupt him and ruin him politically. Ferguson wrote: 'Mr Scrymgeour ... seems to have been a pretty sharp thorn in the side of officials in [Dundee] for a long time, because of his opposition to some of their ways of conducting public business and the publicity which he has given municipal affairs. [The] case impresses us as having been seized upon as an opportunity to "get even".'[5]

Regardless of the veracity of such claims, Scrymgeour still needed to find the vast sum of money or face ruin. But he was savvy enough to recognise that, if he were to succeed, it would be necessary to do more than pester and cajole his relatively impoverished supporters, even those based on the other side of the world. The Scottish Prohibition Party therefore organised ticketed events, such as concerts, to support the Scrymgeour Defence Fund. One 'Grand Concert', scheduled for February in Kinnaird Hall, involved a range of singers, comedians and one George Bryan, who was described as 'an international dancer' leading a 'famous troupe'. But even such enticing offerings were not sufficient to meet the demands of Scrymgeour's creditors, who were growing increasingly sceptical of his ability to raise the requisite funds. In desperation – and no doubt with some moral contortions – he decided to run a lottery. The prize would be 'a valuable gold watch', and tickets could be purchased for three pence. Launched in March, it proved an instant hit. Scrymgeour finally believed he may have found a winning fundraising strategy. But then it came to a crushing halt.

The letter from the Procurator Fiscal – Dundee's prosecutor – arrived at Scrymgeour's Victoria Road home on 22 April. It made grim reading. 'I have to inform [you] that the selling and issuing of such tickets ... is illegal and in contravention of the Lotteries Act 1823,' the prosecutor wrote.[6] Unless Scrymgeour immediately wrote stating his intention to scrap the competition to win the gold watch, he would face the prospect of criminal charges, the prosecutor added. Scrymgeour was understandably incandescent, and the situation reinforced his belief that he was being persecuted by the Dundee establishment for his political views and activities. In his response, after confirming that he would scrap the competition, Scrymgeour listed four other Dundee groups concurrently running similar competitions, before sarcastically closing: 'We, at any rate, quite understand the situation, in which our case has, to say the least, been taken first.'[7]

Scrymgeour's prospects were now increasingly bleak. Even allowing for his own hyperbole, his message to supporters in a 10 May edition of *The Scottish Prohibitionist* strikes a particularly downtrodden tone:

> We are within a few weeks of the time when, according to our anticipations, the final financial settlement might be made with our opponents; but, so far as things have recently gone [in relation to the watch competition], it will not be possible to pay ... the balance of [the] claim standing against us. In these disappointing circumstances, we must just be prepared for the worst, which, after all, will be taken as the best by the other side.[8]

A further message, on 24 May, was even more defeatist, with the Scottish Prohibition Party's supporters bearing the brunt of Scrymgeour's ruminations. 'We deeply regret having to report a scarcity of responses in recent days to our urgent appeals,' he wrote reprovingly.[9] 'This means, after all has been said and done, that numerous professing friends are quite indifferent to what may befall us.' He added: 'With God's help, we nevertheless still persist in believing that all will yet come right sooner or later, although no thanks to those who are shirking their duty.' Scrymgeour, however, was determined not to give up and – like a desperate gambler trying to win back his increasing losses – he raised the stakes yet again. With his settlement date fast approaching, he decided to bet on a spectacle that would not only raise the necessary funds, but also silence his critics. The Scottish Prohibition Party, Scrymgeour decided, would organise Dundee's first ever air show.

'Dundee's Great Event' – as Scrymgeour named it – was announced in *The Scottish Prohibitionist* on 14 June.[10] The city's Fairmuir Park would be the 'centre of attraction . . . not only for the citizens, but for thousands of visitors near and far'. The centrepiece of the event would be 'a series of aeroplane exhibition flights, the first ever made available for the satisfaction of the public in this part of the country'. To deliver the show, Scrymgeour turned to the Spencer Brothers. The firm had been founded by Charles Green Spencer – an early aviation pioneer – in north London, but its primary business was initially manufacturing hot-air balloons, as well as – less reassuringly – parachutes that offered a 'certainty of escape for aviators'.[11] After Charles's death in 1890, the firm was taken over by his six sons, who expanded its offerings to include aeroplane displays, balloon races and parachute descents – and they were enthusiastic to answer Scrymgeour's call. Fencing was leased from the Dundee Horticultural Society, and a tent was procured in which the plane could be viewed by ticketed guests between the two planned displays. The event was scheduled – weather dependent – to take place on Saturday 28 June, and a full front-page advert in *The Scottish Prohibitionist* was given over to its promotion. It was a significant outlay for Scrymgeour, but given the popularity of the event, he stood not only to clear his debts but also deliver a much-needed windfall for the party. Everything, it seemed, was in order.

Scrymgeour initially hoped the Spencer Brothers would provide him with the famed Lewis Turner as a pilot, whom he described as 'one of the most skilful aviators in the world'. He was, however, to be disappointed; Turner was called away unexpectedly and the firm instead offered Sydney Pickles. An Australian by birth, the 19-year-old Pickles was not a household name but was well known on the adrenaline-fuelled circuit of early 20th-century aviation. '[He] is a wonder,' the company effusively wrote in a bid to reassure their client.[12] 'Today he is flying from London to Brighton and back. He will give you a fine show,' they added. The Spencer Brothers could not know it then, but nothing could be further from the truth.

The day of 'Dundee's Great Event' began inauspiciously. The weather in the early morning was stormy with clouds closing in on the city, threatening high winds and rain. Pickles warned he could not fly in such weather, and a devastated Scrymgeour prepared to call off the event. But – and Scrymgeour may have thought miraculously – at mid-morning the skies began to clear and by noon it was a balmy June day, the improvised runway at Fairmuir Park bathed in sunshine.

Pickles was now enthusiastic for the event to get underway but, as he tested his single-seater Bleriot XI monoplane, he discovered an issue with the propeller. Confident he had solved the problem, he persuaded a reluctant Scrymgeour that he should conduct a brief test flight, just to ensure everything would run smoothly once the crowds arrived at 2 p.m. Scrymgeour was particularly concerned that ticketed members might resent their friends and neighbours seeing the plane over the city before they did, but – with so much riding on the success of the event – acquiesced to the expert advice. It was just before 12.30 p.m. that Pickles jumped into the cockpit and started the engine. Despite his earlier confidence, the plane initially spat and spluttered its way jerkily up the makeshift runway in the park. Unable to get enough speed, he turned, tried again and this time successfully achieved lift off.

That was when the trouble really began. As soon as he was in the air the propeller began to whine and crack. The wind, stronger than anticipated, buffeted the lightweight plane from side to side. While still above the park, Pickles's aircraft began to rapidly lose speed and elevation. His undercarriage narrowly missed a telegraph line and, despite furious attempts to pull up, he could not regain control. The plane crashed, ignominiously, into the large chimney stack of a semi-detached house on Muirfield Crescent. There it paused, seemingly suspended mid-air for what felt like an eternity, before sliding down the sloped roof and into the garden. It had flown less than 100 metres.

Remarkably, no one was seriously injured. The owner of the house, John Drysdale, was inside and unharmed; he later said he felt like he was in an 'earthquake'.[13] More seriously, his two young sons and a five-year-old friend visiting from Glasgow were playing in the garden at the time of the crash. The trio narrowly escaped the shower of bricks cascading from the roof as the Bleriot hit the chimney. They were scared, but uninjured. Pickles, despite staying seated in the cockpit throughout, was also able to walk away from the crash. Later that evening he quietly departed the city, telling a reporter he was on his way to France to pick up a plane for the Admiralty.

Scrymgeour, however, faced ruin. 'Dundee's Great Event' had descended – quite literally – into farce. Personally, it was a humiliation that caused delight among Scrymgeour's opponents, who were quick to deride the whole concept. The Liberal-leaning *Advertiser* mocked: 'Aviation as a draw has no power over Dundonians . . . an unfortunate accident, which very easily might have had very serious results, rendered the exhibition a fiasco.'[14] *The Courier* took Scrymgeour to task for the failure of the air show and risk of injury, but also blamed the council for allowing the 'most inappropriate' Fairmuir Park to be used as a location for such a display.

Most importantly given Scrymgeour's precarious position, the debacle of the air show was financially calamitous. Not only had Scrymgeour failed to clear his debts, but he had now incurred additional financial liabilities. In the aftermath of the crash, an effort to persuade people to not seek a refund for their tickets enjoyed only minimal uptake. A dispute over insurance cover also soon emerged with the Spencer Brothers, with both parties seeking to blame the other for the fiasco. Meanwhile, Scrymgeour personally faced additional claims from disgruntled residents. Drysdale, whose house the plane had crashed into, wrote to Scrymgeour demanding £50* to compensate for the 'shock and inconvenience' of the 'mishap'.[15] Other local residents followed suit. One of Drysdale's neighbours lambasted Scrymgeour for the 'serious inconvenience' caused by the workmen repairing the smashed chimney and demanded £10. This was money that Scrymgeour – already deep in the red – simply did not have.

---

* Approximately £3,900 in 2017.

Matters finally came to a head on 10 September, when two bailiffs appeared at the offices of *The Scottish Prohibitionist*. Perhaps sensing the intense vulnerability of his adversary, Thornton had lost patience in waiting for his damages. He now demanded the outstanding £146 be paid in full, within 15 days. The only alternative was for Scrymgeour to declare himself bankrupt. As he wrote in *The Scottish Prohibitionist*: 'It now lies with us to find the money, or intensely gratify the desires of our enemies by being declared bankrupt, with accompanying results, which include compulsory retiral from the council and practical expulsion from public life for several years. We are certainly not going to let our enemies trample over us.'[16] Yet the question of how Scrymgeour would find the money still remained. Generous supporters had so far allowed Scrymgeour to clear about £600* of debt – including the costs of the air show fiasco – but it seemed unlikely their philanthropy would or could extend much further.

As it happened, it was Scrymgeour's least elaborate money-making scheme that eventually proved the most effective: he launched a massive subscription drive for *The Scottish Prohibitionist*. Party activists set about encouraging new subscribers, but also persuaded many already regular readers to simply pay for a year's worth of editions in advance. By offering something tangible in exchange for money – rather than soliciting donations – Scrymgeour was soon on the way to meeting the debt. 'It is satisfactory to find that promises ... and subscriptions are now reaching [us],' he was able to write with some relief. 'We trust that no friend of the movement will fail to most heartily support the very important undertaking.' The boost in subscriptions, coupled with the imminent prospect of bankruptcy, which focused minds and encouraged some additional last-minute donations, finally delivered. On 23 September, Scrymgeour was able – with much relief and no doubt a little glee – to settle his debt with Thornton. More than a year after he first libelled the policeman, *The Scottish Prohibitionist* was able to run the headline 'Sergeant Thornton Vanquished'.[17]

Despite his eventual success, this was a trying period for Scrymgeour which came very close to breaking him personally and politically. As he well knew, a bankruptcy ruling would have ruined his political

---

* Approximately £47,000 in 2017.

prospects. The debacle of the air show was no less of a humiliation for him and his fledgling party. Yet, by forcing him to more aggressively pursue *The Scottish Prohibitionist*'s commercial prospects, the saga also helped him develop a valuable political asset. There were now several thousand subscribers – and probably many more readers – of Scrymgeour's views every week in Dundee. Equally, the entire story had proved something of a *cause célèbre* in the city, raising Scrymgeour's profile among voters. Remarkably, the episode left the reputation of his party and him personally if not enhanced then certainly enlarged. It would be some time before these assets could be fully utilised, but Scrymgeour could look back on the events of 1912 and 1913 with satisfaction. But, with 1914 fast approaching, the whole world was about to be turned upside down.

Chapter 14

War
1914–1916

On 5 June 1915, Churchill enjoyed his greatest ever reception in Dundee. The Kinnaird Hall was 'crowded in every part', with many more waiting outside to try to catch a glimpse of their MP.[1] As he entered the hall, a spontaneous chant of 'For He's a Jolly Good Fellow' sprung up among those lucky enough to have gained entry. His usual companions – Clementine and Ritchie – were by his side, but so too were men who, just a year earlier, would have been considered his political enemies. Among those who warmly greeted Churchill as he strode towards the podium was Sir George Baxter, his erstwhile Conservative/Unionist opponent in the elections of 1908 and December 1910.

Yet – despite the enthusiasm of the crowd – when Churchill spoke, he was dejected, even melancholy. 'I have not come here to trouble you with personal matters,' he began sombrely, 'or to embark on explanations, or to indulge in reproaches or recrimination.'[2] After a pause, he added: 'In war time, a man must do his duty as he sees it, and take his luck as it comes or goes.' And Churchill – who had arrived in Dundee just 10 days after being forced out of his role as First Lord of Admiralty – very much felt his luck had gone.

As First Lord of the Admiralty, Churchill had one of the most important roles in the cabinet on the outbreak of the First World War in August 1914. As the European continent inexorably ground towards conflict following the assassination of Archduke Franz Ferdinand in Sarajevo in late June, Churchill became a vocal advocate of intervention, particularly in the case of a violation of Belgium's neutrality. Since being appointed First Lord of the Admiralty in 1911, he had

The Manchester North West by-election in 1908 was hard fought. Churchill's defeat left his cabinet career hanging in the balance. (Mirrorpix/Reach Licensing)

The outcome of the 1908 Dundee by-election was far from certain, and Churchill was frequently harassed. Here, the Irish suffragette campaigner Marly Maloney uses a dinner bell to drown out Churchill's speech to assembled workers. (Mirrorpix/Reach Licensing)

Above. Churchill's victory in Dundee in 1908 saved his political career. Here, a clearly delighted Churchill waves to his supporters from a landau after the result is announced. A smiling George Ritchie is seated just to his left. (Fremantle/Alamy Stock Photo)

Right. Churchill's by-election victory gained national attention. This cartoon from the *Daily Mirror* portrays Churchill marching in a kilt to the tune of 'Scots Wha Hae', a patriotic song by Robert Burns often favoured by Scottish nationalists. A dog named Bonnie Dundee walks at his side.

(Mirrorpix/Reach Licensing)

Clementine, just before her marriage to Churchill in 1908. During her peripatetic upbringing, Clementine would spend many summers in Scotland, staying with her maternal grandmother in Angus. (Pictorial Press Ltd / Alamy Stock Photo)

Churchill and Lloyd George were dubbed the 'Terrible Twins' by the Tory press in 1910 for their pursuit of progressive social reforms. Churchill recognised these as being of key importance to his electoral base in Dundee. (Pictorial Press Ltd/Alamy Stock Photo)

Dundee's residents suffered a level of poverty and ill-health beyond anything Churchill had previously witnessed, helping to influence his political development. Mary Lily Walker was a pioneer who believed direct action was needed to help alleviate suffering in the city.

(Libraries, Leisure and Culture Dundee)

Churchill with the officers of the 6th Battalion, Royal Scots Fusiliers, on the Western Front in 1916. On Churchill's left is Andrew Dewar Gibb, a future leader of the Scottish National Party, and on his right Sir Archibald Sinclair, his second in command and future political ally. (Fremantle / Alamy Stock Photo)

E.D. Morel had won fame for his humanitarian work campaigning against the abuses of the Congo Free State and was then imprisoned for his opposition to the First World War. During his campaign in Dundee in 1922, he would face xenophobic abuse for his French heritage. (History Collection 2016/Alamy Stock Photo)

A clearly emaciated Churchill is carried into the newly-completed Caird Hall on an improvised litter. Churchill's ill health would contribute to his defeat in 1922, but it was not the biggest issue his campaign faced. (Fremantle/Alamy Stock Photo)

David Coupar Thomson became one of Churchill's most implacable opponents in Dundee. The media group that he founded and to which he lent his name continues to be a major employer in Dundee 100 years later. (DC Thomson & Co. Ltd)

Edwin Scrymgeour and his wife were given a warm send off from Dundee en route to Westminster for the first time in 1922. Scrymgeour would remain MP until 1931 but would be left frustrated by his legislative failures. (DC Thomson & Co. Ltd)

This portrait of Churchill by Sir James Guthrie was commissioned during the early stages of the First World War, when Churchill's political career was at its lowest ebb to date. It currently hangs in the Scottish National Portrait Gallery, Edinburgh, but few other physical marks of Churchill's time as an MP in Scotland remain. (National Galleries of Scotland, given by W.G. Gardiner and Sir Frederick C. Gardiner, 1930)

sought to prepare the Royal Navy for what he increasingly believed was an inevitable confrontation with Germany. In this endeavour he had been largely successful, although it came at the price of antagonising powerful figures in the naval establishment, a fact that would count against him in the not-too-distant future. Nevertheless, in August 1914 he felt confident the Royal Navy could play a decisive role in the coming conflagration.

On the outbreak of war, Churchill quickly prioritised a blockade of Germany and confining the German Navy to the Baltic, as well as supporting the British Expeditionary Force on the continent. Yet what began as a war of rapid movement soon descended into stalemate and trench warfare. The advent of modern weaponry, such as the machine gun, as well as new technology, such as barbed wire, led to mass casualties as both sides vied for minuscule advantage on the Western Front. By Christmas 1914, it was apparent that a seemingly unbreakable deadlock had set in.

It was in this quagmire that Churchill devised a scheme to launch an assault on the Dardanelles, the Ottoman-controlled straits that guarded the entrance to Constantinople – now known as Istanbul – and the Black Sea. The Ottoman Empire, Germany and Austria-Hungary had closed the Dardanelles to British and French shipping, who hoped to resupply their ally, Russia, via the Black Sea. The idea of an assault to reopen the Dardanelles was first mooted at the war cabinet on 25 November, where it was well received but ultimately not acted upon. But, with casualties on the Western Front escalating and the chances of a breakthrough looking increasingly unlikely, Churchill – fatefully – returned to the idea.

Strategically, an assault on the Dardanelles made sense. Further attacks on the Western Front – sending men to 'chew barbed wire in Flanders', as Churchill himself graphically described it – was futile. Equally, opening the straits would allow material support to be provided to Russia and potentially lead to the Ottoman Empire being knocked out of the war. Churchill hoped this, in turn, would encourage neutral powers, such as Italy and Greece, to join the war alongside Britain and France.

The problems with the Dardanelles scheme were tactical and operational. Tactically, launching a successful assault on the straits was difficult if not impossible. It was only four miles across at its widest point

– one mile at its narrowest – and it had significant Ottoman entrench-
ments and fortifications on either side. The strait itself had been heavily mined and the current, flowing from the Black Sea to the
Mediterranean, made the work of minesweepers more problematic.
Operationally, the mission was ill-conceived. All initial planning envi-
sioned a solely naval endeavour but, just six days before the attack
began, the plans were changed to include an amphibious landing of
soldiers. A failure to acknowledge the significant obstacles and a lack
of clear planning meant the operation was doomed from the outset.

Preparatory shelling of the outer forts of the Dardenelles began in
February 1915 – thereby losing any element of surprise – before the
full-scale assault began in March. On 18 March, the Anglo-French
fleet attempted to take the strait, but was forced back with three ships
sunk and three more badly damaged. The forts protecting the straits
were battered by Allied naval artillery, but of 176 Ottoman gun
emplacements, just four were destroyed. Throwing good money after
bad, the Allies then decided to launch an amphibious landing to
capture the Ottoman forts on the Gallipoli peninsula, in order to give
the naval fleet a fighting chance of getting through the straits. When
the troops were deployed in April, the Ottoman commanders –
including a young Mustafa Kemal, who later rose to prominence as
Atatürk, the founder of modern Turkey – were well prepared. The
Allied troops – including many ANZACs – suffered horrendous casualties and soon became irrevocably bogged down in trench warfare, a
bitter irony given that was exactly what the initial Dardanelles operation had been designed to end.

As First Lord of the Admiralty, Churchill was held responsible for
the debacle. The extent that he alone was culpable is still hotly debated,
and Churchill himself remained a passionate believer both in the
operation itself and that he was absolved of any guilt for its failings.
Even when addressing the Dundee audience in June, by which point
even the most optimistic planner would admit the operation had well
and truly failed, he continued to resiliently defend it: 'There never was
a great subsidiary operation of war in which a more complete
harmony of strategic, political and economic advantages were
combined, or which stood in truest relation to the main position in
the central theatre [i.e., the Western Front]. Through the narrows of
the Dardanelles and across the ridges of the Gallipoli Peninsula lie

some of the shortest paths to a triumphant peace.'³ While it is note-worthy that Churchill felt the need to explain his decision-making to his Dundee constituents, these comments are also at least partly an attempt to spread the blame ahead of a public inquiry and, indeed, to prime history to forgive. But Churchill certainly did continue to believe that the concept of the Dardanelles operation was correct.

The political class, however, viewed things differently. In May 1915, concerns over the supply of shells to the Western Front – it was suggested there were not enough shells or that they were defective – precipitated a political crisis.* Amid the ensuing scandal, Asquith decided the only way forward was for the Liberal Party to join with the Conservative Party in a coalition government, creating a united political front to jointly pursue the war to a positive conclusion. The Conservative leader, Andrew Bonar Law, agreed to the scheme – but the price for his support was Churchill being removed from the Admiralty.† Churchill, despite his efforts to persuade Asquith to the contrary, was relegated to one of the lowest cabinet positions, Chancellor of the Duchy of Lancaster. He had become, in the words of one biographer, the 'scapegoat-in-chief'.⁴ The demotion left Churchill in a deep rut of depression. After he lost the Admiralty, 'he thought he was finished', Clementine recalled, several decades later. 'I thought he would never get over the Dardanelles. I thought he would die of grief.'⁵

Despite Churchill's dejection, his constituents in Dundee largely rallied round their embattled MP. *The Courier*, for example, was effu-sive in its praise for Churchill's 5 June speech in the city, which is particularly remarkable given the paper's usually hostile attitude. 'Mr Churchill has rarely spoken to better purpose than he did on Saturday,' read the paper's editorial on 7 June.⁶ His speech, the paper said, 'struck the proper note' and 'no one could find fault' with it. Even on the Dardanelles, where *The Courier* might have felt able to score an easy

* Somewhat ironically given how events proceeded, the scandal was briefed to the newspapers by Freddie Guest, aide-du-camp to Sir John French, commander of the British Expeditionary Force, and Churchill's cousin.

† The Lord Chancellor and former Scottish MP Richard Haldane was also forced out as a result of the new coalition, because of alleged, but unfounded, rumours that he was pro-German.

hit, its opinion was circumspect, even favourable: '[The Dardanelles operation has] proved costly and vexatious; and in the view of many [has] diverted a large army which might have been more usefully employed in France or Flanders. This, however, is merely a superficial view. Mr Churchill is right in saying that the forcing of the Dardanelles would provide a shortcut to peace ... The Dardanelles expedition therefore is not a diversion, but a project with a great object.'[7]

Such warm sentiments were not confined to the response to the Dardanelles but were also expressed about Churchill's other controversial actions during the opening phases of the First World War. Most notable was his behaviour at the Siege of Antwerp. In early October 1914, during the so-called 'Race to the Sea', the Belgian government announced it intended to abandon the city of Antwerp to advancing German forces. This was strategically undesirable for the British, who hoped to keep as many Channel and North Sea ports as possible in Allied hands. Churchill volunteered to go and inspect the situation in Antwerp himself and, if possible, persuade the Belgian government to stand firm. Despite being a somewhat extraordinary proposition – at least to modern readers – it was in fact endorsed by the Secretary of State for War, Herbert Kitchener, and, more reluctantly, the Foreign Secretary, Edward Grey. Alongside the presence of the First Lord of the Admiralty himself, Churchill also deployed the Royal Naval Division – a land unit under Churchill's remit but made up of 'the rawest recruits', a number of which came from Dundee[8] – to aid in Antwerp's defence.

On arrival in the under-siege city, Churchill settled himself in the city's best hotel, which became his battlefield headquarters, and – despite being a civilian – effectively took command of the city's defence. Observers remarked on Churchill's personal courage, which he regularly displayed by visiting the front lines in the afternoon and evening, having spent the morning dictating despatches from bed. In one incident he narrowly escaped serious injury or death when a shell exploded 'in his immediate vicinity'.[9] Churchill had hoped to hold the city for 10 days – after which he expected the British Army to be able to lift the siege – but in the end the Belgian resistance could only survive for half that time before they, along with Churchill, were forced to withdraw amid the German onslaught. Of the British soldiers deployed at Churchill's behest to try to defend the city, 215 were killed or wounded, 936 were taken prisoner and a further 1,500 were interned for the remainder of the war in neutral Holland.

Churchill received some stinging private and public criticism for his decision to try to hold Antwerp. Admiral David Beatty, who served Churchill in the Admiralty, described the decision in his diary as 'mad', while Herbert Richmond, the assistant director of military operations, wrote that it was 'a tragedy that the Navy should be in such lunatic hands'.[10] The reaction in the national press was equally scathing, describing it as 'a costly blunder' or 'a gross example of mal-organization'.[11]

The reaction in Dundee was, however, supportive. Despite being given another potentially easy hit to criticise their MP – particularly given soldiers from the constituency had been lost in the failed defence – the local press demurred and even defended him. The *People's Journal*, which was published in Dundee but read across Scotland, was unrestrained in its praise for Churchill's bravery during the siege of Antwerp: 'Mr Churchill's critics are angry because, with his inexhaustible energy, he has himself been more than once on the Continent, and even, it is whispered, spent a night in the trenches,' the paper's editorial thundered, before adding: 'It is one of Mr Churchill's characteristics that he must know at first hand every aspect, whether by air, land, or by sea, of every problem he tackles. Surely his critics are exceedingly bankrupt of argument when they are reduced to object-ing to his professional activity.'[12]

When considering such articles, it is worth remembering that they were written in a time of war and patriotic fervour. Editors and reporters may therefore have been more reluctant to criticise Churchill and his record, particularly around the detail of military operations. Censorship may also have been a factor. However, this clearly did not impact several national newspapers, who frequently used their pages to chastise the First Lord of the Admiralty. Being fiercely proud of their independence, it seems likely that had Dundee's newspapers wished to be more critical, they certainly would have been.

It was not just the Dundee press that supported Churchill at this time – his fellow Dundee MP, Wilkie, also did. From the outbreak of hostilities, Wilkie was a passionate supporter of the war. 'Defeat in this war would be a calamity worse than death and would be a setback to the human race,' he robustly declared in September 1914.[13] As the war progressed, and even after the Dardanelles debacle, Wilkie declined to criticise Churchill, with a speech after his demotion from the Admiralty being described as 'most consoling'.[14] A sense of patriotic fervour undoubtedly guided these actions, but it is also evidence of the strength of the growing personal and political bond between Churchill, his Labour colleague and his constituency.

Pride in Churchill's actions aside, Dundee did have other good reasons to be upbeat. Economically, at least, the city was having a 'good war'. After the outbreak of hostilities, demand for jute sky-rocketed, reinvigorating the struggling industry and creating an economic boom in the city. In March 1915, Dundee companies were awarded lucrative contracts from the War Office to produce jute sacks, which were often deployed as sandbags in trench warfare. With substantial guaranteed orders, firms not only made significant profits but also increased pay for workers. By 1916 Dundee's jute barons had secured contracts to provide an enormous six million jute bags a month, with one baron remarking that the war meant 'jute fibres turned into strands of gold'.[15] However, emotions were tempered for many in Dundee in 1915 following the Battle of Loos, where the 4th Battalion Black Watch – Dundee's Own – suffered horrific casualties in the failed assault.

One voice in Dundee, perhaps predictably, was unhappy with Churchill's war record. Scrymgeour derided him as 'Dundee's Swashbuckler' and branded him nothing more than a 'dioramic [model] war guide'.[16] Such criticism was not a one-off. A later article in *The Scottish Prohibitionist* branded Churchill 'vainglorious' and, responding to Churchill's suggestion that the Dardanelles operation was 'a legitimate gamble', suggested: 'He has an inalienable and indisputable right to gamble his last sou [penny] at Baden-Baden or at Monte Carlo, or his life in the trenches, in the air, or in the North Sea; but no man, though born with a silver spoon in his mouth or specially gifted by nature, has the right to gamble with the lives of men.'[17]

But such strong criticism was very much the exception. Dundee, despite the Dardanelles debacle and cabinet demotion, was proud of its MP and his efforts to defeat Germany – and a booming economy, spurred by major contracts from Churchill's government, only helped to sweeten the deal. Indeed, the early years of the First World War, when Churchill's political star fell to perhaps its lowest ebb to date, was – somewhat ironically – the time when he was most popular in Dundee.

But Churchill, though warmed by the reception he received in Dundee in June 1915, could not shake the belief that his political career had suffered a major – perhaps irrevocable – setback. 'I am finished,' he told Sir George Riddle, the proprietor of the *News of The World*.[18] As well as the political ramifications of losing his position as First Lord of the Admiralty, there was a significant personal cost: not only was Churchill's salary halved, but he and Clementine now had nowhere to live in London, having previously utilised Admiralty House, a grace-and-favour residence.

Churchill spent the months following his speech in Dundee fighting for influence in the cabinet, but to no avail. Deeply depressed and increasingly despairing of his situation, in November 1915, he wrote to Asquith to resign as the Chancellor of the Duchy of Lancaster. In place of a ministerial career, Churchill declared he would 'place myself at the disposal of the military authorities, observing that my regiment is in France'.[19] The MP for Dundee was going to the trenches.

Chapter 15

On the Front Line
1916

Captain Andrew Dewar Gibb was less than pleased when he discovered Churchill was to take over command of the 6th Battalion, Royal Scots Fusiliers. The mood among the rest of the soldiers was hardly better. They had liked and respected their old commanding officer and there was resentment that a 'prominent outsider' could 'come in and usurp his place so easily'.[1] As word spread among the men of the identity of their new commander, a 'mutinous spirit grew'.[2] 'Why could not Churchill have gone to the Argylls [the Argyll and Sutherland Highlanders]?' Dewar Gibb asked, adding: 'We all should have been greatly interested to see him in a kilt.'[3] As this comment suggests, the implicit concern of many of the troops was Churchill's unsuitability for a command in a Scottish regiment.

Churchill's arrival at the battalion headquarters, just after midday on 3 January 1916, did little to dispel Dewar Gibb's fears. He appeared mounted on a black horse, followed by a caravan of luggage and two grooms. Among the items in the substantial baggage train was a large bath and boiler for hot water. At 2.30 p.m., the men were invited to meet their new commander. Each officer was called forward in turn to greet Lieutenant Colonel Churchill. Having saluted and curtly shaken their hand, Churchill slumped back into his chair and then 'scrutinised [them], silently and intently, from head to foot' as they stood to attention in front of him.[4] The experience of this 'unconventional attack on one's composure', Dewar Gibb later recalled, 'was distasteful'.

The following day, Churchill summoned his officers to a further meeting. After more than 24 hours with his new battalion, and having fully evaluated his men, the commanding officer was finally ready to issue his first instructions. 'War is declared, gentlemen,' Churchill said, 'on the lice.'[5]

Churchill had departed London's Charing Cross station to journey to the Western Front on 18 November 1915. It took more than a month for him to receive command of the 6th Battalion, Royal Scots Fusiliers and, in the meantime, he had a very unconventional experience of the front line. On arrival, he dined with Sir John French – the British Commander-in-Chief, who pledged to find Churchill a larger and more prestigious brigade, rather than battalion, to command – before staying in 'a fine chateau, with hot baths, beds, champagne and all the conveniences'.[6] But as time went on such luxuries became scarcer and Churchill was soon writing feverishly to Clementine requesting additional supplies. By the time he was in the trenches with the Royal Scots Fusiliers, his list of requests was extensive. As well as brandy and cigars, he asked for 'large slabs of corned beef, stilton cheeses, cream, hams, sardines, dried fruits: you might also try a big beef steak pie, but not tinned grouse or fancy tinned things'.[7]

His motivation for seeking a command was two-fold. Firstly, he genuinely enjoyed military matters and – as evidenced by Antwerp – relished martial command. He had a genuine wish to test himself on the front line and prove his strength and courage. As he wrote to Clementine: 'It is satisfactory to find that so many years of luxury have in no way impaired the tone of my system.'[8] In doing so, he also hoped to banish the depression that had accompanied him since the debacle of the Dardanelles. 'Amid these surroundings, aided by wet and cold, and every discomfort, I have found happiness and content such as I have not known for many months,' he wrote to Clementine, with an honesty that was surely meant to be reassuring rather than offensive.[9] Despite such upbeat assessments, Churchill's melancholy still defines his writing, which regularly takes a macabre form. In describing a brief tour with the Grenadier Guards, Churchill told Clementine 'a total indifference to death or casualties prevails', adding: 'What has to be done is done, and the losses accepted without fuss or comment.'[10] Such fatalism is undoubtedly a feature of war, but the desolation of the trenches also well reflected Churchill's personal mood at the time.

Indeed, his second motivation for seeking a command was at least in part to redeem his reputation and restore his confidence. Having lost the political initiative and fallen out of favour, he believed the quickest and most effective way back was via military glory. If it seems extraordinary for a cabinet minister to behave in such a way, that is because it was. But for Churchill there was a precedent: his early political success was partly a result of his military exploits in South Africa and ensuing fame. He hoped that, by proving himself again, it would reignite his political career with similar results.

For her part, Clementine was understandably worried about her husband's safety. Many of her letters express her anxiety that he might be killed or wounded – fears presumably not waylaid by his occasionally morose asides – and implore him to write back with news that he is safe. But, with her husband indisposed on the front lines, she also acted not just as a conduit for political news, but as a prudent and persuasive counsellor. Churchill's melancholy and mood swings since losing the Admiralty meant he was occasionally prone to 'unbalanced' political judgements.[11] Clementine therefore played a crucial role not just as his eyes and ears in Westminster – alive to possible opportunities for a comeback – but also as a moderating influence on his more extreme mood swings.

Despite French's efforts, procuring command of a brigade for Churchill proved impossible. This was not least because of a political backlash in Westminster, where several MPs queried why a recently resigned cabinet minister with only minor military experience should be given such an important post. This was partly pot-stirring on behalf of Churchill's emboldened opponents, but it was also true that it was 16 years since Churchill had last seen combat as a soldier – and that was during the Boer War, a significantly different conflict to the attritional fighting of the current war. Churchill himself came to recognise this deficiency and writing some 15 years after the event, attempted to address it: 'Having been trained professionally for about five years as a soldier and having prior to the [First World War] seen as much actual fighting as almost any of the colonels and generals in the British Army . . . I did not feel incapable of discharging the duties in question, provided I had a month or two in the line to measure the novel conditions of the [First World War] for myself.'[12]

Churchill attached himself initially to the Grenadier Guards, who were moving in and out of the front at the time, to get a feel for trench warfare. But he also spent a significant amount of time hanging around the British Army's general headquarters in 'absolute idleness' waiting to find out where he could serve more permanently. On 1 January 1916, Churchill finally got the news he had been waiting for. He would take command of the 6th Battalion, Royal Scots Fusiliers.

Arriving in such circumstances – a cocktail of defiance and dejection – it is understandable that Dewar Gibb and others in the battalion were sceptical. But Churchill quickly set about reforming, improving and ultimately winning over his Scottish battalion. As well as tackling the lice – Dewar Gibb notes that after four days of 'unsavoury toil ... we were certainly a liceless battalion'[13] – Churchill introduced several practical reforms to help reduce casualties in the battalion. Among these were the essential elements of soldiering in the trenches, such as fitting gas masks, taking cover, trench discipline and other drills.

Churchill coupled these practical aspects by delivering better equipment and rations for his men. The battalion, for instance – and perhaps because of its new, famous commander – was among the first to receive newly issued steel helmets, which substantially reduced head injuries, particularly from shrapnel. Churchill had been an early convert to the benefits of a steel helmet, having been given a French-made steel helmet in early December, before he joined the Royal Scots Fusiliers. Churchill wore the helmet throughout his entire service on the Western Front, hoping it would 'perhaps protect my valuable cranium'.[14] In fact, the unusual helmet almost did the opposite, with it and his other 'queer garments' leading Churchill at one point to be mistaken for a spy by soldiers in another battalion.[15]

During Churchill's four months in command of the battalion, it suffered 15 men killed and 123 wounded, a lower number than expected over the period of time, a fact attributed to Churchill's training and equipment changes. Under Churchill's administration, rations in the battalion also improved and he arranged for disused brewery vats to be converted into baths for his soldiers.* To boost morale, he also introduced sports – from mule races to pillow fights – and concert evenings.

Practical changes were also accompanied by key changes in personnel. The 6th Battalion had – like many Scottish regiments – suffered

---

* Churchill offered fellow officers the use of his own bath.

intense casualties during the Battle of Loos in autumn 1915. This led to a dearth of experience by the time Churchill took command, not to mention low morale among the survivors and new recruits. 'Like all the rest of this Scottish division it fought with the greatest gallantry in the big battle [Loos],' was Churchill's initial assessment to Clementine.[16] But, emphasising the lack of experience – though not willing – he added: '[It] was torn to pieces. More than half the men and three quarters of the officers were shot and these terrible gaps have been filled up by recruits of good quality, and quite young inexperienced officers.'

To improve professionalism and add much-needed experience to the battalion, as well as plug some key gaps in personnel, Churchill recruited a Scottish baronet, Sir Archibald Sinclair, as his second in command. Sinclair – known as Archie – was a career soldier, having been commissioned into the Life Guards in 1910, and proved indispensable at managing the regiment and filling any deficiencies in Churchill's military knowledge. The arrival of this Scottish aristocrat was initially unwelcome. Dewar Gibb noted in his diary: '[Churchill] ... orders Archie Sinclair to be second in command; I feel excessive annoyance ... three officers supplanted.'[17] That Sinclair appeared to usurp the battalion's other officers was bound to cause resentment, but he soon won admiration for his courage and charm.

Sinclair went on to be a lifelong friend and political ally of Churchill's, helping him campaign in Dundee in the general election of 1918 before working as his ministerial aide for several years. In the words of one historian, he acted as Churchill's 'shadow' when he was Secretary of State for War and, after 1921, Secretary of State for the Colonies.[18] Sinclair himself was elected as the Liberal MP for the Highland seat of Caithness and Sutherland in 1922. He went on to lead the Liberal Party between 1935 and 1945, becoming a prominent anti-appeaser and, in May 1940, Secretary of State for Air in Churchill's wartime cabinet – an important position he maintained for the remainder of the Second World War.

As well as appointing a Scottish second in command, Churchill embraced the national and cultural identity of his regiment. On learning of his appointment, he asked Clementine to send him a copy of Robert Burns's poetry, telling her: 'I will soothe and cheer their spirits by quotations from it … You know I am a great admirer of that [Scottish] race. A wife, a constituency and now a regiment attest to the sincerity of my choice.'[19] Churchill's appreciation for Scotland's cultural heritage did not go unnoticed by his men, who came from across Scotland. Dewar Gibb favourably recorded: '[Churchill] however recognized, as many Englishmen do not, that the [bag] pipes are instruments capable of playing definite airs.'[20] At one dinner party given by Churchill for his officers before the battalion headed back into the front line, their piper struck up 'Bonnie Dundee', which Churchill then demanded be repeated.

Of course, Churchill's charm offensive was not limited to poetry and music – it took on a material and distinctly more Churchillian element as well. His generosity in sharing 'peach brandy, whisky and cigars' with his officers was welcomed by Dewar Gibb as 'much needed to counter the horrors of trench warfare'.[21] Such largesse was the norm rather than the exception. 'Last night Archie and I entertained all the officers at a [Royal Scots Fusiliers] Regimental dinner,' he proudly wrote to Clementine several weeks into his command.[22] 'We sat down 20 and had an elaborate feast beginning with oysters and lots of champagne … the pipes played doleful dirges and we sang "Auld Lang Syne" and generally there was a scene of much enjoyment.' The officers, he added, 'were really delighted'.

But such a charm offensive could only go so far in relieving doubts among the soldiers of the battalion about Churchill's suitability for command. Like any military leader, he needed to prove his mettle under fire to properly build loyalty, trust and authority amongst his men. This was a task Churchill took up with an almost reckless relish, reflecting his emotional imbalance at the time. While there were no major offensive – or defensive – operations during Churchill's time on the front line at Ploegsteert – referred to by British troops as Plugstreet – on the Ypres salient, he nevertheless took part in more than 30 forays into no man's land. Typically taking place in the middle of the night, such operations – designed to gain intelligence and generally harass the enemy – were obviously highly dangerous.

Churchill's performances in such operations, which required stealth as well as courage, were initially that of a well-meaning but bungling amateur. One of his fellow officers recalled how, on one early foray into no man's land, a German machine gun team suddenly opened fire on the group: 'We all made a dive for the shelter of the shell crater … [and] suddenly a blinding glare of light appeared from the depths of the hole and with it [Churchill's] muffled request to "put out that bloody light". It was only a matter of seconds before he realised his crouching posture was responsible for pressure on the contact switch of his own flash-lamp, and corrective action swiftly followed.'[23] He was often perceived as being 'far too loud', with a junior officer describing him as being 'like a baby elephant out in no-man's-land at night'.[24] Such potentially catastrophic mishaps did not fail to endear Churchill to his soldiers, however, who were amazed at his bravery under fire and indifference to danger. Dewar Gibb recalled that Churchill seemed to 'revel' in the dangers of war, adding: 'There was no such thing as fear in him.'[25]

By the time Churchill's command of the battalion came to a close he was widely admired, respected and liked. His practical changes, embracing of the regiment's heritage and his courage had won over soldiers and officers alike. 'I am firmly convinced no more popular officer ever commanded troops,' wrote Dewar Gibb in his memoir of the war.[26] He added: 'Work in intimate association with Winston Churchill was the last experience in the world any of us ever expected … [and] at first the prospect frightened us … [but] we came to realize … his transcendent ability. He came to be looked on as really a possession of our own, and one of which we were intensely proud.'[27]

The transformation of Dewar Gibb's view of Churchill, particularly in such a relatively short space of time, is remarkable. But it is even more so when you consider Dewar Gibb's politics. He had always placed himself within the Conservative tradition, but by 1930 he had firmly embraced Scottish Nationalism as well. He was a founding member of the Scottish Party, which later merged with the more left-wing National Party of Scotland, forming – in 1934 – the Scottish National Party (SNP). Between 1936 and 1940, Dewar Gibb served as the SNP's second-ever leader. Yet, despite his politics, he never lost his fondness for Churchill.

The admiration shared between Churchill and his subordinates in the Royal Scots Fusiliers was mutual. He was effusive in his praise for the courage and heroism of the Scottish troops he had served with, and he continued to provide support to the officers and men after he had resigned his command. At his farewell reception with his battalion, he not only thanked the men for their service but told them they had proven themselves 'a formidable fighting animal'.[28] Churchill even spoke up for 9th Scottish Division – of which the 6th Battalion were a part – during a debate on its reconstitution in the House of Commons in June 1916: 'You talk about the Charge [of the Light Brigade] at Balaclava or the Fusiliers at Albuera [an 1811 battle in the Peninsula War], but even these deeds pale before the deeds done in the present day by these new divisions [such as the 9th] raised in the British Army.'[29] The impact of this did not go unnoticed in his constituency of Dundee, either, with *The Courier* running a front-page headline: 'Churchill extols the heroism of the depleted Scottish battalions'. Other stories praising Churchill's bravery on the front line, including his calmness under fire, were also published by Dundee papers during his period at the front line.

Despite his relative success at leading the 6th Battalion – and their newfound devotion to him – Churchill could not stay away from politics for long. His decision to take up a command had been brought on by feelings of depression and despair following his demotion and loss of influence. In the trenches, leading his Scottish soldiers, Churchill had found mental if not physical comfort, as well as a new purpose. It would still take time before he fully recovered from the fallout from the Dardanelles, but his service with the Royal Scots Fusiliers had set him on the road to recovery.

In May 1916, it was announced that the depleted 6th Battalion would be merged into the 15th Division, eliminating Churchill's command. With Asquith facing a political crisis over whether to introduce conscription – the army to this point had been manned purely by volunteers – Churchill was desperate to return and, if possible, use the tumult to navigate a way back into high office. He therefore did not seek another commission, but instead returned immediately to Westminster. In his absence, he would find a lot had changed.

Chapter 16

The Home Front
1914–1917

Inspector Fitch of New Scotland Yard arrested Morel at 9.15 a.m. on 30 August 1917, in the normally quiet hamlet of Jevington, Sussex. Earlier that day – unbeknownst to Morel – detectives had also raided his home in Hertfordshire and his office, just off London's famous Strand. Morel was not particularly surprised – he had, in fact, almost expected this. 'I have nothing to conceal,' he told Fitch after his arrest, adding: 'Everyone knows my work and where I am to be found.'[1]

Morel, the hero of the Congo Reform Association, was used to harassment. He had received threats and intimidation – as well as the offer of bribes – from concerned businessmen and agents of King Leopold. Yet he had never experienced anything quite like this. One of his close friends, the future Labour Prime Minister, Ramsay Macdonald, painted a vivid picture of what he alleged was a government-led witch hunt against Morel:

> I . . . know how the intelligence department has been laying snares for you; how you and I once shared the charming smiles of an *agent provocateur*, paid for from our own taxes, and how the poor thing whom we pitied came to grief when she found she could not ensnare us; how your letters have been opened, read, returned to their envelopes, and then delivered; how officers have tampered with your staff and offered them appointments [jobs] if they would give information against you; how, in short, you have been living in a glass house for years where there has been no privacy, with every action spied upon and reported, and running the risk that your most innocent and ordinary conduct might be converted and perverted into a criminal one.[2]

But now, after all these other tactics had failed, the police finally believed they had laid a successful snare for Morel. When he appeared in the dock the day after his arrest, the government hoped to put him away for a long time.

The reason the British government took such an interest in Morel was because of his role as a founding member of the Union of Democratic Control (UDC). Established in August 1914, as the first shots of the First World War were fired, the innocuous-sounding UDC's primary aim was to 'secure control over their foreign policy by the British people' and to promote 'international understanding'.[3] More specifically, its four 'cardinal points' were that: no country should annex territory after the war without the consent of the people that live there; any treaty agreed by the government must be ratified by parliament; a focus on maintaining the 'balance of power' should be scrapped in favour of promoting international cooperation; and there must be a 'drastic reduction' in the proliferation of armaments after the war.[4] To modern readers, such demands will seem entirely reasonable, if not wholly sensible, but in the fevered atmosphere of imperial Britain at war, they were considered outlandish, even dangerous.

The UDC was initially made up of radical Liberals – including Morel himself, who in 1912 had been selected as the party's candidate to contest the safe Conservative seat of Birkenhead at the next general election[*] – as well as some Labour supporters. The UDC, and Morel in particular, were hard-hitting campaigners. Reigniting the zeal he had shown during his years at the helm of the Congo Reform Association, Morel set about exposing how British foreign policy – and particularly secret treaties with France and Belgium – had led Britain into what he argued was an unnecessary war. He was particularly critical of Sir Edward Grey, the Liberal government's Foreign Secretary, who he attacked with 'renewed vigour' born of a 'deep personal hatred'.[5] Unsurprisingly, these actions led to Morel being scrapped as a Liberal Party candidate and left him, albeit temporarily, politically homeless. But while he may have suddenly lacked a political party, Morel was not completely alone in viewing the war as a

_____

[*] An election had been due to take place in 1915 but was delayed as a result of the First World War.

dubious and thoroughly unnecessary imperialistic exercise. Expressing such a view in 1914 made him more of an outlier, but as the war dragged on such opinions became more commonplace, particularly after the advent of conscription in 1916.

This was a political journey that was familiar to Scrymgeour. Unlike Morel, he was initially supportive of the war as hostilities broke out in 1914. 'Britain, for whose government we have certainly no admiration, could not possibly in [the face of German aggression] have done other, on the grounds of sheer self-defence alone, than challenge sooner or later a force so completely given over to bullying,' Scrymgeour wrote in *The Scottish Prohibitionist* on 4 August 1914.[6] Indeed, he was vociferous in his praise of the British military as well, writing with a rarely-sighted patriotic fervour later that same month: 'At [the Battle of] Mons, the British forces magnificently sustained their credentials, the Germans delivering a vigorous attack, which was resisted with the dogged obstinacy displayed by British squares at [the Battle of] Waterloo.'[7] Even his early prescription for peace – which he argued could only be delivered by 'turning to God with contrite hearts and propagating national and international policies of righteousness'[8] – suggests he viewed Germany at least as culpable as Britain in starting the war.

But as the conflict dragged on and casualties mounted, Scrymgeour became increasingly anti-war. There is little doubt this stemmed from a genuine pacificist conviction, which had admittedly been briefly overwhelmed at the outbreak of hostilities. It was, however, also politically advantageous, given that both Churchill and Wilkie – Dundee's two MPs – were passionate supporters of prosecuting the war to victory.

The introduction of conscription in 1916 was Scrymgeour's breaking point, though he had become increasingly sceptical of the war over the previous year. He – along with former Scottish Prohibition Party organiser Bob Stewart – were key founders of the Dundee Joint Committee Against Conscription (JCAC) in early 1916. By May of that year, a branch of the UDC had opened in Dundee and helped support its work. Scrymgeour – himself too old to be conscripted – and the JCAC were particularly vociferous in their opposition to Dundee's Local Tribunal, which adjudicated exemptions from military service. The JCAC argued Dundee's Local Tribunal was giving 'scant consideration' to conscientious objectors and was acting without 'principle'.[9] In fact, the JCAC was right that Dundee's Local Tribunal was particularly tough on conscientious objectors. In one case in March 1916, it heard 44 applications for conscientious objection and rejected them all.

Alongside his campaign against conscription, Scrymgeour also supported Morel's cause of exposing what he now perceived as the unjust origins of the war. Between the founding of the UDC in August 1914 and the advent of conscription, Morel wrote a number of books — such as *Ten Years of Secret Diplomacy* and *Truth and the War* — which sought to articulate this position and share responsibility for the conflict between Germany and Britain. Scrymgeour was a particular fan of *Truth and the War*, which he urged 'every sincere patriot' to read.[10]

As with much of his career to date, Scrymgeour's opposition to the war and conscription was largely dismissed as another of his eccentricities that would amount to very little of political consequence, if anything at all. But with his renown as a campaigner stemming from his work on the Congo, Morel was taken as a credible threat by proponents of the war, both in politics and the media. By 1915, the UDC was regularly being branded as pro-German in the press, while in one case a meeting of the organisation was broken up by ex-soldiers and supporters of the war. Politicians joined in the denouncing of the group, with one member of the House of Lords — anticipating the attacks that would be made on Morel when he was a candidate in Dundee — calling for the French-born activist to be denaturalised as a consequence of his campaign.

But by 1916, what had begun as jingoism and xenophobia about the UDC, and Morel in particular, evolved into a genuine paranoia. The catalyst for this change was Morel's old colleague and close friend Sir Roger Casement. On Good Friday 1916, Casement was arrested on the west coast of Ireland, having been dropped off by a German U-boat that morning. He had spent the previous 18 months in Germany itself, trying — without success — to recruit Irish prisoners of war into a regiment to join the German Army on the Western Front fighting the Allies. The fact Casement's landing took place just 72 hours before the failed Easter Rising in Dublin only added to the drama and impact of his arrest.

Casement was charged with treason and prosecuted by Churchill's best friend, the Attorney General F.E. Smith, who ruthlessly denounced Casement with vicious irony in a 'brilliant example of destructive advocacy'.[11] The case was, however, more delicate than Smith recognised. Casement – whatever his recent actions – had been an effective and significant servant of the British in Africa, had won fame as a campaigner for reform in the Congo Free State and retained many powerful friends. One consequence of this was that Smith's prosecution of Casement became controversial in itself, particularly as Smith was among the strongest opponents of a united Ireland in the House of Commons.* Casement's many admirers – including Morel, but primarily another friend from his days with the Congo Reform Association, Conan Doyle – started lobbying for clemency, a campaign which accelerated after Smith secured the death penalty for Casement.

Fearing there was growing public sympathy for Casement, the government collectively agreed to leak part of his 'Black Diaries', which had been found in his possession during his arrest, to the press. These diaries† detailed Casement's homosexual liaisons over several years. By selectively briefing passages from the diaries to the press, the government forced many of those calling for clemency, including the Archbishop of Canterbury and the Bishop of Durham, to withdraw. As one historian put it: 'That a promiscuous homosexual with an obsessive interest in boys' genitals could not be simultaneously a hero seemed in 1916 a simple matter of fact.'[12]

Nevertheless, despite its effectiveness at the time, the decision to use the diaries to try to discredit Casement was, and remains, controversial. There seems little doubt that Morel, who had been a close colleague and friend of Casement for more than 15 years, would have been furious at this attempt to blacken his friend's character. Indeed, the experience not only further distanced him from his former friends in the Liberal Party but also would have left him with a particular personal animosity to Smith. But regardless of his personal feelings, the Casement case led to renewed and more aggressive scrutiny of

---

* Smith would point out that, in his role as chief prosecutor for the Crown, he was not expected to be impartial – in fact, quite the opposite.

† Some continue to dispute the authenticity of the diaries, but the vast majority of historians agree they are genuine.

Morel. The police became increasingly fixated with the idea that Morel, too, must be a traitor. After all, if his good friend Casement was plotting against the British government, why not Morel himself?

On 4 September 1917 – and following his arrest five days earlier – Morel pleaded guilty to a charge of contravening Regulations 24 and 28 of the Defence of the Realm Act. During the raid on his home and office in August, the police found evidence that Morel had 'transmitted certain printed matter from the United Kingdom to a neutral country', in this case Switzerland.[13] What this in reality amounted to was Morel sending copies of his books *Ten Years of Secret Diplomacy* and *Truth and the War,* as well as a pamphlet, to the French pacifist and writer Romain Rolland, who lived in Switzerland. The case was technical and spurious, but it was enough to force Morel to plead guilty. If he hoped admitting to such a seemingly inoffensive crime would prompt leniency, Morel had sorely misjudged the national mood and institutional opposition to him. He was sentenced to six months in Pentonville prison.

As news of his sentence spread, so too did a sense of outrage. Josiah Wedgwood, MP for Newcastle-under-Lyme, summed up the mood of many of Morel's friends when he told the House of Commons: 'It seems to me, though I am by no means a pacificist, that it is a real national disgrace that we have put Mr E.D. Morel in prison.'[14]

Morel's captivity almost killed him, and he never fully recovered. After visiting him in prison in March 1918, his friend, the philosopher Bertrand Russell, wrote to his lover, Lady Ottoline Morrell: '[Morel's] hair is completely white – there was hardly a tinge of white before. When he first came out, he collapsed completely, physically and mentally, largely as the result of insufficient food. He says one only gets three quarters of an hour reading in the whole day – the rest of the time is spent on prison work, etc.'[15] When Morel was finally released, in April 1918, he joined the Labour Party, completing a political conversion that had begun with the outbreak of the First World War and the founding of the UDC. It was a conversion that would have a profound effect on Dundee, and on Churchill.

While Morel and Scrymgeour spent 1916 and 1917 campaigning against the war, Churchill prosecuted a campaign of his own.

Reinvigorated if not rehabilitated by his time in the trenches, he returned to the House of Commons determined to re-establish himself in high office. This, however, would not prove to be easy. He lacked a clear strategy and many of his closest advisors, including Ritchie, urged him to stay in France and await more favourable circumstances for re-entry. Even Clementine – usually as tolerant as she was dedicated – found Churchill's obsession with reclaiming his position taxing, writing to him on 25 March: 'These grave public anxieties are very wearing.'[16] His initial forays in the House of Commons in the summer of 1916 did little to dispel the sense his return was ill-advised, with the member for Dundee making a number of poorly conceived interventions on government business.

If the shortest path to victory in the First World War lay in the Dardanelles, so too did the key to Churchill's political recovery. Even more than a year on from the beginning of the operation, it still continued to dog and damage Churchill's reputation. It was therefore a relief when, in July 1916, it was confirmed a commission of inquiry into the debacle would take place, offering Churchill the opportunity to clear his name. This he did with gusto, arguing in his evidence session in September that the operation was properly authorised, had a good chance of success, that it did not compromise operations elsewhere and that it was planned and vigorously executed.

Like most government inquiries, the Dardanelles Commission, when it published its initial findings in March 1917 – the complete inquiry was published in 1919 – was measured and generally sought to avoid attributing personal blame, particularly to individual ministers. From Churchill's point of view, it neither exonerated nor damned him, but was ambiguous enough to effectively dissolve the Dardanelles as an obstacle to his return as a minister. Such an attitude was also shared by the constituency press, which had in any case always been supportive. The *Evening Telegraph* firmly put responsibility for the 'Dardanelles Muddle' on 'Asquith, Kitchener and Fisher'.[17]

Being able to shake off the Dardanelles millstone was the key to Churchill's rehabilitation, but it would take a political revolution to give him a clear path back to office. Here, Churchill was lucky rather than intimately involved – although he did retain key friendships with several of the main actors.

Many in the coalition government were growing increasingly uncomfortable with Asquith's management of the war effort, which was viewed as too hands-off given the gravity of the circumstances. His downfall was precipitated by an absurdly obscure House of Commons vote on 8 November 1916, on whether enemy property seized in Nigeria could only be sold to British buyers or those of neutral countries as well. But this peripheral question was the catalyst for a parliamentary rebellion – with Churchill among the rebels – that had the effect of severely undermining Asquith's authority to head the coalition government. Much horse-trading followed over the next few weeks, but by early December it was clear that Asquith did not have the authority to continue as Prime Minister. Instead, Liberal and Conservative MPs coalesced around Lloyd George, who they hoped would take a more decisive and interventionist approach to managing the war effort. On 6 December, Lloyd George formed a new government.

Churchill had high hopes that Lloyd George – the other half of the 'terrible twins' of the January 1910 election – would return him to high office, but opposition in the Conservative Party initially remained too strong, and Lloyd George prioritised putting his premiership on a secure footing. Churchill, while bitterly disappointed, did not despair and continued to work – this time more quietly – to find a path back to power. The opportunity presented itself in May 1917, amid criticism of Lloyd George's first months in office. Churchill – with the assistance of his cousin, Freddie Guest, now the Liberal Party's chief whip – arranged for the House of Commons to sit in a secret session so the Prime Minister could openly discuss the war effort with MPs, something he was otherwise limited in his ability to do. Not only did this lead to a revival in Lloyd George's fortunes, but Churchill also spoke particularly eloquently on his behalf. A grateful Lloyd George – despite some continued Tory opposition – on 18 July invited Churchill to be his new Minister of Munitions, with a seat in the cabinet.

Churchill's route back to power had been long and difficult. He felt that Asquith had deserted him over the Dardanelles and that there was a lack of appreciation for his talents. Yet he also did not help himself, often acting rashly and ignoring the advice of those with his best interests at heart. He was fortuitous that both Asquith's fall and the Dardanelles

Commission report occurred in quick succession, otherwise it is likely he would have been out of office for a significantly longer period. Nevertheless, it was with great delight that Churchill once again resumed his seat at the cabinet table. The only cloud on his horizon was the fact that – having been elevated from the backbenches to the cabinet once again – he now faced another by-election in Dundee. And, once again, his age-old enemy was ready to face him.

Chapter 17

'Shells versus Booze'
1917–1918

The 1917 Dundee by-election was an international event with potentially major ramifications. Churchill had initially hoped to be unopposed, with his major rivals agreeing to not contest the election in the national interest. 'I now ask you to vote for my former adversary the Rt. Hon. Winston S. Churchill,' wrote Sir George Baxter, Churchill's long-running Conservative/Unionist opponent in Dundee, in an open letter to the city's electorate.[1] Explaining his decision, he added: 'In the time of the country's need there must be no party. In my view, and I hope in your view, we must be united in the face of grave peril to the state.' Given Wilkie's de facto pact with Churchill, the Labour Party also agreed it would not stand a candidate. Explaining his decision, Wilkie bluntly told Labour Party supporters in the city, via the Dundee *Advertiser's* London correspondent: 'Never mind a contest now, just get on with the war.'[2]

By-elections – particularly those involving prominent politicians – are, however, magnets for political eccentrics, and any hope Churchill held of a coronation soon dissipated. This was a cause of serious irritation to Churchill who, now back at the heart of politics, was determined to, in his friend Wilkie's words, 'get on with the war'. But it was also a cause for concern. It was barely nine years since he had suffered his gutting defeat in Manchester North West, and now, having clawed his way back to power, he was even more determined to avoid a similar upset this time.

The first wild-card candidate attracted to stand against Churchill in Dundee was Stuart Richard Erskine. Commonly known as Ruaraidh Erskine of Mar, he was a Brighton-born aristocrat who had learned Gaelic from a childhood nurse who hailed from the Isle of Harris. His love of the language influenced his business career – he was an avid publisher of Gaelic journals – but also his politics. Initially involved in the Scottish Home Rule Association, he quickly became an advocate for independence in the form of a 'self-governing Celtic Scotland'.[3] It was in the aid of this cause that he wished to stand against Churchill. 'It would be a pity to allow the place-man Churchill a walkover. What Dundee could ever have been about to elect such a characteristic complement to his friend, Lloyd George, fair beats me,' Erskine wrote when considering his candidacy.[4] He added: 'These Whigs are poisoning the political life of Scotland and fast reducing it to the province that [Andrew] Fletcher of Saltoun prophesied it would become under the cursed Union of 1707.'

It is tempting to view Erskine's interest in contesting Dundee as evidence that Churchill was perceived as being against the concept of Scottish nationhood – as opposed to statehood – or was contemptuous of Scottish identity. But as we have seen both in his politics and his role in the trenches, Churchill was an enthusiast for the devolution of power within Great Britain and Ireland, and eagerly promoted Scottish culture and identity. Rather than actually believing Churchill was 'poisoning the political life of Scotland', Erskine's real motivation was probably born from a desire for the coalition government to suffer defeat in a crucial by-election, or self-promotion, or possibly some combination of the two. This is best evidenced by Erskine's decision not to stand, when the prospect of other candidates emerged, because he was unwilling to split the anti-Churchill vote.

The second – and even more curious – would-be candidate was Major F.J. Scott.* Scott, born in Aberdeen, claimed to have had both a distinguished military and administrative record. He had served with distinction in the Boer War and held a number of business roles, including as a director of the Eagle and British Dominions Insurance Company, later better known as Eagle Star. On the outbreak of hostilities in 1914, he was gazetted as a captain in the Gordon Highlanders and was twice mentioned in despatches. Invalided out of the front lines a year later, he was appointed to a staff role in the Ministry of Munitions, where he was given the delicate task of requisitioning

---

* To add to the mystery surrounding this affair, his first name is not given in any of the extant reports and correspondence.

skilled workers from among the troops in the trenches to work in munitions factories. He was so effective at this important role that Lloyd George singled him out for praise during a debate in the House of Commons, stating: 'We are beginning to get over these difficulties [in recruiting munitions workers], largely through the pertinacity and tact of Major Scott.'[5]

But Scott was no fan of Churchill's and determined to launch a campaign as an independent against him 'solely [based] on his past war record'.[6] Scott went into no further detail, but it seems likely this was a reference to the Dardanelles and, probably to a lesser extent, Antwerp. While Scott lacked a base in the city, with a reputation as something of a military hero and administrative genius, he would have been a potential threat to Churchill.

The development of Scott's candidature is an unusual mix of the mysterious and the comedic. It began on 24 July, just a few days before nominations closed and a week before polling day, with a visit by three anonymous men to Dundee. The unidentified individuals had travelled up from London to take soundings on whether Churchill could be beaten. *The Courier* reported that 'they were supporters of the government but were opposed to Mr Churchill in view of his political errors, and they considered his appointment as Minister of Munitions as against the public interest'.[7] Another reporter observed they had 'military, rather than legal, instincts' and 'did not seem to wish it known that they were there [in Dundee]'.[8] If all went to plan, however, they promised to return with a 'gentleman of high standing' to take on Churchill in the coming by-election.

No more was heard of this strange, almost fanciful trio. But on the day nominations were due to close, Scott – their 'gentleman of high standing' – scrambled off the sleeper from London and into the sheriff court to get his name on the ballot. Here, however, he struck a problem: he – and his anonymous supporters – had not arranged an agent to manage his campaign, which was a strict legal requirement. With two hours until nominations closed, Scott initially tried to find a Dundee-based lawyer to fill this role, only to discover to his horror that all the local firms had closed for the summer holiday. His candidature then ended before it had begun – at noon on 27 July – with the rather undignified sight of Scott approaching 'likely-looking' strangers in the street and asking them to sign his nomination papers.[9]

Having failed to submit the required documents in time, Scott returned – presumably somewhat sheepishly – to London that evening. But Churchill would still not receive a coronation. One implacable rival remained in the field – and he would not be beaten so easily.

Scrymgeour's decision to stand against Churchill made the contest a straight fight between a negotiated peace and prosecuting the war to victory. It therefore gave the by-election not just a national but also an international significance. Politicians across the globe would be looking to Dundee to judge the mood of the British people and their willingness to commit to 'total war'. As one historian has put it: 'The whole world, and especially those hard grey men in the German High Command, would gauge with studied interest the outcome [of the by-election].'[10]

Of course, Churchill was used to matters of war and peace and relished fighting the by-election on an issue of purely international, rather than constituency, affairs. For Scrymgeour, this was more difficult territory, but it nevertheless represented a significant moment for him as a politician. For the first time, he was fighting a campaign based on more than just the prohibition of alcohol mixed with millennialist bombast and vague socialist platitudes. His experience and views were expanding, and with them so was his appeal.

Scrymgeour clearly set out his stall in the peace camp during one of his first campaign rallies. 'I am for peace by negotiation,' he told the crowd.[11] He added, with somewhat clumsy language perhaps reflecting the unfamiliarity of the subject: 'I am prepared, if returned, to take the effectual step to encourage by direct resolution antagonism to any continuation of war credits and to join the German socialists in refusing to provide additional supplies for continuing the war.' This meant Scrymgeour was advocating cutting off all financial and economic support for the war effort to try to force a negotiated peace. As shown by the treatment Morel received, expressing such pacifistic views was controversial if not outright dangerous. At one point in the campaign, Scrymgeour had to ask for police protection at a rally.

But disruption and controversy also helped Scrymgeour increase his campaigning acumen. At an event in Carnoustie, for example, which included soldiers on leave among the audience, Scrymgeour was heckled as a coward. Such an intervention might have flummoxed him previously, but he now had the confidence and experience to respond: 'Don't you think it takes a lot of courage to come down here and talk to such gallant lads as you?'[12]

Scrymgeour's campaign also gained a valuable ally in the city's most influential trade unionist – John Sime, the secretary of the Dundee and District Jute and Flax Workers Union. While he did not actively endorse Scrymgeour, he wrote an aggressive denouncement of Churchill's record as a constituency MP, which was published in *The Courier*. Much of the letter deals with a personal grievance about Churchill responding to a request from Sime by suggesting he contact the relevant government department. But, with an implicit suggestion that voters should back Scrymgeour, Sime adds: 'In my opinion, founded on experience of Mr Churchill, he is one of the last men in parliament who will do anything for the working classes unless they compel him by vigorous action to do so.'[13] As the leader of the city's most powerful union, this was potentially a blow to Churchill's working-class base. In fact, it had a minimal discernible impact on the election, but it is another example of how Scrymgeour – through doggedness as much as dogma – was gaining traction among the city's socialists.

But it would be wrong to think that, at this stage, working people in Dundee were deserting Churchill or did not respect his progressive record. The leader of the Coalminers' Union, Stephen Walsh, was one of those who wrote a letter in support of Churchill's candidacy, saying: 'For nearly twelve years, I have had close knowledge of work in parliament and no man knows better than I how valuable [Churchill's] services have been for the working classes ... I trust the citizens of Dundee, by an overwhelming majority, will show their appreciation for such a record.'[14]

Given the centrality of his new role to the war effort, Churchill's campaigning in Dundee was limited to visits during the opening and closing stages of the campaign. In the intervening period, electioneering in the city was directed by Clementine, who stood in for her husband at rallies and campaign events. She was supported by two experienced hands: John Pratt and Alexander MacCallum Scott. Pratt had been the Liberal MP for Linlithgowshire since 1913, while MacCallum Scott had represented Glasgow Bridgeton since 1910.

MacCallum Scott was also an early acolyte of Churchill's, publishing the first biography of him in 1905, at which point Churchill was just 29 years old. In 1916, he wrote a second edition of the book, entitled *Winston Churchill in Peace and War*. For his part, Churchill would later return to the idea of sending friendly MPs to support Clementine on campaign in his absence in future elections, but with much less success.

On this occasion, Clementine once again campaigned with aplomb, even braving rallies in the pouring rain and outside public houses. She also showed good political instincts, emphasising that the by-election was an opportunity to show Germany that Britain would continue to prosecute the war. 'I hope very much you are going to give my husband a very big majority ... so that a message will be sent to Germany to show them that over here we have no dissension,' she told a particularly wet open-air meeting on Dundee High Street.[15] She added: '[Victory for Churchill] will be a sign that we want to carry on with the war.' Such performances were well received by the local press who described Clementine as 'an excellent advocate' and someone who regularly 'displayed her skill in public speaking' during the campaign.[16] Indeed, she rather outshone Pratt and MacCallum Scott, who were often shouted down and unsure of how to respond.

Churchill arrived in Dundee on 27 July – three days before polling day – and immediately hit the campaign trail. 'What is the issue placed before the electors of Dundee?' he asked his audience at the Lochee West United Free Church Hall that evening.[17] 'What is the question which those who go to the polling booths ... will answer by the crosses which they put on the ballot paper?' It was amid this swirling rhetoric that a member of the audience cheekily shouted: 'Shells versus booze,' eliciting significant laughter. But Churchill soon corrected him, launching a rhetorical broadside against Scrymgeour's pacifism: 'Every vote for Mr Scrymgeour is a vote for a shameful peace with Germany ... If there is mismanagement, let us try to cure it. If there is profiteering [from the war] let us try to punish it, but do not let it be said that in a struggle of this kind the Germans are able to endure hardship from which the Scottish race recoils.' Drawing on his own experience in the trenches, he added: 'That was not so on the fighting front, for there was no bitter form of war in which the Scottish troops were not the masters of the Prussian.'

He closed by asking his audience: 'Is this the time ... to seek to hold up our hands and cry "Kamarad" to the Crown Prince [Wilhelm of Prussia]? Is this the time to pull down the flag and slink away in cowardly surrender? Is that the kind of job that Dundee – world famous, gallant Dundee – will be associated with?'

This rhetoric was brutally effective, and such speeches – focused on international affairs and delivered with an oratorical flourish – represented Churchill at his most comfortable campaigning in Dundee throughout his entire period as an MP. His candidature also benefited from the appearance of William Brace, the Labour MP for South Glamorganshire, who gave an impassioned defence of Churchill as a progressive politician: 'I cut coal for my living from 12 to 25 years of age and today I am the leader of the men with whom as a boy and a man I worked side by side in the pit ... and if I thought for one moment that this was a violation of the great principles for which I and my people stand I would not be here to support Mr Churchill.'[18]

The only black spot on an otherwise pristine campaign was the occasional reference to Churchill's war record – not the Dardanelles, but Antwerp. On one occasion, he was accosted and asked to explain his role 'in the tragedy of Antwerp when hundreds of young lads, many belonging to Dundee and not much over school age, without proper equipment, were sent across to provide a target for German guns'.[19] The critical question clearly struck a nerve and Churchill, having issued a defence of his actions, closed with a cruel and emotionally insensitive put down: 'There has been no subject which has been made more a parrot cry by people whose brains are smaller than those of the smallest parakeet than the subject of Antwerp.'

Churchill, however, was clearly encouraged by the overall reception he received in Dundee, and – confident of victory – departed for London the night before polling day. As it was, the horror and the anxiety caused by the First World War stripped the vote of any of the gaiety of the previous contests since 1908. Turnout was low, with a total poll of 9,290 – just 43 per cent of eligible voters – but Churchill was nevertheless returned with a majority of 5,266. Clementine, who had stayed to finish the campaign she had begun, thanked the voters of Dundee for 'a great mandate [for] the government to get on with the war'.[20] *The Courier*, usually Churchill's most ardent critic, agreed, and was scathing about Scrymgeour: 'The electors have inflicted upon the advocate of shameful peace a defeat which will have far-reaching effects and which will show to the world the determination of the Scottish people to hold out until Prussianism is destroyed.'[21] Scrymgeour, however, was upbeat, describing his 2,036 votes as 'magnificent' and expressing a belief it would increase again in the future.[22] He did not have to wait long to find out.

Lloyd George called a general election for 14 December 1918, just over a month after the armistice was signed, ending the First World War. It was also almost exactly eight years to the day since Asquith had led the Liberal Party into the second general election of 1910. Then the question at stake had been the power of the House of Lords, but now – with almost a million lives lost in four years of war – the country was facing an existential crisis. As the armistice was signed on 11 November, Churchill summed up the feelings of many when he said he was 'conscious of reaction rather than elation'.[23] There had simply been too much death and destruction for real celebration.

On the home front, besides the devastating loss of life, there were more than 1.6 million wounded, more than 160,000 women widowed and more than 300,000 children left fatherless. Many more men returned from the trenches with invisible, but equally debilitating, injuries, including what would now be recognised as post-traumatic stress disorder. Meanwhile, the economy had been buckled by the requirements of 'total war', there was a growing militancy among industrial workers, global trade was at a standstill and millions of men needed to be demobilised from the armed forces. The perennial question of what to do about Ireland, which had rebelled in 1916, continued. Internationally, there were key questions of what a European peace settlement would look like, how nascent demands for statehood amid collapsing empires would be managed, and how liberal democracies would coexist – or confront – Lenin's Russian Revolution, which was still in its infancy. All of these questions, to a greater or lesser extent, impacted Churchill's remaining years in Dundee.

Lloyd George recognised that he needed a new mandate from the people to tackle these – and many other issues – head on. It was a mammoth challenge but one that he strongly believed he was best placed to meet. Equally, he cynically recognised that it was best for him to go to the country while the glow of victory was still bright.

Lloyd George's only problem was, since the demise of Asquith's premiership, he – and, indeed, Churchill – was effectively without a party. Asquith was still leader of the Liberal Party and rejected a rapproachement with Lloyd George, who he felt – with some justification – had betrayed him in order to advance his own career.

Lloyd George therefore struck a deal with Arthur Balfour and the Conservatives to maintain their wartime coalition into the election and government beyond. Churchill became one of the 159 new 'Coalition Liberals' to receive the letter of endorsement dubbed the 'Coalition Coupon', with the contest becoming known, as a result, as the 'Coupon Election'. Churchill therefore fought this election, as he did in the 1917 by-election, with the effective support of the city's Conservatives/Unionists. The 1918 election was also unique in the respect that it was the first election in which all men over the age of 21 could vote, while the franchise was also extended to all women over the age of 30, with some minor conditions. For Dundee, this meant the franchise was increased almost four-fold to 83,767.

Churchill was, however, not unduly concerned about his position in Dundee. His 18-month period as Minister of Munitions was judged as a great success by all but his most implacable foes. With significant components of the armaments industry based in Glasgow, Churchill had made several visits to the west of Scotland and positively engaged with the workers there. Many of them – given the demands of conscription – were women, and Churchill's experience of dealing with the majority-female workforce in Dundee may have helped him feel at ease in this environment. After the war, Churchill had been promised either a return to the Admiralty or to be appointed Secretary of State for War by Lloyd George, assuming they won the coming election. Churchill's effective wartime administration at Munitions had gone some way to vanquishing the ghosts of the Dardanelles and Antwerp, and he felt confident his record as a progressive would stand up to any scrutiny from the left as well.

Churchill's chief focus, therefore, was on trying to help his friend and colleague Wilkie, who was facing a sustained assault from within the local Dundee Labour Party and feared for his political survival. Furious at his support for the war and the coalition government prosecuting it, local party members resolved to effectively deselect Wilkie. As *The Courier* explained: 'Mr Wilkie has been a consistent supporter of the war since the outbreak of hostilities and has made it plain he wishes to have a satisfactory peace secured. It is just here that the extremists in local Labour circles have been up against Mr Wilkie because they have made it plain that their programme . . . [is] complete opposition to the Coalition.'[24] With this in mind, the local party had already selected James Brown, a 43-year-old Dundee native and trade unionist, to run as a candidate – potentially drawing votes from Wilkie – and hoped to find a second to eclipse Wilkie entirely.

Their top target was Morel, whose pacifist sympathies were more in line with local party members. While Morel seriously considered the idea, he was still recovering from his release from prison six months earlier and felt unable to commit. But the idea of a Morel candidature in Dundee would not be forgotten in Labour circles. In the meantime, given Wilkie had been endorsed by the national party – and a satisfactory alternative could not be readily found – the local Labour Party was forced to back down in its attempts to replace him. But there was still a significant concern his votes could be diverted to Brown.

Churchill, displaying a keen sense of loyalty, leapt to his friend's defence and launched a determined effort to ensure Wilkie was re-elected. In a damning inditement of the local Labour Party's efforts to remove Wilkie, Churchill told a working-class audience in Dundee's Lochee district:

> A man might be a Trade Union leader who had for twelve years in parliament supported advanced legislation and pushed forward on every occasion the interest of his class and the democratic cause. He might be a working man, trusted by other working men. But if he was convicted of backing up his own country against the Hun, if he could be found guilty of having, at every stage, put country before everything else and victory before everything else, [then they say]: "out with him, shout him down, cover him with insults, turn him out of Parliament, reduce him to the ranks". That was the cry that was brought forward . . . by those very pacifist people . . .[25]

The extent to which interventions from such a prominent supporter of the war was actually helpful to Wilkie is questionable. But it does reflect the importance of their friendship and Churchill's desire to work with moderate Labour politicians.

As well as defending Wilkie, Churchill also burnished his own progressive credentials. He chose Dundee to reveal that the government would, after the election, nationalise the railways. When asked a question about nationalisation of transport facilities, he responded: 'The government policy at present is the nationalisation of railways. That great step it has at last been decided to take.'[26] It is not clear whether Churchill deliberately intended to announce such a radical rethink of British transport policy to a crowd assembled in a church hall, or if he accidently let slip what had hitherto been a confidential plan. While the latter seems more likely, it was understandably seized upon by the press, with the *Advertiser* describing Churchill's announcement as 'the most important concerning domestic policy that has been made for many years'.[27] Now fully committed, Churchill elaborated on the plans in Dundee a few days later, expanding the proposal to include not just nationalisation but significant government subsidy: 'It might ... pay the state to run the railways at a loss if by developing industries, creating new ones, reviving agriculture, and placing the trader in closer contact with his markets, they stimulated a great development at home.'[28]

For the rest of the campaign, however, Churchill largely mimicked his strategy in the 1917 by-election, albeit in an updated form. He sought to frame the vote as 'patriotism versus pacifism' and attacked Scrymgeour over his previous desire to negotiate a peace with Germany, an idea Churchill said had been proved a folly by the Allied victory.[29] He contrasted his service in the trenches and as Minister of Munitions aiding the war effort with those who opposed the conflict entirely, while war heroes were drafted in to praise Churchill's leadership qualities – a tactic Churchill would return to again when facing Scrymgeour. Sir Douglas Haig, the British commander on the Western Front, for example, tactically placed a letter in the *Evening Telegraph* thanking Churchill for his service, suggesting it was crucial 'in the success of operations and the final defeat of the enemy'.[*][30]

The electoral atmosphere in Dundee was, however, even more rough than Churchill had previously experienced. Churchill attributed this to the presence of Bolsheviks in the crowds, and it is likely

---

[*] Despite Haig still being a public appointee at this time, there is no evidence of a backlash against him for overtly endorsing a party-political candidate.

that the experience contributed to his growing concern about trade union militancy. In one incident outside the Kinnaird Hall, Churchill and Ritchie were surrounded by a hostile mob, one of whom accosted Ritchie. Churchill, with excitement as much as fear, later recounted what happened next: 'With great agility [Ritchie] seized his assailant by the throat and succeeded in forcing him under the wheels of a motor car.'[31] The man was only saved from being run over by Archie Sinclair, Churchill's former second-in-command on the Western Front, who had volunteered to help with his re-election campaign. This case was extreme, but disruption and vitriol were increasingly common, foreshadowing the campaign in 1922.

The only crisis of the 1918 campaign for Churchill came when he began to lose the city's Irish vote. The immigrant Irish community had been a bedrock of the Liberal Party's base in Dundee even before Churchill's first election in 1908. Now, with the expanded franchise, the Irish vote was estimated at a significant 16,000 votes, about a fifth of the total Dundee electorate. But Asquith's failure to deliver Home Rule, coupled with the brutal treatment of Irish rebels during the Easter Rising – not to mention figures such as Casement – meant the city's Irish community no longer viewed Churchill and the Liberal Party as their natural allies.

Scrymgeour, meanwhile, had been burnishing his own credentials as a Home Ruler in a bid to win over this increasingly powerful block. On 9 December, he was endorsed by the Irish National League of Great Britain and the United Irish League, which had previously supported Churchill. This would not have a great impact at the 1918 ballot, but it meant Churchill's electoral base in the city was increasingly reliant on his longstanding working-class supporters and the Conservative/Unionist voters who supported the coalition government – unless he could win the Irish voters back. Over the coming years, neither would prove particularly resilient.

If Churchill was concerned about these dark clouds on his horizon, he did not show it. In fact, he predicted a resounding victory. 'The general election is going well, the Scottish election is going even better, and the Dundee election is going the best of all,' he told a cheering crowd of supporters two days before polling day.[32] And he was right. Churchill, having topped the poll with 25,788 votes, was returned with a majority of 15,365 – his most impressive electoral victory to date and a majority that was the largest of any member of the coalition. Equally satisfying for Churchill was the return of Wilkie, who received 24,822 votes, with the second Labour candidate, James Brown, receiving just 7,769. Scrymgeour received 10,423 votes, a 9 per cent increase on his performance in the December 1910 general election, which offers a better point of comparison than the two-horse by-election of 1917. He was still some way off victory – the Liberal-leaning *Advertiser* derisively dismissed him as 'the most defeated candidate in Britain'[33] – but he had now at the very least moved himself from eccentric outsider to credible contender.

Churchill was not in Dundee to celebrate his victory. He departed half way through polling day to have dinner in the more cosmopolitan surroundings of Edinburgh, before returning to London by the sleeper train. When he arrived home and learned of the result, he cannot have helped but be pleased. Not only had he been resoundingly returned in Dundee, but the electorate had emphatically endorsed Lloyd George's coalition across the country. More than 500 coalition-supporting MPs were returned to the House of Commons, while Asquith's rump Liberal Party slumped to a crushing defeat. The former Prime Minister himself even lost his own seat of East Fife, which he had represented since 1886.

Nevertheless, despite the encouraging overall picture, the detail showed more cause for concern. The Labour Party had won 57 seats and was increasingly asserting itself as a political force to be reckoned with, while the more nationalist Sinn Fein had decisively defeated the more moderate Irish Parliamentary Party in Ireland. Both these factors would be a cause of increasing concern for Churchill, but that lay in the future. For now, there was major work to be done, not least making peace with Germany.

Chapter 18

Winning the Peace
1918–1919

It was with a sense of trepidation that Scrymgeour waited in the ante-room to the suite at the Hotel Majestic* in Paris. The firebrand Dundonian was not normally lacking in self-confidence, but the plush majesty of his 19th-century surroundings put him ill at ease. It was partly the ostentation of the Louis XIV furniture, which he found grotesquely extravagant, but he was also disorientated by a new language and culture. He travelled infrequently and, with literally no French to speak of, had already endured a difficult stay since his arrival two weeks earlier. He frequently got lost, found Parisians rude – '[their] tendency is . . . to take advantage of even Allies as if they were Germans'[1] – and had struggled to get the necessary access to conduct his journalistic assignment. The man he now waited for, he reflected ruefully, was his last hope.

Scrymgeour had decided to travel to Paris in February 1919 to cover the peace conference taking place in the city. 'The Big Four' major powers – Britain, France, the United States and Italy – had all sent substantial delegations, while dozens of smaller nations also had representatives present. Meeting at the French Foreign Ministry in the Quai d'Orsay, on the left bank of Seine, the victorious politicians and diplomats intended to carve out a post-war settlement for Europe. In this effort, they did not have their troubles to seek.

For people in Britain there was tremendous interest in the proceedings – the result of the deliberations would, after all, be what they had fought and sacrificed for. Of chief concern to many was the issue of reparations – the British public wanted to ensure Germany paid for

---

* Now known as the Peninsula Hotel.

the war – as well as what to do about Kaiser Wilhelm, who had nominally led Germany throughout the conflict.

Among the Allies, France wanted financial and territorial compensation, as well as heavy restrictions on the size and scope of Germany's
military, while President of the United States Woodrow Wilson
wanted countries to sign up to his peace-keeping brainchild, the
League of Nations. The collapse of the Ottoman Empire, which had
dealt such a heavy defeat to the Allies at the Dardanelles, also meant
there was a power vacuum across its former empire in the Middle East
– a void Britain and France hoped to fill.

Scrymgeour, showing audacious journalistic instincts if not hubris,
decided to go and scrutinise the decisions on these matters and many
others for himself. Having been influenced by figures such as Morel,
he believed that the war had been started by duplicitous British politicians and their secret diplomacy, and he was not about to allow that
to happen again.

Covering an international conference of this magnitude was not,
however, easy, and Scrymgeour soon ran into bureaucratic and logistical issues. It took over a month of negotiation and a 10-hour office
visit in London to secure the correct accreditation. He was then
unable to find a crossing from Dover to Calais, eventually having to
travel on an overnight ferry between Southampton and Le Havre,
before journeying on to Paris. As he watched the full moon shining
upon the English Channel, he reflected on the many young men who,
over the previous four years, had travelled a similar journey, only never
to return.

When he finally arrived, Scrymgeour's first impressions of Paris
were not good. He reported, somewhat callously, that the 'congestion
of people is ... overwhelming' despite France being 'tremendously
bereft of her young manhood'.[2] The Parisian railway system was
'particularly dirty' while the taxis 'look as if they had been at the very
front with the myriad of machine guns and German tanks'. Difficulty
in securing a hotel room – they were presumably all stuffed with
diplomats – did little to alter his mood.

Even the famous Tuileries Gardens and the Champs-Élysées failed
to move him. 'The monumental and general statuary of Paris are
indeed ponderous, splendidly dignified and richly ornamental,' he
wrote in his despatch back to Dundee, 'but owing to heavy winter

conditions ... the scenic effects are not by any means entrancing.'³ He
then added, in a piece of analysis that – even in a Paris afflicted by four
years of war – is hard to take seriously: 'Whatever the task of Dundee's
City Engineer in putting our streets right, the job is not a patch on
what the Parisians have to face.'

Scrymgeour's intention had been to link up with George Lansbury,
the editor of the *Daily Herald*, a Labour Party-supporting newspaper.
It is not clear how well – if at all – the two knew each other, but the
fact that Scrymgeour wished to associate with such a senior Labour
figure is reflective of his growing closeness to the party. But, despite
his best efforts, Lansbury could not be located. His attempts over the
rest of the week to cover the conference itself fared little better.
Despite his accreditation, the correspondent of *The Scottish Prohibitionist*
was not afforded as much support or access as the international media
outlets present. Understandably, officials clearly viewed placating this
niche publication as a low priority. Struggling to settle or find his
friends, Scrymgeour ended his first week in Paris with a downbeat
assessment: 'Whatever other experiences I may yet have in Gay Paree
– as seen at the cafes and other places of popular patronage – the
awful war and severe winter conditions from which the city has
suffered terribly will make our remembrance of the visit [as] one of
seeing Paris in sombre attire.'⁴

Having exhausted all his other options, Scrymgeour then made his
way to the 'palatial' Hotel Majestic, which was almost adjacent to the
Paris Peace Conference itself. This was where the most important
members of the British government delegation to the peace conference were staying. Scrymgeour had not made an appointment but,
after a wait, was shown into a 'charming boudoir' to meet his would-
be saviour. Then, 'after several minutes,' Scrymgeour wrote in his
despatch to Dundee, 'the British Minister of War extended a most
courteous reception to his Prohibitionist opponent of five
elections.'⁵

Churchill's reaction to having Scrymgeour turn up, unannounced,
at his hotel suite in Paris is not recorded, but it is hard to believe that
it was not surprise bordering on incredulity. They were around 700
miles from Dundee and – as Scrymgeour himself points out – political opponents. If Churchill was taken aback, however, he did not show
it. In fact, he did everything he could to assist Scrymgeour who,

having recognised he was getting nowhere at the peace conference, had decided to attempt a feature on the recently silenced battlefields of the Western Front.

Having listened to his proposed article with interest – Churchill himself was, after all, no stranger to war reporting – he set about helping Scrymgeour with his logistics. Churchill gave him use of his private vehicle and driver and arranged the necessary passes to visit the former front, access to which remained strictly controlled. At 9 a.m. the following morning, Scrymgeour was being whisked towards Meaux – site of the first Battle of the Marne – by a government chauffeur called Matthews, military pass in hand. Scrymgeour noted with some pride that the 'splendid car' had been used to convey 'Mr Lloyd George, Mr Balfour, Mr Churchill and other distinguished visitors' around Paris.[6]

It is easy to view Churchill's assistance as a cynical ploy. Scrymgeour was, after all, professionally if not financially destitute. In such circumstances, Churchill may have seen an opportunity to place his most implacable opponent in his debt and perhaps hope to nullify his animosity in the future. But this seems unlikely, not least because Churchill – now with a 15,000 majority in Dundee – failed to perceive Scrymgeour as a genuine political threat. Equally, if he wished to help Scrymgeour only for cynical purposes, he need not have given over his own time – in the midst of the most important treaty negotiation to date in history – to help him. It seems most likely that, if Churchill really did despise Scrymgeour, he simply would have refused to see or assist him in any way.

That Scrymgeour also sought out Churchill to seek his assistance is equally significant. Reading his speeches and articles on the senior member for Dundee, it is easy to perceive nothing but hostility bordering on contempt. Yet he clearly thought enough of Churchill to seek him out in his time of need, and to be genuinely grateful for the assistance, offering him his 'heartiest thanks'.[7] In fact, the whole episode suggests Churchill and Scrymgeour – despite their considerable political and personal differences – had a more genuine and respectful relationship than has previously been assumed.

Like Scrymgeour, Churchill was also enduring a frustrating time in Paris. While he was not closely involved in the drafting of the Treaty of Versailles or other associated agreements – Lloyd George considered this very much his own remit – he was tasked with trying to negotiate a common Allied position on Bolshevik Russia and the ongoing civil war since Lenin's revolution in 1917. Churchill was in favour of supporting the White Russians – a coalition of anti-Bolshevik forces – by supplying them with weapons or even troops. But Lloyd George was unwilling to support the latter proposition and there were considerable divisions among the Allies – particularly the United States – over how to respond. After four days of intense nego-tiation – interrupted only by the visit from Scrymgeour – Churchill had failed to persuade the Allies to reach an agreement on how to respond to the Bolsheviks. Churchill was infuriated, but it was a subject he would return to.

The Paris Peace Conference ended in the signing of the Treaty of Versailles on 28 June 1919. Despite – or perhaps because – of his limited involvement in it, Churchill thought it a deeply unsatisfactory document. He was particularly agitated about the strong economic penalties and indemnities placed on Germany, which he believed were too severe. Churchill presciently believed that crippling Germany economically – as well as substantial losses of territory – would stoke resentment and be a constant barrier to peaceful coexistence.

But the question of compensation was a significant issue in Dundee where, as in many other places in Britain, voters wanted Germany to be financially punished. Churchill had promised as much during the 1918 general election, suggesting a £2 billion* penalty, but his constit-uents were soon demanding more. 'Twelve thousand million, fifteen thousand million,' Churchill noted, 'everywhere on the lips of men and women who had the day before been quite happy with the two thousand million [two billion] and were not anyhow going to get either for themselves.'[8]

The response in Dundee to the news of the signing of the treaty was therefore 'quietly dignified' rather than boisterous, with the ring-ing of church bells and flying of flags from public buildings and some private homes, including those 'in some of the city's most humble streets'.[9] The *Evening Telegraph* summed up the mood succinctly, suggesting that Dundonians might not like the terms of the treaty

* Approximately £58 billion in 2017.

were they to read them, but most were ultimately too relieved the war was definitively over to care: 'What is to follow the signing of peace may be problematical [but] it was enough for the public to know that the sealing of the treaty must surely mean the end of war in our time, if not for all time.'[10]

Morel's reaction to the treaty was among the strongest and most controversial of any politician. Like Churchill, he feared that humiliating Germany would not lead to a lasting peace. But rather than reparations, Morel was most concerned with the occupation of the Rhineland and specifically the French government's use of black colonial soldiers as a contingent in the occupying army. This concern was overtly racist – Morel believed that insatiable black troops were sexually assaulting German women, girls and boys and that they had been deliberately placed there to do so as a punishment for the German people. As a result of these apparent atrocities, Morel said, it would be impossible for France and Germany ever to be reconciled, thereby risking further European conflict.

Articulating his views in a 10 April 1920 article entitled 'Black Scourge in Europe: Sexual Horror Let Loose On The Rhine' for the Labour-supporting *Daily Herald*, Morel wrote: 'The results of installing black barbarians among European communities are inevitable and are known to be inevitable by those responsible for doing so ... The African race is the most developed sexually of any. These levies [troops] are recruited from tribes in a primitive state of development. They have not, of course, their women with them. Sexually they are unrestrained and unrestrainable.'[11] These sexual assaults by black troops, Morel argued, were 'nearly always accompanied by serious injury and not infrequently ... fatal results' because of 'well-known physiological reasons'.[12] This piece was not a one-off but was followed up with a series of further articles and even a pamphlet entitled *The Horror on the Rhine*, which ran to eight editions.

Morel himself admitted these views were not based on evidence. In the same *Daily Herald* article, he noted 'my information is not as complete as I should wish' and that 'the abundance or otherwise of specific reports is immaterial'.[13] Nevertheless, Morel's article caused a sensation and became an accepted argument against the Treaty of Versailles in Labour Party circles. On one occasion it fell to Churchill to explain, in response to a question from a Labour MP, that only

7,500 of the 95,000 French troops stationed in the Rhineland were colonials, of which only one brigade was Senegalese. The Women's International League for Peace and Freedom invited Morel to speak on the subject to an audience of women's political and trade union groups, which later passed a motion calling for 'troops belonging to primitive peoples' to be removed from Europe.[14]

Such views were not particularly controversial in the early 20th century but are understandably shocking to contemporary readers. They may also be particularly surprising in Morel's case, given his pivotal role in ending the horrors of the Belgian Congo. Indeed, he went to some lengths to insist his views were not racist or prejudicial, even arguing that he in fact supported removing black troops from the Rhineland to alleviate possible racial tension. This argument is flimsy at best and certainly does not excuse the definitively derogatory language he used. From a contemporary perspective, the only possible mitigating case for Morel's argument is that it stemmed from the worthy desire of avoiding another Franco-German conflagration, but this well-intentioned motive clearly does not justify his language or views. The solution to the dichotomy of Morel's Congo activism and later views on the Rhineland is perhaps best summed up, however, by the *Daily Herald's* editorial that accompanied his initial article: 'We champion the right of the African native in his own home, [but] we deplore that he should be used as a mere instrument of revenge by an imperialist power.'[15] Such views are of course unacceptable today, but – as evidenced by their ready acceptance even in apparently progressive circles – were more commonplace in the early 20th century.

The signing of the Treaty of Versailles formally ended the First World War, though the repercussions both of the war and the settlement itself would be far-reaching. For Churchill, however, the Paris Peace Conference had been a frustration. As has been noted, he failed to secure an agreement among the Allies to support the White Russians, who were rapidly losing ground to Leon Trotsky's Red Army. But the Bolsheviks were not only on the march in Russia, but on the dockyards and railway depots of Scotland and England as well. A revolutionary fervour was in the air across the country – and Churchill was determined to stop it.

Chapter 19

Revolution
1919–1922

The war cabinet listened in silence as Andrew Bonar Law, the de facto deputy Prime Minister, read out the telegram from the Lord Provost of Glasgow. For many around the table – among the most powerful ministers and civil servants in the state – it was the sum of their worst fears. Glasgow, the Lord Provost warned, was teetering on the brink of major industrial unrest. The workers' demand was for a 40-hour week and, by the time the war cabinet met on 30 January 1919, the dispute had been building for several days. As well as walk-outs by engineers and shipbuilders, the Lord Provost warned electricity workers could now also strike, cutting all but essential electrical power to the city. In this void – and with other employees unable to work even if they wanted to – it was clear there was a real risk of a breakdown in law and order.

Many of the major trade unions were still in negotiations with employers and had therefore refused to join the strike. But this had allowed more 'extreme' elements to hijack the process and press on with a wildcat action.[1] The hope according to one of the leaders of the strike, Councillor Emmanuel 'Manny' Shinwell, was that their unauthorised action would then 'spread' across Glasgow and beyond, into a general strike.[2] But the strike leaders were also under pressure to deliver and had asked the Lord Provost to demand the British government deal directly with employers in an attempt to resolve the dispute. They asked for a response to this demand by 31 January, the following day.

For the war cabinet, this was not viewed as a mere obscure industrial dispute, but a possible precursor to a violent uprising. The Russian Revolution had begun less than two years previously, while the nascent German republic had only just managed to violently suppress a left-wing insurgency led by Karl Liebknecht and Rosa Luxemburg. With the First World War now concluded, the government feared a similar reaction was possible if not likely in Great Britain and Ireland.

Bonar Law, who was MP for Glasgow Central, told his fellow ministers he believed it was 'vital' that there was 'a sufficient force in Glasgow to prevent disorder'.[3] His specific desire was – given that the strike was not backed by many trade unions – to protect those who wanted to continue to work. The problem was exacerbated by the fact that the manpower of Glasgow's police force – along with others across the country – had been badly depleted by the demands of conscription during the First World War.

Amid this shortage of manpower, General Sir William Robertson, the Commander-in-Chief of British Home Forces, gave his view on the possibility of military support. After pointing out that Scotland had its own commanding officer, he said: 'The military part of the question is quite simple. The civil authorities [in Glasgow] are responsible for law and order, and the military could not step in except at their requisition in accordance with King's Regulations.'[4] He then went on to explain there were 19 infantry battalions in Scotland, 18 of which were formed of Scottish soldiers. The troops, he warned, were in a mixed state of readiness. The officers, he declared, were 'not very efficient' while the soldiers themselves were a cocktail of 'old, young, convalescents and men with wounds'.[5] Hardly a crack squad of hardened killers then, but a group that could potentially keep the peace. Without an imposition of martial law, however, there was little the military could do without the express request of the authorities in Glasgow.

It was then Churchill who suggested that the war cabinet should not 'exaggerate the seriousness of this disturbance', before adding, perhaps with his mind drawing back in part to Dundee in 1911: 'In times of peace we had had to go through strikes just as dangerous as this one.'[6] While Churchill argued that a 'confrontation' between the government and illegal strikers was inevitable, he argued for restraint when considering sending troops, telling the war cabinet: 'We should be careful to have plenty of provocation before taking strong measures. By going gently at first we should get the support we wanted from the nation ... the moment for [troops to be] use[d] has not yet arrived.'[7] Later in the same meeting, he would add: 'Before taking any action in dealing with the strikers we should wait until some glaring excess has been committed. The moment the revolt advances over the line of a pure wage dispute, and the strikers are guilty of serious breach of the law, then is the moment to act.'[8]

At the conclusion of the meeting, the war cabinet accepted that it had neither the authority – that rested with the local government in Glasgow – or the need to send troops to Glasgow at this stage. It did, however, agree to put the nearby military in a state of 'readiness' should they be needed, instructed the Lord Provost to prioritise keeping the electricity running, and urged the local authorities to take 'firm but not provocative action' to 'put down disorder and prevent intimidation'.[9] Finally, Bonar Law sent a telegram to the Lord Provost responding to the strike leaders' demand that the government intervene directly with employers. This he refused to do as 'the precise question [of a 40-hour week] ... is being dealt with at the present time between employers and the duly elected representatives of the trade unions chiefly concerned'.[10] If he were to intervene, it 'could only undermine the authority of those who have been chosen by the men to represent them and would destroy the cooperation between employers and employed'. In making such an argument, Bonar Law correctly judged that, in the words of one newspaper, 'the question at issue is not one between employer and workman, but between a revolutionary section of trade unionists and their fellow trade unionists'.[11] The telegram would be read out in Glasgow's George Square at noon the following day, 31 January.

The exact cause of the rioting in George Square on 31 January is still disputed. What is clear is that a large crowd – estimated around 25,000 – had gathered to hear Bonar Law's response, which was read out at noon. The disorder and violence began shortly afterwards, possibly with police using the blocking of trams in the square as an excuse to try to disperse the crowd. Baton-charges and serious disorder then followed, with injuries among both workers and the police.

The war cabinet met again at 3 p.m. that day, several hours after the rioting had begun. The Secretary for Scotland, Robert Munro, described the events as an attempted 'Bolshevist rising', but suggested they gave 'the appearance of breaking up at an early date, and that there was a strong feeling against the leaders [of the strike]'.[12] The Lord Advocate – Scotland's top legal officer – also suggested that it would be possible for the army to arrest the strike's leaders under the Defence of the Realm Act, assuming necessary authority could be issued. Churchill then made his only recorded comment at the meeting, suggesting the Lord Advocate's request could be arranged 'in a very few minutes, if necessary'.[13] Finally, the war cabinet was updated on the logistical arrangements for getting troops to Glasgow – a request for which had been made earlier that day by the local sheriff of Lanarkshire.

The troops began arriving in Glasgow later that night – after the rioting had ceased – and played no active role in the suppression of the strike. Six tanks were sent in support but arrived several days later and never left their depot. Local press reports even welcomed the arrival of the soldiers. 'The week has finished very quietly in Glasgow,' wrote a reporter for the *Sunday Post* on 2 February, 'due in very large measure to the presence of large bodies of the military.'[14]

Despite Churchill's peripheral role in the response to the 1919 Glasgow strike, he is often portrayed as the villain of the so-called Battle of George Square. In particular, he is personally accused of 'sending in the troops' to suppress the strikers. The historian Gordon Barclay has attributed this to Shinwell's memoir of events, published in 1973, which is the first known reference to Churchill being responsible for the deployment.[15] 'Churchill,' Shinwell wrote, 'persuaded the Cabinet that troops, machine guns and tanks should be deployed in the Clydeside area.'

This claim is directly contradicted by the war cabinet minutes at the time. It can also be refuted by the fact no troops played a role in confronting strikers, and the fact that tanks were never 'deployed'. Indeed, as we have seen, of all the members of the war cabinet present at the 30/31 January meetings, Churchill was the one most arguing for restraint. This should not be entirely surprising. While Churchill enjoys a bellicose reputation, his response to pre-war industrial unrest was generally cautious. As one historian has put it: 'There is little on the record to show that as Secretary of State for War [Churchill] was a military hothead in industrial disputes or diverged significantly from the cautious but firm approach of his colleagues.'[16] Nevertheless, and despite the efforts of historians, Churchill's role in the Glasgow Strike of 1919 continues to be mythologised, embellished and falsified, with inaccurate narratives even being repeated in Scottish school history textbooks.

What is true is that, from the end of the First World War through to the general election in 1922, Churchill became ever more obsessed with trying to 'strangle' the Russian Revolution 'near to birth'.[17] As he showed during the Paris Peace Conference, he was determined to provide material and – if possible – physical military support to defeat the Bolsheviks, which he viewed as an international menace. He described them as creating 'a Russia of armed hordes smiting not only with bayonet and with cannon, but accompanied and preceded by swarms of typhus-bearing vermin which slew the bodies of men, and political doctrines which destroy the health and even the soul of nations'.[18] This description is clearly verbose and colourful to excess, but it accurately reflects Churchill's outlook at the time.

By early 1919, Britain had several thousand troops in eastern and northern Russia, part of a contingent of Allied forces in the country that numbered more than 100,000. These troops were sent to support the White Russians – native opponents of the Bolsheviks – who had a similar number of troops based around Siberia. With these, Churchill hoped to defeat the nascent Red Army of Leon Trotsky, but the operation ended in ignominy and retreat by early 1920, with a substantial bill for taxpayers as well.

The debacle was reminiscent of Antwerp and the Dardanelles – though with significantly less loss of British and Imperial life – and Churchill was somewhat fortunate to escape it without furthering his reputation as a dangerous military adventurer. But there were several other areas where Churchill's crusade against the Bolshevik's did have a decisive impact. Personally, it reconnected him with the right-wing of the Conservative Party, who had largely shunned him for the previous 15 years, but who were equally alert to the alleged Red Menace. Lloyd George had no interest in fighting the Bolshevik regime and instead was determined to recognise and trade with it. This lack of interest from his leader in an issue of the upmost importance to Churchill helped begin his drift back towards the Conservatives.

Concurrently to this, his strong anti-Bolshevik sentiments alienated many of his working-class supporters in Dundee. The level of support for the Russian Revolution there is difficult to gauge, but it is likely that some in Dundee were supportive and many more were sympathetic. News of Bolshevik atrocities did filter out, with newspapers in the city including a despatch from Helsinki outlining how 61 people had been executed in Petrograd (St Petersburg) after being implicated in a 'plot' against the regime.[19] But the extent to which such accounts were believed or dismissed as anti-Bolshevik propaganda is unclear, and left-wing supporters could also temper such reports by pointing to White Russian atrocities on the other side. At the very least, Churchill's support for the aristocrats and militarists among the White Russians is unlikely to have been a major vote winner among the city's jute workers and dockers. Even among those opposed to the Russian Revolution in Dundee, there is likely to have been significant opposition to his enthusiasm for military action. The country had, after all, only just emerged from the First World War, and the Spanish Flu pandemic was also currently ravaging cities around the world.

This bellicosity towards Bolshevik Russia was particularly damaging to Churchill in Dundee because it was effectively exploited by his political opponents. Scrymgeour said Churchill's behaviour proved he was 'the man particularly associated with Imperialism and war', while Sime, the secretary of the Dundee and District Union of Jute and Flax Workers, branded Churchill 'one of the most dangerous men to the peace of the world'.[20] Morel also got in on the act, telling a Dundee audience in 1921: 'His appeal was to the prejudices, intolerances, conceits, common to every people, and more potent perhaps to people like themselves who had for years exercised dominion over others . . . his call was to mastery in armaments over everything except their own ruder passions . . . mastery for mastery's sake, mastery for the ruling British caste . . . over the minds and bodies of the common people in this and in lands beyond the sea.'[21] Such views about Churchill were not new and would have been unpopular during the war. But post-1918 – and particularly after the Treaty of Versailles – there was a feeling that Churchill was out of step with the new order and that, rather than working for peace, he was determined to rush again into war.

For Dundee, however, Churchill's Russia policy was not just a moral question, but also an economic one. Morel – displaying an astuteness and worldliness perhaps lacking in Scrymgeour – cleverly sought to link Churchill's Russia policy to a decline in the sale of jute to Moscow. In particular, he identified a large shipment of jute bags bound for Russia that had been 'stopped at Constantinople by the British navy' as part of Churchill's blockade to deprive the Bolsheviks of resources.[22] This revelation was leapt upon in Dundee Labour circles, who utilised it as a way to effectively illustrate how Churchill's views were harming the city's main industry. Sime even tracked down the affected firm, the directors of which he noted were 'feeling sore' about the lost trade.[23] Morel's investigation would have particularly resonated because the jute industry – having enjoyed a massive boom during and immediately after the First World War – was by 1920 in one of its periodic and increasingly severe slumps. Many were put out of work and some of the blame could now – fairly or not – be placed at their own MP's door.

Churchill did not resign himself to these and other attacks but engaged in a typically robust defence of his behaviour. In late 1921, for example, he convened a meeting in Dundee specifically to discuss unemployment and to hear from local government and business in the city what more could be done to support job creation. He had earlier insisted at a post-Armistice meeting with the city's jute barons that it was his 'earnest desire' to 'do all he could for the special interests of his constituents', adding:

> One of the popular illusions about Dundee is that it lives only on marmalade. When they consider that the staple trade of Dundee, like the cotton trade of Manchester, established under purely artificial conditions, and depending for its existence upon the markets of the world, and, when they consider that the whole of this great industry depends on efficiency of production and enterprise, and the skill of the workers, it is wonderful that it should have resisted the competition of the world, and the shock of Armageddon [the First World War], with undiminished strength and vigour.[24]

Yet, despite this stirring rhetoric, Morel's attacks stuck. The unfortunate reality for Churchill was that his opposition to Bolshevik Russia – while entirely genuine and morally justifiable – began to alienate him from his working-class base in Dundee, just at it began to alienate him from the Liberal Party itself. With the loss of an increasing number of working-class voters, Churchill's electoral room for manoeuvre was rapidly diminishing. His main option to rebuild a broad electoral coalition was to win back the significant Irish block vote that – loyal for so many years – was now dissipating almost as fast as his working-class support. But achieving that would be easier said than done.

Chapter 20

Resolution
1916–1922

Churchill was the first member of the cabinet to arrive at Inverness town hall on 7 September 1921. It had been a difficult drive from his lodgings at Brahan Castle, south-west of Dingwall, to the capital of the Highlands. Despite the journey being just 15 miles, the Highland roads were in poor condition and Churchill's vehicle broke an axle *en route*. His colleagues travelling from London had an equally trying 15-hour journey by sleeper train, with Austen Chamberlain, the Leader of the House of Commons, describing Lloyd George's decision to 'drag us to Inverness' as 'outrageous'.[1]

For the people of Inverness, however, the meeting of the cabinet at the city's town tall was a major event. Not only was it a chance to see many famous politicians, but it was also the first ever meeting of the cabinet in Scotland. As news of the meeting spread, thousands of local people gathered in the vicinity of the town hall, while many more were spotted 'at every convenient window and roof in the vicinity'.[2] More dramatically, a few 'clung to parapets and chimneys at dizzying heights in order to obtain better views' of the government ministers as they arrived.[3]

The emergency session was taking place in Inverness because – despite Chamberlain's grumblings – it was actually the most practical place for the majority of the participants to reach. Lloyd George initiated the meeting but was isolated on his summer holiday near the small village of Gairloch, on Scotland's north-west coast. The house had no telephone and only one car to reach the post office, about a mile away, which had just a single telegraph transmitter. The nearest railway station was four hours' drive away. It is not recorded whether or not his colleagues thought it prudent for the Prime Minister to have placed himself incommunicado in such a way, but it was clear that calling a full cabinet meeting at Gairloch was neither prudent nor practical. Equally, it was determined that having the Prime Minister travel back to London – regardless of whether he was willing to cut his holiday short – was equally redundant. Only a handful of his cabinet colleagues were in the city, with the majority using the parliamentary recess to take holidays around the UK. As was typical, many – including Churchill – had chosen to holiday in Scotland. Inverness was therefore settled on as the location for this crucial cabinet meeting. But even if the surroundings were new, the topic for discussion was hauntingly familiar to all present: Ireland.

The Easter Rising in Dublin in 1916 – despite its relatively limited support at the time – sent shockwaves through the British establishment and signalled the start of significant repression in Ireland. Almost 100 prisoners were shot under martial law in Ireland itself while other supporters, such as Sir Roger Casement, were tried and executed in London. But rather than breaking the resolve of Irish separatists, this repression helped turn public opinion against the British state.

The extremist Sinn Fein – meaning 'Ourselves Alone' – movement quickly claimed ownership of the 1916 Rising and grew in popularity, soon supplanting the more moderate Irish Parliamentary Party, which had been led by John Redmond, who had shared a platform with Churchill to promote Irish Home Rule in 1912. In the 1918 general election, Sinn Fein won 73 of the 105 Irish constituencies, albeit on less than half of the Ireland-wide vote. In contrast to the Irish Parliamentary Party who had supported Irish Home Rule, Sinn Fein now advocated only total independence and had the support of the Irish Republican Army (IRA) – previously known as the Irish Volunteers – commanded by the famous Michael Collins.

Following their victory at the ballot box in 1918, Sinn Fein refused to take their seats in the House of Commons, and instead called a parliament – known as the Dáil – in Dublin, effectively declaring independence unilaterally. By 1919 Ireland was therefore torn between two jurisdictions and governments – Irish and British – vying for legitimacy and control. The British government – consumed by a plethora of other issues after the end of the First World War – was initially unsure of how to respond and attempted to agree a new settlement. The Government of Ireland Bill proposed dividing the island into two separate territories, governed from Dublin and Belfast respectively, which would both be offered a version of Home Rule. While this was accepted in Belfast, which in 1921 got its own local administration and parliament, it was rejected in the south of Ireland, and a violent conflict, known as the Irish War of Independence, soon ignited between the British state and the IRA.

After the Easter Rising of 1916, it had been hoped the Royal Irish Constabulary (RIC) could be used to maintain law and order, but over the following years the RIC was much depleted and demoralised by IRA attacks and assassinations. As the violence between the British and Irish sides intensified in late 1919, Churchill, in his role as Secretary of State for War, proposed recruiting former soldiers as a 'Special Emergency Gendarmerie' to support the work of the police and army.[4] Clad in khaki uniforms with black belts, this force became known as the Black-and-Tans and quickly gained a reputation for indiscriminate ferocity. He also recruited an auxiliary force for the RIC, known as the 'Auxis', to 'strike down in the darkness those who struck from the darkness'.[5] In reality, however, the brutal tit-for-tat attacks of both forces were counterproductive, alienating local people with wholesale reprisals and excessive violence.

More importantly from Churchill's political perspective, these actions made him a villain not just among the Irish in Ireland, but also among the Irish in Dundee. News of the atrocities committed by Churchill's new recruits in Ireland were widely reported in the local press in Dundee, while letters of complaint about Churchill's seemingly bellicose stance even made it into local Conservative-leaning newspapers, who otherwise would probably be sympathetic to his position.

Churchill vigorously defended his strategy of meeting terror with terror to his Dundee constituents, arguing at a particularly rowdy meeting in the city on 18 October 1920:'[The IRA] has so terrorised the Irish population that not a single one of these murderers has been brought to justice and hung – not even by accident. Having no redress, the soldiers and policemen broke from the bonds of discipline and executed reprisals upon notorious members of the Sinn Fein army [the IRA] or organisation in the neighbourhood of the murders.'[6]

It is a sign of how widespread knowledge of the Black-and-Tan atrocities was in Dundee that Churchill did not even attempt to dispute them, but rather solely rationalised them on the basis of summary justice. It also seems highly unlikely the large portion of Irish voters in the city would have accepted Churchill's justification as legitimate or necessary.

Events in Ireland also brought trouble for Churchill even closer to home, with Clementine writing to him on 18 February 1921:'Do my darling use your influence *now* for some sort of moderation or at any rate justice in Ireland – put yourself in the place of the Irish – if you were their leader, you would not be cowed by severity and certainly not by reprisals, which fall like the rain from Heaven upon the Just and upon the Unjust [original emphasis].'[7] Here, Clementine again showed that she often had a better feel for a situation than her husband, who could allow his passions to overwhelm his better judgement.

By July 1921, the British state and IRA had fought each other to a standstill. Lloyd George was told it would take 100,000 troops to win the war – a number that was unacceptable to the public – while Collins privately confessed that, due to a lack of weapons and ammunition, the IRA's ability to keep fighting would cease within a month. A truce was therefore signed on 11 July. But in the following weeks, little progress towards a lasting peace agreement was made, with arguments raging over the preconditions needed for negotiation. As Ireland teetered once again on the verge of all-out conflict, Lloyd George decided to call the meeting of the cabinet in Inverness to get a full mandate to begin negotiations without delay.

Despite the views of his constituents or even the pleas of his wife, Churchill remained resolute in his opposition to giving ground to the Irish nationalists. He suggested they had 'fear in their hearts' and could still be militarily defeated, which, given Collins's later confession that the IRA was at this point rapidly running out of supplies, may have been accurate.[8] Churchill made such an assertion not because he had changed his views on Irish Home Rule or was any less of a devolutionist, but rather because he resented the tactics of the IRA 'murder gangs' and believed a better and more lasting solution to the Irish question could be achieved if they were first defeated, or at least a clear military superiority was gained over them.[9] Indeed, there is no reason to think Churchill was being insincere; he had strong form for showing magnanimity to defeated foes, such as the Boers, and had opposed punitive settlements on Germany in the aftermath of the First World War.

Churchill, however, was in the minority and, at the close of the cabinet meeting, a letter was agreed and sent to Éamon de Valera, the American-born leader of Sinn Fein. It asked if he would be 'prepared to enter a conference to ascertain how the association of Ireland with the community of nations known as the British Empire can best be reconciled with Irish national aspirations'.[10] By authorising such an offer, the extraordinary cabinet meeting in Inverness holds an important place in the history of Anglo-Irish relations and the peace process. If the answer to the cabinet's letter was affirmative, Lloyd George offered to hold initial discussions in Inverness two weeks later. That meeting did not happen but – under pressure to reach a settlement domestically – de Valera kept the channel of communications with Lloyd George open. The matter was further discussed among some members of the cabinet who made the arduous journey to see the Prime Minister at Gairloch – including Churchill – and it was agreed to organise a peace conference with Sinn Fein in London that October.

Churchill was selected as one of the negotiating team for the British government, but by his own admission he performed a secondary role in the conclusion of a deal. He did, however, play an important if not decisive part by befriending Collins, showing him a poster from Pretoria in 1899 offering £25* for his own capture, and comparing it humorously with the £5,000 bounty now offered for Collins. The pair became respectful mutual admirers if not close friends, with Collins later claiming: 'We could never have done anything [in the negotiations]' without Churchill.[11]

After an arduous and at times confused negotiation – but one deftly handled by Lloyd George – an agreement was eventually reached, and the Irish Treaty signed in December 1921. The deal between the Sinn Fein representatives – de Valera was not among them – and the British government effectively granted southern Ireland the status of a dominion, equivalent to Australia or Canada, which it would enjoy until the Statute of Westminster in 1931. It was, however, not

---

* Approximately £2,000 in 2017.

universally welcomed in Ireland itself and pro- and anti-Treaty factions soon began a bloody civil war for control of the state. Collins, murdered in August 1922 by de Valera's anti-Treaty faction, was among the highest profile casualties.

By helping to negotiate the Irish Treaty, Churchill actually handed southern Ireland status and powers far beyond what was advocated by the Home Rule movement. The Irish Free State had complete control over its own internal affairs and was no longer subject to the parliament at Westminster. It also had a greater sense of nationality and nationhood than ever would have occurred under Home Rule alone. Yet, it is something of an irony that Churchill got little credit for this among the Irish voters in his constituency, who had backed him at multiple elections on the basis he supported Home Rule. But now he had delivered more than that, they could no longer vote for him. He was simply too closely associated in the public mind with the Black-and-Tans, the Auxis and their atrocities, and that was something Irish voters could not forgive.

The post-war period therefore saw Churchill alienate – either by accident, design, or a mix of both – two of the most important elements that had formed his base in Dundee over the preceding 14 years. With the working-class and Irish vote slipping away, Churchill would struggle to retain his 'life seat'. Going into the next general election, he needed to build a new and different electoral coalition to the one that had sustained him since 1908.

While Churchill's electoral base was evaporating, there were also ongoing difficulties with his local party. The Dundee Liberal Association had accepted the need for the coalition government in the 1918 general election, but many members were increasingly dissatisfied with Lloyd George and wanted to return their allegiance to Asquith, who was continuing to lead a rump Liberal Party that sat in opposition to the coalition. Matters came to a head in Dundee when trying to find a running mate for Churchill, after Wilkie confirmed he was standing down. Ritchie struck a particularly downbeat tone in a letter describing the process to Churchill: 'We had a long and merry fight to keep the unity of our party. Had it not been out of personal loyalty to yourself I would have given it up.'[12] He also reported that party members were dissatisfied with the direction of the government, which he branded 'arrogant', and warned he believed a credible opposition party would win the next election by a landslide.[13] The sum of the 'strictly personal and confidential' letter – though Ritchie did not explicitly say it – was that he believed, on the current national and local trajectory, that Churchill was at serious risk of losing his 'life seat' at the next election.

In reply, Churchill was equally candid about his view of the government, saying he 'quite understand[s]' Ritchie's views before noting sombrely, with a rare lack of confidence: 'I do not know whether these difficulties could be better dealt with by other men.'[14] Hinting at his own frustrations with Lloyd George, not least over Bolshevik Russia and Ireland, Churchill added: 'If I thought [another party could do a better job] I should certainly not regret a change of administration, as personally I would far rather at this juncture and after all these years be free from the burden and obloquy of public office.'[15]

The suggestion that Churchill was weary of public office must have stung Ritchie, who had done so much to promote his career, but it may also have been designed purely to shock and to show Ritchie in no uncertain terms how far he agreed with his views and wanted them addressed. Churchill then closed his letter by thanking Ritchie 'once again most warmly for all the support you are giving me and the great tact and skill with which you steer our party fortunes in Dundee throughout the difficulties of these exceptional times'.[16] It was one of the last letters he ever sent him.

Ritchie's sudden death from a brain haemorrhage, in early December 1921 at the age of 72, was a personal and political tragedy for Churchill. Personally, he lost a close friend and confidant, someone who had always had confidence in his abilities and supported him unwaveringly through some of the most testing times of his career. He was loyal and wise, and Churchill had both enjoyed and benefited from his company. Politically, Churchill had lost his keenest and most effective advocate in the Dundee Liberal Association at a time when party disunity was rife. With Ritchie's death, he also lost a substantial institutional knowledge of Dundee and its politics, as well as the energy of a formidable campaigner and organiser. With an election expected within months, it was also a loss that Churchill had little time to recover from.

The importance of Ritchie to Churchill's political and personal life in Dundee and beyond is reflected in the tribute he gave after his death. It is a particularly moving piece of writing and reflects some of the strong personal bonds Churchill built with people in Dundee over his near 15 years as an MP in the city. It is worth quoting at length: '[Ritchie] was a man who was an honour to his native town. His firm grasp of principle and loyalty to political doctrines in no way hampered a strong practical common sense. His perfect integrity was the foundation of shrewdness and deep sagacity ...This combination fitted him to guide the political affairs of large numbers of his fellow citizens through the difficulties of these anxious years.'[17]

Churchill then adds an emotive personal note: 'His kindness to me was boundless and unceasing. From the first moment when he sat over the telephone awaiting the result of the Manchester [by-]election in order to send me an invitation from the Liberals of Dundee down to the last time we were together a few weeks ago, he has been one of the best friends I have ever had and one of the most able and far-seeing counsellors.'[18]

He closed the tribute in a more distinctly Churchillian tone: 'Dundee is sensibly the poorer in the loss of this upright man and Scottish worthy, for in such types of character reside [the] imperishable riches of the Scottish race.'[19]

Lloyd George's downfall as Prime Minister came following a meeting of Conservative MPs at the Carlton Club, at its former location on London's Pall Mall, on 19 October 1922. Here, the gathered politicians – tired of Lloyd George's leadership – voted, by 186 votes to 87, to end the coalition agreement and fight the election as an independent party. Lloyd George was left with little choice but to dissolve parliament and fight a general election, which would take place on 15 November 1922.

Churchill had spent the previous week attempting to persuade his Conservative partners not to turn their back on the coalition, but on the morning of the Carlton Club meeting he began to feel severely unwell. Churchill was initially seen by his long-standing GP, Dr Thomas Hartigan, who thought he might be suffering from gastroenteritis and ordered a 'watching brief' and strictly confined him to bed.[20] As the coalition collapsed around him, Churchill was therefore hauled up at home, unable to contribute to events, a circumstance that he undoubtedly found as – if not more – excruciating than his illness.

But by 18 October, it became clear that Churchill's condition was far more serious. The splendidly named surgeon Sir Crisp English was called to Churchill's bedside and immediately diagnosed appendicitis. Emergency surgery was now necessary. At 9.45 p.m. in a room at number 4 Dorset Square, London, Churchill was placed under general anaesthetic to undergo life-saving surgery. As a five-inch-long incision was cut across his side, there were just four weeks left until voters in Dundee would go to the polls to decide Churchill's fate.

Chapter 21

Clementine's Campaign
1922

Clementine left the Caird Hall in a hurry. It had been a particularly rowdy meeting, with a crowd of more than 3,000 filling the city's newest venue, which had been bequeathed by the eponymous jute baron, philanthropist and Churchill supporter Sir James Caird, who had died in 1916. The crowd had been boisterous from the start. James Robertson – Ritchie's replacement as chair of the Dundee Liberal Association – had already been shouted down by a variety of hecklers. The situation was so severe that his peroration amounted to threatening – and failing – to evict hecklers from the hall. On one occasion a steward was so cowed by the disruptors he was trying to remove that he was forced to withdraw in humiliation.

Clementine – dressed in a dark dress offset with a bright pearl necklace – was received a little more respectfully but was soon facing jeers about her wealth and status. The Dundee crowd – always combative – had now taken on a distinctly radical and classist tone. Reporters from *The Courier* identified the 'meeting-wreckers' as 'communists'.[1] By the time David Macdonald – Churchill's Liberal running mate – tried to speak there was full-scale pandemonium in the hall and no further orations could be made. Sensing trouble, the Liberal entourage decided to beat a hasty retreat. As they left, several women spat on Clementine. '[She was] like an aristocrat going to the guillotine in a tumbril [an open cart used to convey prisoners to the scaffold during the French Revolution],' an admiring General Edward Spears – another of the Liberal campaign team – reported back to Churchill.[2] He added: '[Her] bearing was magnificent.'

★   ★   ★

Clementine had arrived in Dundee on 5 November, 10 days before polling day, to campaign in lieu of Churchill himself, who was still convalescing after his operation. His doctors had successfully removed his 'black gangrenous perforated appendix', but ordered him to rest and avoid strain for several weeks.[3] Churchill was, understandably, reluctant to follow this advice and was determined to get to Dundee as soon as possible.* But in the meantime, it would be down to Clementine to fight the seat.

This was not a new experience – she had campaigned in the city before and been well received. Indeed, in her letters back to Churchill outlining the campaign to date, she showed a clear-sighted understanding of the electorate and the key issues facing the campaign. It was a crowded field, with six candidates in total. Churchill – along with his running mate Macdonald – represented the National Liberal Party, the home for Liberal supporters of Lloyd George and the coalition government. Opposing them was an Asquithian Liberal candidate and a Communist candidate. Hoping for victory on his sixth attempt, was the indefatigable Scrymgeour. The local Labour Party, meanwhile, had in early October finally persuaded Morel to assume the Dundee candidacy he had turned down on grounds of ill health in 1918.

'The idea against you seems to be that you are a "war monger" but I am exhibiting you as a Cherub Peace Maker with little fluffy wings round your chubby face,' Clementine wrote to Churchill, most likely on 9 November, with a mix of affection and sagacity.[4] She added, trying to temper Churchill's more electorally self-destructive political inclinations: 'I think the line is not so much "Smash the Socialists" as to try with your great abilities to help in finding [a] solution [to] the capital and labour problem.'

But while she was a willing stand-in, the campaign was not easy for her. Just two months prior – on 15 September – she had given birth to Mary, her fifth child, who was still so young that Clementine had to bring her to Dundee and look after her in-between campaign sessions. Mary's presence also did not go unnoticed by Churchill's

---

* Immediately on waking from his anaesthetic, his first request was to read the latest newspapers. Despite this being denied, his doctor returned a short time later to find Churchill once again passed out, but now surrounded by four newspapers.

opponents in Dundee, with a common heckle being 'does your bairn [child] live on a shilling?'.⁵ Having her young child brought into the campaign as part of a personal attack is bound to have been unsettling, particularly without the reassuring presence of her husband or Ritchie.

Meanwhile one of her other daughters, Sarah, was suffering from tubercular glands in her neck – Clementine had to leave her in the care of doctors in order to travel to Dundee. Such a sacrifice would be heart-wrenching for any mother, but it was particularly so for Clementine. The previous year her daughter Marigold had died aged two-and-a-half having suffered from sepsis in her throat. Marigold's death understandably devastated both Churchill and Clementine, and the memory of it cannot have been far from her mind as she left Sarah under medical attention to head for Dundee. If Clementine ever felt any resentment towards Dundee in later life – and there is no evidence that she did – the harshness of the campaign and the involvement of her children may serve as at least part of an explanation. Certainly, leaving a sick husband and child to campaign on the other side of the country with a baby in tow was an enormous emotional, as well as physical, drain.

Clementine's public performances were, however, widely praised in a press that was generally far from supportive of Churchill's cause. *The Courier*, for example, highlighted Clementine's reposts to the 'silly sallies' of interrupters, concluding that she 'met with success in her latest ordeal'.⁶ Some of these glowing reviews may be in part influenced by an Edwardian deference towards women in general in interwar British society, and wealthy women in particular, but it is clear that Clementine largely held her own. The transcripts of public meetings, for example, show that Clementine was an adept debater who could think on her feet and provide witty put-downs to often determined and aggressive disruptors. She was not there merely as a talking head with the right surname, but a genuine campaigner and evangelist for her husband's cause.

Of course, the gruelling campaign schedule also took its toll – not least as a new mother – and, on one occasion, Clementine was forced to absent herself from an evening rally. But she showed an endurance beyond even seasoned politicians, not only campaigning in place of her husband but also his running mate, Macdonald, who was confined to his bed midway through the campaign with a bronchial infection. Clementine was then representing not one but two National Liberal candidates.

Her only major misstep came when she allowed her remarks to descend into xenophobic innuendo, questioning Morel's birth in Paris – a trope that was repeated and amplified by Churchill's entourage as the campaign went on. 'Is it a fact that Mr Morel is not an Englishman but was born a Frenchman?' she asked a crowd in the city on 8 November.[7] 'Is it true he became an Englishman to avoid military service in the land of his birth? Did he, during the war, render any service to Britain?'

The error in this attack was not its prejudicial tone. While that would rightly be controversial today, it elicited no critical response at the time. Rather, it was an error because it was patently false, ineffectual and actually served to strengthen Morel, as evidenced in his devastating response:

> Regarding Mrs Churchill's questions, I am always willing to oblige a lady. My father was a Frenchman, my mother was an Englishwoman, and I was born in Paris. We do not select our parents or our place of birth. I am no more responsible for the fact my father was French than Mr Churchill is responsible for the fact his mother was American. What has all this to do with the issues before the country? ... My mother sent me to school in England when I was eight [and] in England I have lived ... ever since.

He added, to much laughter from the crowd: 'Very clever of me to come over here when I was eight in order to escape military service, wasn't it? A kind of juvenile precocity of a remarkable kind.'[8]

It is not clear how comfortable Clementine felt using this line of attack on Morel but, particularly given her own time living in France, it seems an unusual choice. In fact, in her private letters to Churchill, she offered a favourable view of Morel, describing him as '*very moderate* [original emphasis]'.[9] She also took a great deal of interest in the poverty in Dundee – 'the misery here is appalling ... some of the people look absolutely starving'[10] – and it is on these issues that she was most comfortable campaigning.

Clementine's performances were a bright spot in an otherwise increasingly chaotic and unfocused campaign. Some of this was not Churchill's fault. He was recovering from major surgery – an arduous process today, let alone in the 1920s – and was right to follow the

advice of his doctors and rest. But his absence, however justified, did
serve to embellish his reputation as an absentee MP who was out of
touch with the city he represented. Even the press release explaining
his absence was unlikely to have elicited much sympathy among his
constituents, who struggled to access any proper form of healthcare:
'Mr Churchill's medical advisers, Lord Dawson, Sir Crisp English and
Dr Hartigan, have consented to his fixing provisionally Saturday
November 11, as the date when he can address a public meeting in
Dundee. Whether in fact Mr Churchill will be able to fulfil this
engagement must depend upon the progress made in the next four or
five days, when a further consultation will be held.'[11]

As well as reinforcing the perception that Churchill was detached
from the city, his absence also affected his political judgement of the
situation on the ground. While he reluctantly followed the advice of
his esteemed medical team not to physically campaign, he nevertheless relentlessly fired off missives attacking his political opponents
from his bed in Dorset Square. But the distance – coupled with the
absence of actionable insight from Ritchie – meant these despatches
were at best shots in the dark, and often actively damaged Churchill's
position.

His chief error was to misunderstand the political position of his
opponents. The Asquithian Liberal candidate, Robert Pilkington,
risked pulling away some of his votes. But Churchill also faced three
candidates to the left: Morel, Scrymgeour and William Gallacher, a
candidate of the Communist Party of Great Britain. Gallacher had
been involved in the 1919 Glasgow strikes and was also an opponent
of British involvement in the First World War. In 1935 he would be
elected to represent the constituency of West Fife, where he remained
MP for 15 years. Yet Churchill misread Gallacher's role in the contest,
believing he was acting as a running mate to Morel, when it was
Morel and Scrymgeour who had in fact built an informal partnership.
This meant Churchill spent significant energy attacking the fringe
candidate Gallacher, who was only likely to pull votes away from
Churchill's actual rivals, Morel and Scrymgeour. 'A predatory and
confiscatory programme fatal to the reviving prosperity of the country, inspired by class jealousy and the doctrines of envy, hatred and
malice, is appropriately championed in Dundee by two candidates
[Morel and Gallacher] both of whom had to be shut up during the

late war in order to prevent them further hampering the national defence,' Churchill angrily wrote in one missive.[12]

In reality, Morel was not only '*very moderate* [original emphasis]' – in Clementine's words – and 'in favour of only constitutional methods', but he also would not have minded Churchill banishing the ghost of the inoffensive Wilkie and ingratiating him with Dundee's more radical elements. Meanwhile, Scrymgeour – Churchill's longest-running opponent who had enjoyed a 9 per cent swing in the 1918 general election – was largely ignored.

The biggest issue the campaign faced, however, was the choice of Churchill's stand-ins who, with the exception of Clementine, were singularly unsuited to electioneering in Dundee. Some were too aristocratic – John Wodehouse, the 3rd Earl of Kimberley and an Olympic polo player – or too militaristic – General Edward Spears – and actively put off working-class constituents. They were also almost wholly ignorant of politics or campaigning. Wodehouse had a stint as the 22-year-old MP for Mid Norfolk after winning the seat in 1906, but stood down just four years later, while Spears was about to be elected unopposed as the MP for Loughborough. 'I knew nothing about politics,' Spears candidly admitted some years later.[13] He added: 'Jack [John] Wodehouse knew nothing about politics. There we both were – rivals in ignorance.'

By far the biggest disaster, however, was F.F. Smith's appearance on 9 November in the Caird Hall. Churchill's best friend – and a heavy drinker – had arrived earlier that morning, via the sleeper train from London, and spent the day enjoying the hospitality of the city's Conservative Eastern Club. The electoral logic behind his appearance was to strengthen the Conservative/Unionist vote for Churchill, although the extent to which this was worthwhile – given the Conservative/Unionist vote had nowhere else to go – is questionable. By the time of the meeting itself, Clementine reported that Smith, having spent the day imbibing with his party colleagues, was 'drunk' and 'no use at all'.[14] Dressed in a grey tweed suit, Smith stumbled onto the stage before 'owlishly' surveying the 3,000-strong audience.[15]

Smith was renowned for performing when inebriated, but in this instance the material seems to have badly let him down. He focused his attacks on Morel and built on Clementine's earlier allusions to the Labour candidate's French heritage. Putting on an exaggerated French accent, he extravagantly elicited Morel's full name, 'Mr George Eduard Pierre Achille Morel de Ville'.[16] After this yielded some laughs, Smith – apparently bereft of other material or jokes – continued to repeat it a further four times through the course of the speech, with increasingly diminished returns.

Further gaffes also followed, not least his suggestion that Churchill was among the bravest fighters in England, leading one Dundonian in the audience to point out Smith presumably meant Britain. More cruelly, Smith also made a pointed reference to the 'late Sir Roger Casement' – the man he had just six years ago secured the death penalty for – to whom he gave entire credit for the work of the Congo Reform Association. Morel, he suggested, had merely piggybacked on Casement's 'humanitarian' work in order – somewhat fancifully – to ensure the Congo was removed from King Leopold's control and handed over to Germany.

Apart from Clementine's personal criticism of Smith's inebriated state, the newspapers were also unimpressed. The Courier's editorial suggested euphemistically that the speech was delivered with 'great heartiness' but was 'completely devoid' of 'any constructive policy for getting the nation out of its present mess'.[17] It added: 'These Coalition apologists have remarkable affrontery.' A number of prominent local people also wrote in to local newspapers defending Morel, while Morel himself dismissed Smith's attack as a 'third-rate music hall performance'.[18] But – on realising the extent of the backlash – Morel quickly sought to directly associate Churchill with it, branding that 'unbalanced and violent individual' as the 'inspiration' for Smith's comments.[19]

Throughout this, Clementine had tried to reassure her convalescing husband that he still stood a chance of retaining the seat and that any missteps in the campaign could be remedied by his reappearance. 'The situation here is an anxious one ... Of course I feel the minute you arrive the atmosphere will change and the people will be roused,' she wrote encouragingly, most likely a couple of days before Churchill's arrival in the city.[20] But she also made it clear that this was unlike any campaign Churchill had previously fought in his 'life seat' – it would require a substantial effort amid a hostile atmosphere. She sought to prepare him not just for the extra effort, but also the likelihood of a difficult reception: 'If you feel strong enough, I think besides the Drill

Hall meeting, which is pretty sure to be broken up, you should address one or two small open meetings. Every rowdy meeting rouses sympathy and brings votes, and especially as you have been so ill.'

It is a sign of how difficult votes were to find – and how convinced Clementine was that Churchill would be shouted down – that she sought to persuade him that weakness in front of the electorate would in fact be a vote winner. She added wistfully, but also in a sensible attempt to manage expectations: 'I am longing to see you and so is Dundee – I shall be heartbroken if you don't get in.'[21]

Churchill boarded his private coach of the sleeper from London to Dundee on the evening of 10 November. His doctors had finally but reluctantly given him the all-clear to travel. At his side was a private nurse, as well as Detective Sergeant Walter Thompson, his Scotland Yard-assigned bodyguard. Clementine had already instructed her husband to make sure to tell Thompson to 'conceal himself tactfully as it would not do if the populace thought you were afraid of them'.[22] But by now Churchill had few illusions about the difficulties he faced or the reception he would get. Emaciated and with an only partially healed incision across his stomach, he knew it would be a struggle, but also that he could make a decisive impact. He knew he was likely to be heckled and shouted down, but that many in the city still had sympathy for his position. He knew, above all, that he had four days left to save his 'life seat'.

Chapter 22

The Final Round

1922

Four men, dressed in flat caps and thick tweed suits, carried Churchill into the Caird Hall. Each clutched the end of two wooden poles that had been lashed to the bottom of an armchair, creating an improvised litter. As they stooped forward under the weight, the regal head of their charge could briefly be glimpsed, while his feet – a foot off the ground – gently swayed back and forth. In his left hand, he clutched a silver-topped cane. If it was not for the trademark Homburg hat and bow tie, he could well have been confused with a Caesar. Despite taking an unexpected route to avoid the waiting mob, a small crowd had still managed to find the door to the hall he intended to use. As his litter-bearers strode decisively forward, a shout was heard from the waiting throng: 'Ah'll gie ye twa pound tae drap him [I'll give you two pounds to drop him].'[1]

Churchill had arrived in Dundee earlier that morning, Saturday 11 November, Armistice Day. Clementine, his brother Jack and a small gang of well-wishers were there to meet him, and many were shocked at his sunken appearance. As he was helped down from the carriage by his private nurse, he produced a smile of greeting that could just have easily been a grimace. Unable to take the stairs, he was helped up to the street via the goods lift and then whisked away in a waiting car to his hotel. He paused briefly for reflection as the signal gun heralded the two-minute silence, and then began his fight to retain Dundee.

Despite his condition, Churchill threw himself into the campaign. As well as the meeting that afternoon at the Caird Hall, he agreed to preside over a 'Workers for Churchill' meeting later that evening. A truce had been agreed between the candidates for Remembrance

Sunday, but two further mass meetings were announced for Monday 13 November – two days from polling day – at the YMCA and the Drill Hall. A further four meetings were arranged for 14 November.

This gruelling schedule clearly reflects Churchill's own recognition that something drastic had to be done to rescue the campaign, but it also shows the strength of the desire he had to remain the MP for Dundee. This was not purely a question of maintaining a foothold in parliament to further his own career. Churchill could have – given his illness – perfectly respectably stayed away from the campaign entirely and then looked for another, safer seat. He need not have sent his wife and their newborn child to the city in his stead or risked his recovery by travelling and electioneering so soon after dangerous surgery. As he noted confidently later: 'The whips will find me a seat if I want one.'[2] Therefore, the desire to win in Dundee was not just an issue of keeping a constituency, but also a result of his genuine association and feeling for the city. He had represented Dundee for nearly 15 years and wanted – if the electorate allowed him – to continue to do so.

Churchill's first meeting at the Caird Hall that day, however, exposed what a challenge this gruelling schedule would be. As well as having to be carried into the hall on the litter – an optic that did little to dispel his patrician image – he had to speak sitting down and, initially, could hardly be heard by the 3,000-strong crowd. The event had been ticketed in order to avoid heckling – a soft launch for Churchill's reappearance – but there was still occasional shouting and barracking from the crowd. But Churchill grew into his oration, speaking for an hour and a half and even managing to stand for his closing remarks.

The speech itself showed the extent to which Churchill had heeded Clementine's political advice. He outlined the policy achievements of the coalition government, presented himself as a supporter of peace internationally and said that he 'rejoiced' at the progress made on the Irish question.[3]

When he did attack his opponents, it was with a respect and subtlety that had been devoid in his campaign thus far. Morel, he said – and borrowing Clementine's exact language – was a man of 'constitutional means', as well as a 'man of intellectual eminence and distinction'.[4] Incorrectly referring to Morel as a 'conscientious objector', he added: 'If a man faces hardship and imprisonment for his opinions, you do not deny him at all the reputation of being conscientious, but if a man is conscientiously bent on my destruction, although I may admire his methods, I resist his actions.' On Scrymgeour, Churchill said he admired 'the persistency and his fidelity to the principle which he advocates' but that a vote for the prohibitionist will not 'have any direct bearing on the great issues fought out in Dundee'.[5] When Clementine leant over and pointed out that Scrymgeour was in fact in the audience, Churchill smiled at him warmly before changing the subject.

The fact that Churchill was able to speak for such a long period – as well as moderate his tone – meant the Caird Hall meeting was a success. It was, however, an address to an audience largely made up of Churchill supporters. It therefore did not fully introduce Churchill to the hot temper of meetings littered with communist disruptors. Even Scrymgeour left Churchill's remarks unanswered despite being present, a situation the firebrand later somewhat lamely and unbelievably attributed to his desire not to 'breach political etiquette'.[6] Equally, preaching to the almost wholly converted could only have a minimal impact on the direction of the campaign, which continued on a downward trend. The Remembrance Sunday truce provided some respite, but also halted any momentum gained by Churchill's first day in the city. When campaigning restarted, matters went from bad to worse.

On Monday morning, it was reported that Robertson – Ritchie's replacement as chair of the Dundee Liberal Association – had made a bungled approach to see if Scrymgeour would stand on a joint ticket with Churchill. Not only had Scrymgeour categorically rejected the approach but, in the process, he tricked Robertson into revealing that he believed the prospects for Churchill's re-election were at best uncertain. The fact these conversations were revealed in a prominent article in *The Courier* only further enhanced their damage to the credibility of Churchill's campaign and any momentum it had gained from his arrival in the city.

Whether or not the story was factually true was disputed at the time, but it seems highly likely that it was. Robertson categorically denied it – although by that point he had no other option – and the only source for these revelations was Scrymgeour himself. Clearly Scrymgeour had obvious motives in having the discussion made public – it simultaneously made Churchill's campaign appear weak and made him seem more credible. It would also sow disarray in the National Liberal camp given the party apparatus was apparently willing to discard the (admittedly lacklustre) Macdonald – Churchill's nominal running mate – mid-campaign.

But, despite a clear motive, it seems unlikely Scrymgeour would have completely invented the meeting, even if the supposedly verbatim account he gave the newspapers may have been misremembered or – much more likely – embellished for dramatic effect. At the very least, it is probable that Robertson held a meeting with Scrymgeour to discuss the election and during it attempted to recruit him on a joint ticket. Whether or not he actually said to Scrymgeour he was unsure of Churchill's chances is a moot point – the fact the meeting took place at all was evidence that he thought it. In any case, it was highly naïve of Robertson to hold such a meeting with Scrymgeour without first being certain he was open to the offer. It is hard to fathom Ritchie making such an error and, as he read down the columns of *The Courier*, Churchill must have regretted his absence more than ever.

That evening, Churchill addressed a rally at Dundee's Drill Hall but, unlike the Caird Hall event, this was almost entirely unticketed. A few seats near the front of the auditorium were reserved for special guests, but behind them was a free-for-all. In the hours before the event, substantial crowds began gathering and the venue was soon filled to capacity. 'No smoking' signs were torn down and an increasingly rowdy atmosphere prevailed as the hall filled with a fog of tobacco smoke. Supporters of Gallacher and Scrymgeour were prominent among the guests crowding the back of the hall, with boisterous renditions of the socialist anthem 'The Red Flag' and evangelical hymn 'Tell me the old, old story' competing to be heard.

Outside the hall, however, the situation was even worse. Crowds continued to gather despite the hall being full. The pressure on the padlocked gates by the venue was so great that one soon burst open. Dozens of police then launched a baton charge to try to disperse the mob, with the situation rapidly descending into a riot. It seems likely that Churchill had been informed of these events before his arrival – his party prudently diverted to enter via the back door – but chose to press on anyway.

Having made his surreptitious entrance and with the crowd refusing to pay any heed to the chairman of the meeting, Churchill – with considerable effort – stood up to speak. If he had hoped that the sight of his weakened condition might at least bring silence, if not – as Clementine once suggested – sympathy, he was mistaken. 'I was struck by looks of passionate hatred on the faces of some of the younger men and women,' Churchill recalled of the meeting, some 10 years later, adding: 'But for my helpless condition I am sure they would have attacked me.'[7]

'You'll be bottom of the poll,' screamed one member of the audience, to which Churchill responded, with good humour but bite: 'If I'm to be bottom of the poll, why don't you allow me one dying kick?'[8] It was, however, little use. He continued, despite the strain, to try to speak, but the constant interruption made it impossible – even for a speaker in rude health – to be heard. A final attempt to ditch the speech and move straight to questions proved equally futile, with Churchill facing a cacophony of questions on an extraordinary array of subjects, from the Black-and-Tans to ministerial pay to the Balfour Declaration, with only a few answers being heard.

Despite the atmosphere, Churchill seemingly remained in a good mood. When he was heard, his comments elicited some laughter, and he held a smile – as candidates are trained to do – throughout. Still, there was more than a hint of irritation in his voice as the meeting was finally abandoned: 'We will not submit to the bullying tyranny of featherheads, we will not submit to be ruled. We will stand up for . . . the rights and liberties of British citizens against the supporters of the Socialist candidates who, if they have their way, would reduce this great country to the same bear garden to which they have reduced this great meeting.'[9] With that – and some warm nods to those supporters he had in the room – he left.

The experience probably had little bearing on the outcome of the election. After all, most attendees had already made up their mind how to vote – albeit not for Churchill – and were only there to make things difficult for him. Yet, while Churchill maintained a brave face throughout, it was a frustrating and to an extent, frightening, experience.

Once the meeting finished, Churchill and his entourage repaired to the Royal Hotel for a champagne supper, with General Spears reporting – tongue in cheek – that 'every time a cork popped, we thought it was Winston being shot'.[10] But behind the bonhomie there was a genuine concern, with Churchill, a veteran of the Boer War and the trenches, instructing his bodyguard to sleep across from his hotel room door that night. Politically, the meeting was a frustration, particularly with just a day left of the campaign. He had hoped to make a positive impact, if not in the meeting itself then with the press reporting it, but instead awoke to headlines such as 'Churchill Howled Down: Drill Hall Meeting Wrecked'.[11]

But it was, in fact, an editorial in the supposedly Liberal-supporting *Advertiser* that really concerned Churchill. 'The Liberal who supports Mr Churchill in the present situation is merely perpetuating the factionalism which has sterilised his party,' the article read, continuing: 'The Unionist who does so is providing a sinister form of opposition for his own chief . . .'[12] The piece also claimed Churchill was 'enraptured' with 'self-admiration'. It was the final straw for the increasingly beleaguered Churchill, who had already been dissatisfied with the press in Dundee for some time.

The vast majority of the newspapers were owned by David Couper (D.C.) Thomson after he acquired the city's rival publishers, John Leng & Co, in 1905. This gave Thomson a practical monopoly on news in the city, controlling the Conservative-leaning *Courier* and the Liberal-leaning *Advertiser*, as well as the *Evening Telegraph*. The company also published several national titles, including the *People's Journal*, the *Sunday Post*, the *Weekly News* and *The Scots Magazine*, which it is claimed has been in print since the Jacobite Rising of 1745. D.C. Thomson would later achieve international fame as the publisher of the *Dandy* and *Beano* comics.

While the Thomson family had begun building its business empire in shipping it was, under D.C. Thomson's leadership, becoming a publishing powerhouse. Thomson himself – 61 years old in 1922 and sporting a bushy moustache – was a shrewd and uncompromising businessman, but he shared with Churchill a stubbornness and a determination not to be cowed. Initially, their relationship had been cordial if not close. While *The Courier* was broadly critical of Churchill, the *Advertiser* was broadly supportive, meaning Churchill could be satisfied he was getting a fair hearing in the city. But, with the advent of the coalition and the split in the Liberal Party, this happy equilibrium effectively broke down and both papers took a more critical line. D.C. Thomson had always been wary of what he perceived as Churchill's 'greed for glory' and the events of 1916 to 1918 – with Churchill's stint in the trenches followed by his attempts to regain office – seeming to have reinforced this opinion.[13] This breakdown in relations culminated in the editorial in the supposedly supportive *Advertiser* the morning before polling day, which Churchill – probably accurately – was convinced had been dictated by D.C. Thomson himself.

With the campaign faltering and seemingly under attack from all sides, Churchill was in a particularly bellicose mood when he summed up his views at a rally in Broughty Ferry later that day on 14 November:

> Here we get in the morning the Liberal Mr Thomson through the columns of the Liberal *Advertiser* advising the Liberals of Dundee to be careful not to give a vote to Mr Churchill because his Liberalism is not quite orthodox ... [and] at the same time ... you have the Conservative, the Diehard, Mr Thomson, through the columns of the Conservative *Courier* advising the electors of Dundee to be very careful lest in giving a vote to Mr Churchill they should run the risk of building up opposition to the new Conservative government.
>
> Behind these two [newspapers] ... you get the one single individual – a narrow, bitter unreasonable being, eaten up with his own conceit, consumed with his own petty arrogance, and pursued from day to day and from year to year by an unrelenting bee in his bonnet.[14]

Turning to the respective reporters present, he closed, with words he would come to regret: 'Now put that down for the *Advertiser* and the *Courier*.'

Such a public attack by a politician on a respected newspaper proprietor would be extraordinary even in normal times, but during an election campaign it was positively foolhardy. Churchill, by this point, appears to have practically given up hope that he can retain the seat, and is instead choosing to lash out at his enemies – real and perceived – with the remaining time he has left, regardless of the consequences. Of course, as a constituency MP it would be understandably frustrating to have a hostile local media, but this was clearly not the best way to go about changing that fact. The strength of Churchill's attack is such that it made his relationship with Thomson unsalvageable, which is not a course he would have embarked upon had he been confident of being returned as the MP for Dundee the following day.

As Churchill retired to bed at the Royal Terrace Hotel later that evening, he wondered how this election – his sixth contested in Dundee – would turn out. There was no doubt it had been a difficult campaign. In many ways he had been unlucky, his life-threatening illness at the start of the campaign being just one example. But he had also made missteps, not least in his chosen proxies who – with the notable exception of Clementine – had generally made bad matters worse in Dundee. The erosion of his working-class and Irish base was not his sole responsibility, but he had failed to fully realise the danger and respond to it. Even his own arrival, he increasingly believed, might not be enough to turn it around. With his rivals boisterous and the local press turning against him, Churchill closed his eyes and wondered just how many years were really left in his 'life seat'.

Chapter 23

Last Orders

1922

It was a sign of Churchill's nervousness that he was the first candidate to arrive at the count on 16 November. He had suffered a night of 'exhaustion and suspense' contemplating the possible outcomes of the election.[1] His decision to arrive early was evidence of this, breaking his own maxim that it is 'wise not to go [to a count] too early' and try to divine the outcome as the ballots are sifted and piled.[2]

But whatever Churchill's inner fears, he maintained a cheerful demeanour as he walked into the city's ornate Marryat Hall, which formed part of the Caird Hall complex. With Clementine at his side, he wished a cheery 'good morning' to the more than 120 assembled volunteers and exchanged laughs and jokes with the officials already present. This was Churchill's sixth election in Dundee, and by now he was on familiar terms with many of the city's functionaries. Spotting a prominent Liberal supporter, Churchill confidently offered odds of three to one on his coming success, although the bet was not taken.

Six long counting tables extended down the hall and the enumerators steadily assembled on either side. As the morning went on, other candidates began to arrive and – despite the animosities of the campaign – a civil atmosphere reigned. Each candidate brought their wife and, in the case of Macdonald and Morel, their children as well. The different parties greeted each other cordially and Scrymgeour may have thanked Churchill for the autograph he signed for his niece, Flora, the previous day. By the time the ballot boxes finally arrived, having been kept under lock and key in the basement of the city's sheriff court overnight, the room was alive with political rivals, party functionaries, electoral officials, press, volunteers and families.

The Dundee contest, however, was the third vote to be tallied – counts for the nearby and smaller Montrose Burghs and Forfarshire were dealt with first – and as the delay in getting the count underway grew, so too did Churchill's apprehension. When the moment finally arrived, he joined the other candidates in marching up and down the long tables, watching the tens of thousands of ballot papers being sorted. As the counting proper began, he pulled up a chair at the end of one table and stared intently as the piles of votes for each candidate steadily grew. As he watched the votes being tallied – and his future decided – he reflected on the last 24 hours and whether, despite the difficulties of the campaign, he might just be able to pull off victory.

Polling day – 15 November – began quietly. Much of the city awoke to the cold darkness of the November morning and swiftly made their way to work, opting to vote later. The party activists, however, got underway swiftly. One new phenomenon – a particular favourite of the Communist candidate, William Gallacher – was to graffiti slogans such as 'Don't be silly, vote for Willie' down the centre of the city's tram lines.[3] This tactic was later the cause of some irritation when it emerged the calcium carbide solution used was almost impossible to remove.

Not to be outdone, Scrymgeour's supporters soon adopted the same tactic, but with less rhythmical flourish, daubing slogans such as 'Wallace struck his first blow for liberty in Dundee – let Scrymgeour strike his first blow for liberty [today].' The reference to William Wallace – a hero of the Wars of Scottish Independence who it is claimed began his revolt after killing the son of Dundee's English governor – drew ridicule from his opponents, although not Churchill, against whom it was presumably directed. Gallacher remarked: 'Scrymgeour is over sixty years of age – rather late in striking his first blow.'[4]

More conventional campaigning was also underway, with motorcars emblazoned with the colours of the various political parties shipping voters to polling stations. In an ill portent for the superstitious, one car driven by a volunteer for Churchill ran over and killed a black cat. Given schools were closed to act as polling stations, groups of children joined adults in electioneering, chanting songs about their favoured – mostly left-wing – candidates. The rather improbably named Prohibitionists' Pipe Band at one point had a crowd of several hundred following it towards the city centre as it played 'Bonnie Dundee'.

Supporters gathered outside polling stations in a last-minute bid to persuade people to back their chosen candidate. At one polling station, the police had to be called to ensure voters could actually access the voting booths. *The Courier* reported that 'hundreds' of supporters of various parties were 'buttonholing' voters and had to be reminded by officers not to trespass into polling stations. In another, more controversial incident, a female activist offered to 'buddy' an older – and, she claimed, confused – voter into the booth to help her cast her vote. But this apparently 'kindly act' was a mere front to 'properly instruct' the older woman on how to vote.[5] A row then ensued between the pair and, following the intervention of polling station volunteers, the older woman was able to cast her vote unimpeded.

Polling day also featured a new form of campaigning. While it was not 'getting out the vote' in the modern sense, each campaign did have activists delivering leaflets and pamphlets to houses and tenements. Such efforts were unscientific and not targeted but designed purely to remind those that had not yet voted that there was an election on. This change stemmed from a recognition that the vast majority of the electorate was still inexperienced in possessing the right to vote, and therefore needed to be reminded to do so. Even many of the men who had the right to vote in the 1918 general election would have still been conscripted and overseas when that ballot took place. For them – and many more who had reached voting age since – this would be their first time voting in Dundee. Certainly, the strategy of campaigns going door to door to remind people to go the polls can help explain the high turnout in Dundee at this election.

The atmosphere on polling day was in complete contrast to the tenor of the campaign. Churchill and Clementine enjoyed a warm reception as they travelled the city and visited polling stations, waving and smiling as cheering crowds greeted them. Only one observer thought he noticed Churchill sporting a 'corrugated brow', but he attributed this to Churchill's ongoing pain following his surgery.[6] Indeed, given their reception, it is probable that Churchill felt his chances of re-election might be improving. Certainly, there was every reason to assume the vote would be close, with everyone remaining tight-lipped and suggesting it was too close to call. Churchill's personal feelings at this point, however, are perhaps best deduced from his decision to stay and campaign in Dundee right until the close of polling – there were no trips to play a round of golf at Carnoustie or departures to enjoy a lavish dinner in Edinburgh. He clearly felt his personal presence was necessary – and might just be enough to get him over the line.

The only black spot of the final stage of the campaign was Churchill's ongoing row with Thomson. Unsurprisingly, rather than changing Thomson's opinion, Churchill's diatribe against him only hardened his resolve. 'Whatever maybe his chances at the poll today, there can be no doubt that Mr Winston Churchill is in a vile temper,' the polling day editorial of *The Courier* began ominously.[7] It continued, using a rather curious analogy: 'Like the disappointed man on the station platform he kicks out at anybody who happens to be near him. For those not within immediate reach he has buckets of calumny.' After suggesting Churchill's outburst was only due to Thomson's refusal to support the coalition, the editorial concludes: 'We would again advise the Dundee electors to give attention to the candidature of Mr Pilkington [the Asquithian Liberal] and Mr Macdonald.'

While this article pertains to be written by someone else – it refers to Thomson in the third person – it seems certain it would have been published with his approval. Churchill, of course, could have few objections given the strength of his attack. But he will have been surprised that, alongside this negative editorial, the newspaper published a verbatim transcript of his attack on Thomson, under the headline: 'Churchill in a temper: attacks Dundee newspapers'.[8] Thomson, whatever his personal animosity towards Churchill, was clearly at pains to ensure that his readers received both sides of the story, even if he advised them on what conclusions should then be drawn.

The row escalated further in *The Courier* the following day, just as the count was due to get underway. Thomson published a transcript of letters between himself and Churchill over the previous six months, which he said proved Churchill's attempts to influence the position of the Dundee newspapers under his control. Specifically, he alleged that he was offered an honour by unnamed 'Coalition sources' in exchange for giving Churchill favourable coverage.[9] He does not implicate Churchill in this approach, and in a later letter Churchill himself states:

'I know of no emissaries who were sent to you to suggest you being bought with Coalition gold, and I am certain that no person had had any authority to make such a suggestion.'

On first reading, it seems less than credible to suggest that the coalition government would have been so concerned about local media coverage – even in the region of one of its most prominent MPs – to attempt to bribe the proprietor. Yet, it was the common practice of Lloyd George's administration to use honours as political leverage or for financial gain. Between 1916 and 1922, an astonishing 120 hereditary peerages and a further 1,500 knighthoods were created. The situation became so severe that the Honours (Prevention of Abuses) Act of 1925 was passed after Lloyd George's fall to try to prevent the sale of honours.* With that in mind, Thomson's claims become much more credible. Equally, in a separate letter, Churchill does clearly imply that, if the Dundee newspapers do not reconsider their 'damaging hostility' to him and the Coalition, his party would be forced to 'secure newspaper representation ... which would enable its case to be stated and attacks upon it to be rebutted'. Such a threat – in effect to set up a pro-Coalition rival publication – can only have been empty given the costs, manpower and logistics involved in such an enterprise. But it certainly helps to explain the clear souring of relations between the two men.

Crucially, however, Thomson only chose to publish the letters – which incriminated the coalition, if not Churchill himself – after the polls had closed. This is notable given that he presumably had the letters readily in his possession and could have, should he so have wished, published them on polling day itself to try to influence the outcome of the vote. Instead, he waited until they could have no direct bearing on electoral events. This suggests that, while Thomson was anxious to confront Churchill, he was also cognisant of not appearing to try to influence how people voted, which, of course, was Churchill's central charge. For Churchill's part, as he made his way to the Marryat Hall for the count, he must have been relieved – if not grateful – that Thomson had delayed.

*   *   *

---

* Maundy Gregory, Lloyd George's fixer, is so far the only person to have been convicted of selling honours under the Act.

The counting at the Marryat Hall proceeded slowly and it was difficult for Churchill, seated on his perch at the end of one table, to get a clear sense of how things were proceeding. The room was filled with the muted whispers of candidates and their agents trying to judge how the count would go. Party volunteers scuttled nervously back and forth as the enumerators, working in pairs, tallied the votes from their boxes. Slowly, as the ballots were verified and placed in receptacles at the far end of the room, the picture became clearer.

Though Clementine continued to smile brightly, Churchill's face became flushed and the easy bonhomie with which he had started the day was replaced with a withdrawn, forlorn slump. Oblivious to the chatter around him, Churchill suddenly stood up and made his way through to the Caird Hall. He crossed the marble floor of the connecting corridor alone and tried to enter the main hall itself, violently shaking the door. It rocked back and forth on its hinges, but the lock would not yield.

Denied one final look at the auditorium where he had made his dramatic return to Dundee just five days previously, Churchill turned back and asked a passing, bemedalled porter to bring him a chair. Then he sat down and lit a cigar. The final result would not be announced for another three hours, but he had seen enough.

Chapter 24

Closing Time
1922

At 5.10 p.m. on 16 November 1922, Churchill's defeat in Dundee was finally confirmed. He had held the seat for almost 15 years and won the previous five elections decisively, but he could not do it a sixth time.

Having left his solitary seat in the grand marble corridor, he proceeded slowly one floor down, where the sheriff was waiting at a large window to announce the figures to the expectant crowd of thousands below. Churchill already knew his fate – the piece of paper he had been handed had confirmed he had received 20,466 votes, only enough to place him fourth. Scrymgeour, who five elections ago had lost his deposit with just 655 votes, had now topped the poll with 32,578. He was now the first – and to date, only – prohibitionist MP ever elected to the House of Commons. Morel came a close second with 30,292 and was also elected.

Having read the results, Churchill immediately walked over to Scrymgeour, took his hand and offered his congratulations. The pair had been adversaries since 1908 and were, in almost every way, complete opposites. Yet, while he disagreed with him, Churchill held no animosity towards him.

As the sheriff announced Scrymgeour's victory, a huge roar could be heard from the crowd. Standing just to his right, Churchill's eyes filled with held-back tears. Clementine, who had been a bastion of smiling composure all day, was suddenly overcome and actively wept. She was naturally distraught for her husband, but would have also felt the defeat personally, given the direct effort she had put into the campaign and the individual sacrifices she had made.

After Scrymgeour thanked God for his victory – and Morel thanked the people for his – the sheriff turned to Churchill and asked if he had anything to add. Choked with emotion, he could merely shake his head. As the Communist Party candidate Gallacher – who had secured 5,906 votes – got up to say a few words, Churchill, accompanied by Clementine, strode from the room and left the building.

Churchill's defeat in Dundee was sudden and decisive. It came immediately after the election where he had secured his biggest ever vote and seemed – to all except Scrymgeour – unassailable. Yet just four years later, his support had been massively eroded. The precise result was (with 1918 tallies in brackets, where relevant):

1. Scrymgeour (Scottish Prohibition Party) 32,578 (10,423)
2. Morel (Labour Party): 30,292 (Wilkie, 24,822)
3. Macdonald (National Liberal Party): 22,244
4. Churchill (National Liberal Party): 20,466 (25,788)
5. Pilkington (Liberal Party): 6,681
6. Gallacher (Communist Party of Great Britain): 5,906

Churchill had, in the words of one historian, 'taken a two-to-one victory and [seen it turn into] a worse than three-to-two defeat'.[1] While the fact it is a two-member seat complicates analysis, it seems likely he suffered one of the biggest swings against a National Liberal candidate in the whole of the country. Certainly, there was no question of anyone suggesting the result was close, but it is worth noting that, even in defeat, more than 20,000 Dundonians continued to back Churchill.

As is the case in almost all electoral defeats – or, indeed, victories – there is no one factor that can be pinpointed as the cause, but rather multiple, competing issues that are generally responsible. In the case of Churchill's defeat in 1922, these were threefold: personal, local and national.

Personally, and most obviously, Churchill was unable to be physically present in Dundee for much of the campaign due to his appendicitis. When he was able to finally come to the city, he was still in a recovery phase and unable to campaign at a normal pace. Churchill had proved over the previous five elections that he was a fantastic platform speaker and charismatic campaigner, bringing with him energy, dynamism and enthusiasm. His absence was therefore a significant loss to the campaign, while also contributing to the perception that he was an absentee MP. Amid the vacuum left by Churchill's absence, he was ably supported by Clementine, but there was only so much she could do. The arranged professional political stand-ins failed to deliver the necessary impetus and, in at least one case, actively undermined the campaign. Some of this could have been avoided with more judicious planning, but a lot of it was simply down to the vagaries of luck and timing, over which Churchill could have little influence.

Locally, however, the question is more complex. Churchill well knew since he first won the seat in 1908 that his electoral base was in the working-class and immigrant Irish communities in the city. This was the electoral coalition on which his 'life seat' was based and, for the majority of his time as MP for Dundee, he worked to improve the lives and deliver the aspirations of these two groups, often at significant political cost or in the face of personal danger. Yet, by his actions through 1918 to 1922, he actively antagonised and alienated these two rungs of his support. Of course, it would be absurd to suggest that he should have prioritised his electoral coalition in Dundee when you consider the issues – the Russian Revolution and the Anglo-Irish War – that were at stake. Yet there is no disputing that his policies, such as support for the Black-and-Tans or the blockade on Russia, helped erode his base.

At the same time, he lost key local allies and made new local enemies. The death of Ritchie undoubtedly undermined the effectiveness of the Liberal Party in Dundee and robbed Churchill of an invaluable political counsellor. Many of his early missteps – such as believing Morel was partnering with Gallacher rather than Scrymgeour – could have been avoided with Ritchie's actionable advice. Robertson, for all his efforts, lacked either the experience or the ability – possibly both – to effectively manage the campaign. Equally, Wilkie's decision to stand down in the face of local opposition robbed Churchill of his erstwhile running mate. This set the Labour Party in opposition to, rather than in cooperation with, Churchill, for the first time. Meanwhile, the National Liberals' second candidate, Macdonald, despite his marginally higher vote share, simply was not up to the task.

Then there is the case of Churchill's spat with Thomson. As we have seen, this came too late in the campaign to have a substantial impact on the outcome. Indeed, Thomson seems to have actively avoided publishing the letters that could have damaged Churchill until after polls had closed. But the row with Thomson may help partially explain why Macdonald – who, after all, was endorsed by *The Courier* despite being a National Liberal – gained more votes than Churchill himself. Conversely, if Churchill had developed a better relationship with Thomson over the preceding years – and been successful in his attempts to alter his coverage – it is likely this would have helped Churchill gain and retain support in the 1922 general election. This is a counterfactual argument and as such cannot be proved, but it is impossible to think of a scenario where positive media coverage could negatively impact a campaign.

Nationally, the momentum was also against Churchill. The failure of the competing Liberal leaderships to reconcile in advance of the 1922 general election was unhelpful, while the continuing rivalry between Lloyd George and Asquith was unappealing to voters. The aphorism that voters do not support divided parties is true – but it is even worse when the party splits into two competing factions that run against each other. This was compounded by the fact that Lloyd George – having suffered the unexpected and unwanted demise of the Coalition – had little to offer the public. He failed to issue a National Liberal Party manifesto and boldly told an audience of voters he had no 'great slogan' to offer them.[2] Churchill therefore was left to represent a divided party that had no real policy platform. Given the scale of the defeat, it seems unlikely he would have won even if the Liberal Party had been reunited under a single leader and vision, but it was undoubtedly an unhelpful factor in his campaign. As it was, the National Liberal Party under Lloyd George suffered a disastrous result across the country, losing 74 seats and retaining just 53. Asquith's Liberal Party fared only slightly better, winning 62 seats.

Even if the returns for both parties are combined, however, it still only yields a total of 115 MPs – leaving the Liberal vote comfortably in third place. Indeed, the 1922 general election is noted for the emergence of the Labour Party as a national political force. It gained 85 seats – taking its total to 142 MPs – and established itself as the main opposition to the Conservative Party. This was particularly the case in Scotland, where the Labour vote was even higher than in England. This was partly the result of the vacuum created by Liberal infighting, but it was also a natural consequence of the expanded franchise, which brought increasing numbers of working-class voters into the electorate. Churchill's result should therefore be seen in the context of a national swing against the National Liberal Party specifically and the Liberal vote in general, which had now been largely if not completely supplanted by Labour. Personal and local factors played a key role in the outcome, but it was part of a broader – and almost unstoppable – trend. Churchill was an example of the rule, not the exception to it.

The other major contributing factor in his defeat, which had nothing to do with Churchill, was the strength of his opponents. Morel was an able and experienced campaigner, who skilfully related Churchill's record in government to the struggles of Dundee's industry and workers. His opposition to the First World War and post-war settlement may also have increased his appeal to voters who were – with the distance of four years since the conflict ended – starting to reassess the conflict's validity and purpose.

But it is the indefatigable Scrymgeour who deserves particular praise. Churchill could have rightly expected that any other candidate would have given up after the first, second, third, fourth or even fifth humiliating defeat. But Scrymgeour stayed the course, and at each contest slowly raised his profile and increased his relevance, diversifying his offering from raw prohibition to a more broadly socialistic platform. Even outwith elections, he was relentless in expanding his base of support through sales of *The Scottish Prohibitionist* and his social campaigning. As Churchill himself recognised with admiration: 'During the fifteen years of his efforts to gain the seat he had visited several times almost every household in the city.'[3] In the end, it was his persistence that won him the seat.

After leaving the count, Churchill and Clementine made their way by car to the city's Liberal Club. It was a location Churchill knew well and was a fitting place for a final farewell. After waiting for the party's supporters to arrive back from the count, Churchill composed himself and rose to give some impromptu remarks that were laced with emotion:

Fifteen years is a long time for our association to have endured. I would like at this moment to tell you how profoundly I will feel in the debt of Dundee. My heart is devoid of the slightest sense of regret, resentment, or bitterness. On the contrary, looking back over these eventful years in which we have lived and fought through together, I feel I could have done nothing in these stormy times without your loyal and sustained support. All my life I will look back with feelings of the deepest regard for Dundee and for those in it who stood faithfully by me.[4]

Churchill then continued to praise the democratic process, noting – with his Drill Hall meeting in mind – 'there is no need for violence and no need for silencing the voice of reason by clamour.' He then closed with words of warmth and magnanimity for his victorious opponent:

> In Mr Scrymgeour's victory you see the victory of a man who stood for endurance and also for moral, orderly conceptions of democratic reform and action. You will find Mr Scrymgeour will have a useful part to play in representing Dundee, where there is such fearful misery, distress and such awful contrast between one class and another. I do not in the least grudge Mr Scrymgeour his victory ... I carry with me only the kindest thoughts of Dundee, and all my life you will find in me a sincere friend and well-wisher of the city and its inhabitants irrespective of class or party.[5]

As he stepped down from the platform, spontaneous cheers erupted before the crowd began to sing 'For He's a Jolly Good Fellow' as he slowly, pausing to shake the hands of his supporters, made his way out.

Churchill's final speech in the city reflects his understandable emotion at losing the Scottish constituency he had held for nearly 15 years. He was disheartened, but his language was far from embittered or angry. Indeed, it was respectful and, at points, almost effusive, showing nothing but fondness for the city and magnanimity towards Scrymgeour, in particular. This is significant as Scrymgeour was not present at the time, so if Churchill did not have any genuine desire to say something warm about his opponent, he need not have bothered. Indeed, even with the space of an intervening decade, Churchill would still praise Scrymgeour in his memoir, *Thoughts and Adventures*: 'I felt no bitterness towards him. I knew that his movement represented after a fashion a strong current of moral and social revival ... He was surrounded and supported by a devoted band of followers of the Christian-Socialist type. He lived a life of extreme self-denial; he represented the poverty and misery of the poorer parts of the city ...'[6]

Certainly, Churchill's praise of Dundee and Scrymgeour is a far cry from his mythologised last words to the city, which allegedly were that, with his defeat, 'the grass would grow green through its cobbled streets, and the vigour of its industry shrink and decay'.[7] This quote has become fixed in the popular imagination and is still occasionally cited even today. However, there is absolutely no record of it ever having been said – and certainly not by Churchill. Indeed, it would be an extraordinary remark for any defeated candidate – let alone one as experienced and long-serving in Dundee as Churchill – to make. In fact, as we can see, Churchill's final remarks in the city were of an entirely different – and much warmer – tone.

Some of Churchill's friends and acquaintances were less accommodating as news of his defeat spread. 'I am more sorry about Winston than I can say,' T.E. Lawrence – of Arabia fame – wrote to Churchill's assistant, Eddie Marsh, on 18 November.[8] He added: 'What bloody shits the Dundeans [sic] must be.' But, even in his private correspondence, this was not a view Churchill shared. As he wrote to another friend the same day: 'If you saw the kind of lives the Dundee folk have to live, you would admit they have many excuses.'[9]

Having collected their belongings from the Royal Hotel, Churchill and Clementine made their way to catch the 9.40 p.m. sleeper train to London for the final time. There was, of course, a different atmosphere to the journey than they had hoped for or imagined, but Churchill was able to smile and wave at passing crowds, nevertheless. At the station, a group of red-gowned students caught up with the Churchills' car and soon a large crowd had gathered to wish them off. Many were singing and chanting, with the atmosphere curiously reminiscent of Churchill's arrival in Dundee almost 15 years before. Such was the clamour to shake Churchill's hand that one man had his glasses knocked off and trampled underfoot. A young Irish student meanwhile shouted: 'Collins believed in you, and we believe in you.'[10]

Having shaken hands with as many of the crowd as possible, Churchill climbed up into the train before leaning out of the window of his compartment to thank the crowd: 'I appreciate from the very bottom of my heart you boys coming down to see me off. You are very kind.'[11] He added: 'I have always been a democrat and have always believed in the right of the people to make their own institutions. I bow to that now even though I think it is misguided.' Then, as the train slowly chugged its way out the station, Churchill lent out of the window and shouted one last goodbye. It was the last time he ever set foot in Dundee.

Chapter 25

Hangover
1922–1947

On the evening of 7 October 1943, Dundee councillor Robert Blackwood stood up at a council meeting to propose awarding the Freedom of the City to the wartime Prime Minister, Winston Churchill.

He was already anxious about how the meeting would proceed. When the giving of the Freedom had been initially floated two weeks before, there had been mutterings of opposition, though then they had amounted to nothing. But now the moment of decision was at hand, Blackwood remained uneasy. 'It has been a tradition in Dundee,' he determinedly told his audience, '[since] at least from the days of Asquith, that the reigning Prime Minister be invited to accept the honour of being admitted to the Freedom of the City.'[1] Pointing to Churchill's decisive role in saving not just Great Britain but much of the democratic world from the horrors and bestiality of Nazism, Blackwood said: 'If ever a man in politics deserves that approbation from his fellow countrymen it is Mr Churchill.' But Blackwood clearly remained fearful that Churchill's pivotal role in 1940 – and in the prosecution of the war since – might not be enough to persuade his colleagues, so he added, somewhat lamely: 'We will do ourselves and the community a great honour by making him a Burgess of the city.' Even this self-serving sweetener was not, however, enough.

As Blackwood resumed his seat, Arthur Bayne, a Labour councillor, stood up to oppose the motion. Employing a somewhat curious argument for a Labour politician, Bayne criticised the proposal out of an apparent concern for the state of the city's finances: 'This is not a time to waste the corporation's money on ceremonies of this kind. The best course is to defer the matter until the end of the war …'[2] Bayne was supported in his opposition by Lila Clunas, the suffragette who had been deviously locked out of Churchill's Lochee rally as far back as the January 1910 general election and had recently been elected a Labour councillor. But she, too, made her opposing case not in terms of politics, but cost. 'There will be a casket, luncheon, people coming to the Caird Hall and buses running [at a time of fuel rationing],' she said.[3]

Others from the Labour benches stood up and stated their opposition and, to Blackwood's horror, it became clear that the decision to confer the Freedom, far from being unanimous, would in fact be split down party lines.* When it came to the vote, 16 councillors voted in favour of granting Churchill the Freedom of the City, and 15 against – a majority of just one for their former MP. Nevertheless, Blackwood had the authority – if not the mandate – he wanted, and a letter inviting Churchill to accept the honour, at his own convenience, was drafted and sent.

This letter reached Churchill on 12 October, but it had already passed through several other hands. It had first arrived at the Scottish Office on 8 October, where it had been evaluated by Churchill's Secretary of State for Scotland, Tom Johnston, 'a tall, dark and gallicly handsome polymath'.[4] The Scottish Labour MP was no stranger to Dundee or its politics, having represented the constituency for five years from 1924 to 1929. He had begun his career as a left-winger – launching, in 1906, Scotland's premier socialist newspaper, *Forward* – and was also an avid teetotaller who had opposed the First World War. He had also enjoyed good relations with Scrymgeour, with the pair exchanging warm letters on prohibition. On that basis, he should have had a shared sympathy with Churchill's 1922 opponents, but he was appalled when he read of the divisions on Dundee's council over whether to give Churchill the Freedom of the City. He sent the invitation on to Churchill's office but pointedly included a press cutting recounting the debate and the fact there was only a majority of one in favour, pertinent background information that was understandably omitted from the council's invitation. Johnston's office also attached a note to the report of proceedings, stating: 'Comment is superfluous.'[5] The Secretary of State for Scotland, in light of the

---

* This was something of an irony as Blackwood himself had, in the 1922 general election, acted as the agent for Pilkington, the Asquithian Liberal candidate who stood in opposition to Churchill.

division among Dundee councillors, was advising Churchill to reject the invitation.

This was then passed on to Churchill, but not before his Principal Private Secretary, John Miller Martin, had more explicitly stated Johnston's case for rejection:'[Prime Minister], the press cutting below shows that there was considerable opposition to [the award of the Freedom of the City] in the Town Council and the proposal was only carried by 16 votes to 15.'[6] Three days later – and having followed the advice of his Secretary of State for Scotland and Principal Private Secretary – Churchill agreed to reject the offer, given its half-hearted nature, and the following reply was sent from his office on 15 October: 'I am desired by the Prime Minister to acknowledge your letter of October 8 inviting him to accept the Freedom of the City of Dundee, and to thank you for your courtesy. Mr Churchill regrets he is unable to accept the honour which you have proposed to confer upon him.'[7]

The rebuff sent shockwaves through the Dundee council, which called an emergency meeting to hear Churchill's response. As the letter was read out, it was said that 'a pin might have been heard to drop in the stunned silence'.[8] Dundee's current MPs were also agitated and implored the Prime Minister to explain his rejection of the offer, which they said had caused a 'good deal of disappointment among those responsible [for it]'.[9] They were particularly concerned that the rejection looked as if it was due to 'past political history [i.e., Churchill's defeat in 1922]' rather than 'the division of opinion on the Town Council and the large vote against the invitation'. Churchill, however, privately wrote to the MPs that he had 'nothing to add to the reply which has already been sent'.[10]

Churchill's decision to reject the offer of the Freedom of the City of Dundee has remained controversial and has helped contribute to the narrative that he held a grudge against the city as a result of his defeat in 1922. It certainly was a stiff and exceptional rebuke. Churchill, for instance, was enthusiastic to receive the Freedom of the City of Oldham – the city where he was first elected an MP in 1900 – when it was offered in 1944. He also received similar honours from other Scottish cities, such as Edinburgh and Perth.

But, as we have seen, the decision to reject Dundee's offer was not Churchill's alone. Indeed, he received strong advice from respected colleagues that, as a result of the division on the council, the offer should be rejected. In 1943, at the height of the Second World War, Churchill relied heavily on such counsel, particularly on matters of domestic and, in the context of total war, trivial issues. To go against such advice would have required a good reason and there were innumerable other, far more pressing, matters at hand.

Equally, it is understandable that Churchill, by now in his third year of prosecuting the war, felt stung that Dundee was unable to unanimously agree to confer this honour upon him. He might – with some justification – have felt that this was the least he was due, not only as the city's MP of almost 15 years but also the leader of the war against Nazi Germany. This was certainly a view expressed by one Dundee resident, who wrote to Churchill in outrage after the council's split decision: 'I write ... to thank you for refusing what to my mind was an insult in the offering [of] the freedom of this godforsaken town with its inept council and ridiculously (?) self-satisfied councillors.'[11] The language used in this letter, which was sent to Churchill's private office, was extravagant and offensive, but it seems likely many Dundonians would have shared the author's embarrassment over the failure to unanimously offer Churchill the Freedom of the City. Certainly, there was no such controversy around the unanimous offers other cities made, and these Churchill readily accepted, so it seems likely that if the offer of the Freedom of Dundee been made unequivocally, he would have accepted it as well.

The final point is the message sent in response to Dundee's MPs in 1943, who had wanted Churchill to elaborate on his reasons for rejecting the Freedom of the City. His curt response is often cited as a public rebuke, in some cases after Dundee's city fathers had attempted a second approach to ask him to reconsider and accept the honour.* This is, however, inaccurate: it was a dictated, private response to a note from George Harvie-Watt, Churchill's Parliamentary Private Secretary – effectively the Prime Minister's eyes and ears in the House of Commons – at the time. Not only was it not public, but it was not even directly made to any of Dundee's elected representatives.

Of all the characters who played a part in the 1922 general election in Dundee, the continuation of Morel's story is the saddest. He was

---

* There was no such second approach.

– completely naturally – initially delighted with his victory. 'I feel I can never say enough in appreciation to the magnificent devotion and enthusiasm of my friends in Dundee, which were responsible for the great victory we managed to pull off together,' he wrote with undisguised glee to the secretary of the Dundee Labour Party from the House of Commons in the aftermath of his victory.[12] He added, with a flourish of rhetoric that Churchill, ironically, probably would have approved of: 'I have no personal animus to Mr Churchill ... but I cannot help feeling more and more that Dundee has placed the whole Commonwealth under an obligation by giving him his Elba, although it would be too much to hope, I suppose, that Dundee has also given him his St. Helena.'

Yet Morel's delight with being an MP was short-lived. He found Scrymgeour a difficult colleague and their relationship soon descended into acrimony. In this, Morel was not unique – his predecessor as the Labour member, Wilkie, had frequently suffered from Scrymgeour's ire – but Morel seems to have taken it particularly personally. By the 1923 general election, their electoral alliance had completely collapsed, and open hostility reigned. 'It is notorious that during the whole course of the [1923] General Election I was subjected to a running fire of malevolent personal criticisms from Mr Scrymgeour,' Morel wrote to the secretary of the Dundee Labour Party a few weeks after the vote.[13]

In particular, Scrymgeour lambasted Morel as an absentee MP who was more interested in foreign affairs than those of his constituents – the exact same attacks he would have previously reserved for Churchill. Morel dismissed Scrymgeour's allegations as 'frankly grotesque', but, despite his best efforts, he could not ignore them and defeating Scrymgeour became something of an obsession. 'This whole Scrymgeour business has got to be thoroughly tackled,' he wrote to another party official.[14] Even a man who had fought King Leopold to protect an area the size of western Europe found Scrymgeour too much. One solution Morel openly discussed to 'tackle' the 'Scrymgeour business' was running a Labour candidate against him to try to force him out at the next general election. Only the intervention of John Robert Clynes, the deputy leader of the Labour Party, stopped this occurring. He sought to get a guarantee from Scrymgeour to be civil in order to protect the electoral coalition in Dundee. 'If Scrymgeour would definitely commit himself to a written undertaking to cease

attacking me privately or publicly in a personal sense, and at the same
time agree to support the Labour Party programme in the House [of
Commons], it might produce a new situation,' Morel grudgingly admitted to Clynes.[15]

This rapprochement, however, had little time to take effect. On 12
November 1924, Morel suffered a massive heart attack while walking
with his sister-in-law and died. He was just 51 years old, and the strain
of his imprisonment during the First World War had taken a toll on
his health. But he was also deeply disappointed. On the ascension of
the first Labour government after the general election in 1923, Morel
had hoped that the party leader, Ramsay Macdonald, would make
him Foreign Secretary. It was a role, given his experience and interests,
to which he would have been singularly suited, but – perhaps because
of this, and wary of creating a powerful rival – Macdonald instead
chose to keep the position for himself. Willie Gallacher – the
Communist Party candidate in Dundee in 1922 and in several subse-
quent contests – suggested Morel was the naïve victim of dirty tricks
by Macdonald, who manoeuvred Morel into publicly supporting him
retaining the role of Foreign Secretary, on the basis he would give it
to Morel at some unspecified later date. How Gallacher could know
this is not clear, but there is no doubt that – however the decision
came about – Morel was left bitterly disappointed by it.

Morel was given substantial memorial services in London, New
York and his constituency of Dundee. In the ensuing by-election
following his death, Johnston – the man who would go on to join
Churchill's wartime cabinet as Secretary of State for Scotland, and
who would advise against Churchill accepting the Freedom of the
City of Dundee – won the seat for the Labour Party.

Scrymgeour's career after 1922 was significantly longer, but perhaps
no less frustrating. Certainly, like many politicians, it is likely he found
the journey to elected office more rewarding than the destination.

Almost on arrival at the House of Commons, he introduced a
Private Member's Bill on prohibition. His 1923 Bill for Liquor Traffic
Control was typically draconian and uncompromising: all public
houses were to be banned, alcohol was only to be sold for medicinal
purposes – and was to be marked 'poison' – and anyone caught traf-
ficking in liquor was to be sentenced to five years' imprisonment.

Members of the House of Commons – particularly those in the Labour Party – were not without sympathy for Scrymgeour's sentiments, but the bill was simply too extreme to attract widespread support and was rejected by 236 votes to 14. While prohibition had then only been introduced in the United States three years earlier, there was already evidence emerging of its difficulties, which further accelerated over the ensuing decade. This undoubtedly did not help Scrymgeour's second attempt at introducing a prohibition bill, this time in 1931, which was equally unsuccessful. Despite these failures, Scrymgeour continued to campaign on a number of other issues, including various versions of Home Rule for Scotland and pacificism.

While his national legislation failed, so too did prohibition on a local level in Scrymgeour's constituency of Dundee. The Temperance Act of 1920 gave the option for local communities to ban the sale of alcohol – go 'dry' – via a referendum. These contests were generally badged up as 'no change' – those that wanted alcohol to continue to be sold – versus 'no licence'. Dundee held three of these referendums throughout the 1920s while Scrymgeour was MP, but on each occasion 'no licence' was defeated. In 1923, for example, 'no licence' was rejected in Dundee with more than two-thirds of voters turning out, with as many as 75 per cent of voters backing 'no change' in some wards. Seeking to explain Dundee's refusal to back a ban on the sale of alcohol, Scrymgeour rather lamely suggested it was because 'people did not like class legislative action' and that there was a greater chance of success for the cause of prohibition by getting candidates that supported that position elected to the House of Commons.[16] Nevertheless, having his constituents so resoundingly reject the chief cause of its MP must have hurt, even for a man as thick-skinned as Scrymgeour.

Despite this, however, Scrymgeour continued to retain his popularity with the very same voters who rejected his anti-alcohol platform. This confirms that his support was never much based on his prohibitionist views – his socialism, commitment and unique character were what attracted voters to him. He was returned as the city's MP at four elections, one fewer than Churchill. In the 1929 general election he reaped the benefits of his work among the jute mills with the city's female workforce, who turned out for him in large numbers after being granted suffrage for the first time.

Like Churchill, however, his electoral apogee came just before his fall. In 1931, after almost 10 years as the city's MP, Scrymgeour was defeated, his share of the vote falling by 10 per cent. Although still a nominally independent 'Prohibitionist and Socialist', Scrymgeour's association with the Labour Party – which was unpopular as a result of the National Government – is likely to have counted against him. The two-member seat was won by a Liberal and a Conservative/Unionist. The Liberal, who topped the poll, was Dingle Foot, the elder brother of future Labour Party radical Michael Foot. The Conservative victor was Florence Horsbrugh, who went on to be the first woman to hold cabinet rank in a Conservative government.*

But Scrymgeour characteristically remained indefatigable despite his defeat and drew solace from his religious faith. 'For those who believe, as we do,' he said after the 1931 result was announced, 'in the Second Coming of Christ, there is instead of cause for relaxation, stronger reasons than ever for lifting up a standard, casting up the stones, and preparing the way of the people.'[17] But despite this defiant cry, he was – now at the age of 65 – at the end of his political career and he did not stand in Dundee again. He had contested a remarkable 10 elections in the constituency, winning four of them and confirming his place in history as, to date, the only prohibitionist ever elected to the House of Commons.

In 1933, he took on a chaplaincy role at East House and Maryfield Hospital, where he worked until his death on 1 February 1947. His wife, Mary, passed away just a few months later. More than 200 people packed the Methodist church on Dundee's Ward Road for his funeral, with many more having to be turned away due to the closure of the church's gallery, which was undergoing repairs. It was a suitably austere and moving occasion. A blizzard blew outside and, as his coffin was carried out of the church on its journey to the city's Eastern Cemetery, the congregation sang Scrymgeour's favourite hymn, 'Fight the Good Fight'.

Churchill's career after his defeat in Dundee is well known. In the years after he lost the constituency in 1922, Churchill was drawn back

* After Horsbrugh, the next woman to hold cabinet rank in a Conservative government was Margaret Thatcher.

into the folds of the Conservative Party and served as Chancellor of the Exchequer – the summit of Lord Randolph's political career – between 1924 and 1929. He then endured a period in the political wilderness before becoming a prominent opponent of the Conservative government's policy of appeasement towards Nazi Germany. In May 1940, he became Prime Minister, prosecuting the Second World War to a victorious conclusion. The defeat of his government in the Labour Party landslide of 1945 did not mark the end of his political career, however – he returned as Prime Minister between 1951 and 1955. He died, aged 90, in 1965.

His relationship with Dundee remained controversial, with his decision to reject the Freedom of the City of Dundee exacerbated by the fact he never returned to the city following his defeat in 1922. Taken together, these incidents are viewed as irrefutable evidence that Churchill resented Dundee. Certainly, it seems clear that Churchill had no desire to relive the trials and tribulations of his final months as the MP there. The 1922 general election campaign was extremely trying for both him and Clementine, and he clearly had little desire to be reminded of it.

Nevertheless, it would be a mistake to draw too much inference from this omission. After 1922, Churchill had little reason to visit Dundee, which was still relatively inaccessible and of no strategic significance during the Second World War. But, more importantly, Dundee represented for Churchill a very specific part of his political character – and one which he finally jettisoned after he lost the seat. By 1924, he had re-joined the Conservative Party and was a very different figure to the social reformer – Lloyd George's 'terrible twin' – who had been first elected the city's MP at the dawn of Asquith's premiership. As well as going on to serve two terms as a Conservative Prime Minister, he also held numerous senior cabinet positions in that party and became increasingly synonymous with the Tories.

Of course, he did not change his opinions completely. He remained, for example, a fervent supporter of a form of devolution for Scotland. In 1949, he supported John MacCormick's Covenant petitioning the UK government for a Scottish parliament, which received more than two million signatures. But it is clearly the case that, after Churchill left Dundee, he was simply a very different political beast to the one who had arrived on the cusp of his first cabinet appointment in 1908.

As a result of this evolution, Churchill may have viewed it as unnecessary or unpleasant – or perhaps both – to return to the city to see his friends and former colleagues who knew him as a radical Liberal.

Naturally, as a two-time Prime Minister, Churchill continued to engage with Scotland more widely. Many of these interventions were positive and reflected Churchill's appreciation for Scotland's distinct character and heritage. During his second term as Prime Minister, for example, he deftly delt with the so-called Pillar Box War, a row over which cypher the new Queen Elizabeth should be known as in Scotland, given Queen Elizabeth the First had only reigned as Queen of England and Ireland. The furore centred on post boxes, which initially bore the cypher 'EIIR', drawing ire from some – one such post box in Edinburgh was even blown up, its smouldering wreckage then covered in a lion rampant, the Royal Banner of Scotland. But, recognising the offence that had been caused, Churchill's government quietly arranged that post boxes in Scotland should only be decorated with the crown.

Certainly, Churchill's public utterances on Dundee and Scotland post-1922 do not give the impression of animosity. While he is most famously remembered for quipping that he left the city 'without an office, without a seat, without a party and without an appendix', many of his less-remembered remarks are more positive.[18] The best came during a speech in Edinburgh in 1942, and it sums up, as much as anything, Churchill's relationship with Dundee. He said: 'I sat for 15 years as the representative of Bonnie Dundee, and I might be sitting for it still if the matter had rested entirely with me.'[19] He then added: 'I still reserve affectionate memories of the banks of the Tay.'

Afterword to the Paperback Edition

Exactly a year to the day after the first edition of this book was published, the International Churchill Society (ICS) held its 40th annual conference in Edinburgh for the first time. This landmark event was a splendid, significant and naturally Scottish spectacle.

Despite unprecedentedly heavy rain for early October, more than 200 delegates travelled from around the world to Scotland to discuss, debate and – on occasion – defend Winston Churchill's life and legacy. Talks and events – taking place across some of the most iconic locations in Scotland's capital, including Edinburgh Castle and the Royal Yacht *Britannia* – were on topics as varied as Churchill's leadership in 1943 to his legacy as First Lord of the Admiralty and its relevance today. But the ICS conference could not take place in Edinburgh without significant debate about Churchill's relationship with Scotland and, in particular, his legacy here today.

There is little physical to show for it. The epicentre of Churchill's relationship with Scotland – Dundee, which is undergoing a remarkable renaissance – would be almost unrecognisable to him. While many of the street names still exist, the jute mills and many of the tenements have been knocked-down or – in some cases quite dubiously – redeveloped. The dock and waterfront, which for Churchill would have been alive with industry, are now the subject of a £1 billion regeneration, with the new V&A Dundee at its heart. Gazing down on this is the Caird Hall, which has stood the test of time, but little else remains. The jute industry has also disappeared, but journalism – in the form of Churchill's eponymous nemesis, D.C. Thomson – continues to thrive.

More specifically, the city itself has been reticent about its ties with Churchill and, while the ICS encouraged delegates to visit the city during the annual conference, there were only a handful of relevant sites that could be recommended.

In 2008, Mary Soames – Churchill's youngest daughter, who as a two-month-old baby was brought on campaign with Clementine in Dundee in 1922 – travelled to the city to unveil a plaque commemorating the 100th anniversary of his original victory. At its unveiling Churchill's preeminent living biographer, Andrew Roberts, said: 'This is the moment, I think, when the hatchet [between Dundee and Churchill] can finally be buried.'[1] A second, privately funded plaque was installed around the same time in the Queen's Hotel, where Churchill often stayed during his constituency visits, particularly during the early part of his period as an MP. In a charming act of self-depreciation, the hotel has also put up a copy of Churchill's letter to Clementine, where he complains of finding a maggot in his kipper.

Away from Dundee, there was even less for the ICS delegates to see: Sir James Guthrie's portrait of Churchill – commissioned during the First World War while he was still member for Dundee – hangs in the Scottish National Portrait Gallery, Edinburgh, while a four-foot bronze sculpture of Churchill by David McFall can be seen at Glasgow's Kelvingrove Art Gallery and Museum. There are smatterings of other physical recollections of Churchill across Scotland, including hotel rooms where he once stayed.

In many ways – and particularly in Dundee itself – this is a natural state of affairs. It is unusual, if not unheard of, for constituencies to prominently laud their former MPs. Certainly, it would be a niche attraction, even if your former MP is as well-known as Churchill. Indeed, it is hard to think – beyond the two existing plaques – what else physical people in Dundee could do to mark the fact Churchill once represented the city, even if they wanted to.

Nevertheless, there is a sense that people in Scotland have, in the words of one commentator, 'forsaken Churchill'.[2] This was also reflected in the balance of the attendees at the ICS conference, with only a handful of the more than 200 delegates coming from Scotland, despite the location and the fact the event was openly accessible. Similarly, while there was noted press interest in the 100th anniversary of Churchill's defeat in Dundee in 2022, it did not herald a new era of understanding of his near-15 years as a Scottish MP.

To understand why Churchill's legacy in Scotland continues to be so contested, it is necessary to look not at the politics of his time – as we have in this account so far – but the politics of our time. Clearly, in the wake of the Black Lives Matter protests in particular, Churchill's views on race and empire have been subject to renewed scrutiny. Symbols – particularly statues – of Churchill have been vandalised and he has been increasingly vilified, including in Scotland.* In 2019, a Scottish Green Party Member of the Scottish Parliament branded Churchill a 'mass murderer'.[3] As such, these questions clearly feature in discussions of Churchill's legacy in Scotland, but it is not the primary motivator. Instead, Churchill's legacy in Scotland is impacted by more conventional left versus right political debates, as well as, more recently, the question of Scottish independence.

In this respect, Churchill is something of the victim of his own success. In the popular Scottish imagination, he is the bulldog Churchill of 1940, strong and Conservative. The reforming, progressive, Liberal Churchill that we know from this account is largely forgotten. Churchill's legacy in Scotland, therefore, has often been a question of left versus right, Labour versus Conservative. For those of a left and centre-left persuasion, Dundee's rejection of Churchill in 1922 can represent a Scottish rejection of Conservatism. Conversely, for those of a right or centre-right persuasion, the fact Churchill represented Dundee for almost 15 years shows Scotland is not anti-Conservative. This argument of course ignores the fact Churchill was a Liberal when he sat for Dundee but, because he is generally always viewed as a Conservative in the popular imagination, this is relatively inconsequential. Both arguments are also overly simplified but are useful to give a sense of the tone of the debate.

A good case in point took place in 2002. To mark 80 years since Scrymgeour was first elected, Iain Luke, the then Labour MP for Dundee East, put down an Early Day Motion (EDM) commemorating the result. The timing of the EDM is significant as the Conservative

---

* The aforementioned plaque unveiled by Mary Soames in 2008 has been vandalised, although in this respect, it benefits from its relative obscurity and – at several meters off the ground – inaccessibility.

Party then had just one MP in Scotland – having been completely wiped out in the 1997 General Election – and was generally considered to be finished as a political force in Scotland.* The EDM asked MPs to recognise the significance of the 1922 General Election in Dundee, both because Scrymgeour was the only prohibitionist elected to the House of Commons, and because he defeated Churchill. It then calls, somewhat ambitiously, for 'Scrymgeour's unique contribution to the House [of Commons] to be recognised and commemorated by, for example, the bars refraining from the sale of alcohol on the anniversary of his election'.[4] The EDM was sponsored by, among others, the Labour grandee Tam Dalyell and all ten of its signatories, bar one - Plaid Cymru - came from that party.

Such EDMs are commonplace, and it undoubtedly would have been intended as an amusing way to highlight the constituency's notable political history, as well as – of course - the MP behind the EDM itself. Yet it also prompted a heated discussion about Churchill's legacy in Scotland. Explaining his decision to bring forward the EDM, Luke said: 'Churchill is rightly given a lot of attention, but I feel it is about time that Neddy Scrymgeour's unique contribution to British political history is noted. He should be remembered as a principled politician who sought to represent the people of Dundee to the best of his ability.'[5] But others strongly disagreed. A Conservative Member of the Scottish Parliament, Mary Scanlon, who grew up in Dundee, said: 'I think we have to look at Winston Churchill over the years and not the few drams he drank in Dundee. We live in a country now that owes more than we'll ever know to him and to commemorate his defeat by a prohibitionist is small-minded, petty and parochial. We have a freedom today that is very much a result of Winston Churchill.'[6]

Here, Churchill's legacy in Scotland is divided on clear left versus right grounds, but Scottish politics has, of course, evolved since then – and with it the battle over Churchill's legacy has too. In 2014, a referendum was held on Scottish independence, which resulted in more than 55 per cent voting to remain part of the UK. Yet the debate over Scotland's place in the UK – particularly post-Brexit, which a majority of people in Scotland opposed – continues to dominate political discourse.

---

* It has since largely recovered.

Churchill's relationship with Scotland has become an unfortunate casualty of this constitutional conflict, with both pro- and anti-independence activists seeking to use his legacy to promote their cause. This is understandable. Churchill, more than any other figure, is synonymous with British history and, in many ways, the archetypal representative of Britain itself. There is no greater recruiting sergeant for or against a cause than the man who was in 2002 voted by BBC viewers as the Greatest Briton. For Nationalists, therefore, the fact that Dundee rejected Churchill in 1922 is a useful metaphor for Scotland rejecting Britain. The impact of this metaphor is accentuated by the fact that Dundee was the most emphatically pro-independence district in the 2014 referendum. Equally, for those who oppose independence, the fact that Churchill was elected in Dundee and served as the city's MP for nearly 15 years is indicative of Scotland's proud place as a constituent part of Great Britain.

None of these issues are unique to Scotland. Churchill's legacy has been regularly appropriated by different sides in other contemporary political debates, most recently in the 2016 EU referendum. But what is also clear is that none of these narrative frames – left versus right, or Scottish versus British – serves any useful purpose in terms of understanding Churchill's legacy in Scotland or the history of the period as a whole.

The greatest threat to properly understanding Churchill's legacy in Scotland, however, lies in the myths and outright falsehoods that have grown up around his time as MP for Dundee and beyond. Some of these inventions are innocuous. Churchill is perhaps the most misquoted person in recent history, and Scotland is again no exception. Many websites specialising in quotations, for example, will claim Churchill declared that 'of all the small nations of this earth, perhaps only the ancient Greeks surpass the Scots in their contribution to mankind' – but, despite its distinctly Churchillian ring, there is no record of his having said this.

Other misquotes are more deliberately misleading and are propagated by people who, at least in theory, aspire to higher standards. Tony Cox in his book *Empire, Industry and Class: The imperial nexus of jute, 1840–1940* claims – as mentioned previously – that Churchill on his defeat in Dundee remarked: '[That in Dundee] the grass would go green through its cobbled streets, and the vigour of its industry would shrink and decay.' Cox's source for this quotation is given as Tony Paterson's *A Seat for Life*, although Cox does not – as he does in other footnotes – give the page number. For good measure, Cox, a Trotskyist and Scottish independence activist, adds in his footnote that it was his grandfather – who he says attended anti-Churchill demonstrations and described Churchill as a 'pig' – who 'first made me aware of this prophecy. It is correct that this quote features in Paterson's book, but only in the context of Paterson pointing out that Churchill *never* said it. As Paterson writes: '[This quote is] a myth incidentally which has not a shadow of foundation of truth.'

Many more of these falsehoods go beyond throwaway quotations and into an active rewriting of historical events. The false narrative that has become entrenched over the events of George Square in 1919 has already been noted, but it is only one example. In 2013 – a year before the referendum on Scottish independence – a story emerged that 'in 1940 Scotland was to be sacrificed to the Nazis in the event of a German invasion, in order to protect England'. This story was based on selective quotation from a Scottish historian who would later note: 'The book and my research suggest no such thing.' Another case is that of the 51st (Highland) Division, which it is alleged Churchill 'sacrificed' or 'abandoned' at St.Valery-en-Caux in June 1940 'because they were Scots'. Such a notion is clearly absurd, but still continues to gain traction.

At the heart of these falsehoods is a desire to promote the view that Churchill hated Scotland or Scottish people, or at least valued England and English lives over Scotland and Scottish lives. Like the proliferation of fake news, this fake history did not emerge in isolation, but rather is a deliberate attempt to alter facts in order to persuade the public of a particular political point of view. Again, like fake news, social media has been used to spread this fake history, often snaring unsuspecting members of the public and thereby organically growing a false narrative. In some cases – such as the aforementioned events of George Square in 1919 – this distortion becomes so entrenched and widely-held that it replaces the reality, becoming the accepted truth in schools and the correct answer in exams.

If we agree – as we should - that disinformation and fake news are a threat to our democracy, then so too is this fake history. Just as fake news undermines and distorts our understanding of the present, so too does fake history undermine and distort our understanding of the past – which is certainly as, if not more, dangerous. Churchill's legacy in Scotland has clearly already suffered as a result of this, and there is a burden on politicians from across the political spectrum – as well as social media companies themselves – to act responsibly and to treat fake history as seriously as fake news. The cocktail of contemporary politics and social media has already allowed the proliferation of alternative facts, but we should not allow it to create alternative history.

It is my fervent hope that the new edition of this book – with a new title and cover to widen its appeal still further – can help contribute to that effort and promote a greater understanding of Churchill and Scotland in the future.

Andrew Liddle
Edinburgh
April 2024

Notes

Abbreviations

CHAR – Chartwell Papers at the Churchill Archives, Churchill College, Cambridge

DNB – Oxford Dictionary of National Biography

ES – Edwin Scrymgeour Archive Collection, Dundee Local History Centre, Dundee

MOREL – E.D. Morel Archive Collection, London School of Economics, London

1. 'What's the Use of a W.C. Without a Seat?'

1 Shelden, M., *Young Titan*, p. 125
2 Cesarani, D., 'The Anti-Jewish Career of Sir William Joynson-Hicks', p. 462
3 *Manchester Courier and Lancashire General Advertiser*, 25 April 1908
4 Paterson, T., *Churchill: A Seat for Life*, p. 44
5 Ibid.
6 *Manchester Courier and Lancashire General Advertiser*, 25 April 1908
7 Churchill, W.S., *Thoughts and Adventures*, p. 154
8 Paterson, *A Seat for Life*, p. 44
9 Ibid.
10 Churchill, *Thoughts and Adventures*, p. 158

2. The Road to Scotland

1 Soames, M., *Speaking for Themselves*, p. 9
2 *The Courier*, 27 April 1908

3　Miskell, L., Whatley, C.A. and Harris, B. (eds.), *Victorian Dundee*, p. 154

4　CHAR 5/24

5　*The Courier*, 27 April 1908

6　*The Courier*, 24 April 1908

7　Paterson, *A Seat for Life*, p. 45

8　*The Courier*, 27 April 1908

9　CHAR 2/43

10　CHAR 28/27

11　*The Courier*, 28 April 1908

12　Ibid.

13　Rhodes James, R. (ed.), *Churchill Speaks 1867–1963*, p. 145

14　Ibid.

15　*The Courier*, 1 May 1908

16　*The Courier*, 28 April 1908

17　*The Courier*, 30 April 1908

3. 'I Chose Dundee'

1　*Evening Telegraph*, 1 May 1908

2　Ibid.

3　*The Courier*, 2 May 1908

4　Ibid.

5　Jenkins, R., *Churchill*, p. 20

6　Churchill, *Thoughts and Adventures*, p. 151

7　Ibid., pp. 151–152

8　Ibid., p. 151

9　CHAR 5/12

10　CHAR 5/21

11　*Evening Telegraph*, 4 May 1908

12　CHAR 5/12

13　*Evening Telegraph*, 4 May 1908

14　Ibid.

15　*The Courier*, 1 May 1908

16　*The Courier*, 6 May 1908

17　Churchill, *Thoughts and Adventures*, p. 158

18　*The Courier*, 30 April 1908

19　Ibid.

20　Ibid.

21　*The Courier*, 5 May 1908

22　Churchill, *Thoughts and Adventures*, p. 158

23　Paterson, *A Seat for Life*, p. 68

24　Ibid., pp. 70–71

25　*The Courier*, 9 May 1908

4. A Seat for Life?

1 Churchill, *Thoughts and Adventures*, p. 159
2 Ibid., p. 154
3 *The Courier*, 11 May 1908
4 Churchill, *Thoughts and Adventures*, p. 153
5 *The Courier*, 11 May 1908
6 Ibid.
7 Churchill, *Thoughts and Adventures*, p. 159
8 Ibid.
9 *The Courier*, 11 May 1908
10 *Evening Telegraph*, 11 May 1908
11 *The Courier*, 11 May 1908
12 *The Courier*, 25 May 1908
13 *The Courier*, 11 May 1908
14 Ibid.
15 Ibid.
16 CHAR 2/34
17 Ibid.
18 *The Courier*, 14 May 1908
19 *The Courier*, 11 May 1908

5. Vote as You Pray

1 *The Scottish Prohibitionist*, 10 June 1911
2 *Evening Telegraph*, 7 December 1908
3 Ibid.
4 Ibid.
5 Norrie, W., *The Life of James Scrymgeour*, p. 21
6 Walker, W.M., *Juteopolis*, p. 335
7 Ibid.
8 Ibid. p. 345
9 Small, E., *Mary Lily Walker 1853–1913*, p. 11
10 Paterson, *A Seat for Life*, p. 48
11 Ibid.
12 Walker, W.M., *The Scottish Prohibition Party and the Millennium*, p. 357
13 ES/16
14 *The Scottish Prohibitionist*, 10 June 1911
15 Stewart, B., *Breaking the Fetters*, p. 44

6. Enter, Clementine

1 Jenkins, *Churchill*, p. 129
2 Purnell, S., *First Lady*, p. 28

3   For example, Purnell, *First Lady*, p. 14, and Jenkins, *Churchill*, p. 134

4   Soames, *Speaking for Themselves*, p. 3

5   Ibid., p. 7

6   Purnell, *First Lady*, p. 52

7   Soames, *Speaking for Themselves*, p. xv

8   CHAR 1/73

9   Shelden, *Young Titan*, p. 182

10 Bonham Carter, V., *Winston Churchill as I Knew Him*, p. 15

11 Jenkins, *Churchill*, p. 138

12 Shelden, *Young Titan*, p. 189

13 Bonham Carter, *Churchill as I Knew Him*, p. 217

14 *The Courier*, 11 September 1908

7. 'Not at Home'

1   *The Courier*, 27 May 1909

2   *The Courier*, 29 May 1909

3   Soames, *Speaking for Themselves*, p. 32

4   CHAR 1/87/21

5   CHAR 5/21

6   CHAR 5/12

7   CHAR 5/6

8   CHAR 5/12

9   CHAR 5/14

10 Ibid.

11 CHAR 1/74/81

12 Lough, D., *No More Champagne*, p. 95

13 Churchill, R.S., *Winston S. Churchill (Vol. II): Young Statesman 1901–1914*, p. 112

14 CHAR 5/20

15 CHAR 5/5

16 CHAR 5/6

17 Ibid.

18 *The Courier*, 28 May 1909

19 CHAR 5/6

20 *The Courier*, 1 June 1909

21 CHAR 5/6

22 Ibid.

8. Our Man in Dundee

1   Stafford, D., *Oblivion or Glory*, p. 204

2   Tomlinson, J. and Whatley, C.A. (eds.), *Jute No More*, p. 1

3 Ibid., p. 29
4 Jenkins, *Churchill*, p. 107
5 Walker, *Juteopolis*, p. 85
6 Small, *Mary Lily Walker*, p. 80
7 *Evening Telegraph*, 2 April 1906
8 Churchill, R.S., *Young Statesman*, p. 31
9 *Hansard*, 5th Series, Vol. 4, Cols. 388–389
10 Paterson, *A Seat for Life*, p. 81

9. The Peers versus the People

1 https://winstonchurchill.hillsdale.edu/dundee-election-1910/#_ftn1
   (Retrieved on 20 November 2021)
2 Tomlinson and Whatley, *Jute No More*, p. 5
3 Lee, G., *The People's Budget*, p. i
4 Jenkins, *Churchill*, p. 160
5 Paterson, *A Seat for Life*, p. 83
6 Ibid., p. 84
7 Ibid., p. 87
8 https://winstonchurchill.hillsdale.edu/dundee-election-910/#_ftn1
   (Retrieved on 20 November 2021)
9 *The Courier*, 7 January 1910
10 Miskell, Whatley and Harris, *Victorian Dundee*, p. 167
11 *The Courier*, 14 January 1910
12 Miskell, Whatley and Harris, *Victorian Dundee*, p. 161
13 *The Courier*, 29 December 1909
14 *The Courier*, 17 January 1910
15 *The Courier*, 19 January 1910
16 Ibid.
17 https://winstonchurchill.hillsdale.edu/dundee-election-1910/#_ftn1
   (Retrieved on 20 November 2021)
18 *Hansard*, 5th Series, Vol. 26, Cols. 508–509
19 Paterson, *A Seat for Life*, p. 95
20 Ibid.

10. The Strike before Christmas

1 *The Courier*, 20 December 1911
2 Ibid.
3 Ibid.
4 Ibid.
5 CHAR 12/12
6 Jenkins, *Churchill*, p. 199

7   *The Courier*, 20 December 1911
8   *The Scottish Prohibitionist*, 30 December 1911
9   *The Courier*, 25 December 1911
10 CHAR 12/12
11 *The Courier*, 25 December 1911

11. HOME RULE

1   Jenkins, *Churchill*, p. 234
2   Addison, P., *Churchill on the Home Front 1900–1955*, p. 64
3   Rhodes James, *Churchill Speaks*, p. 216
4   Ibid.
5   Roberts, A., *Churchill: Walking with Destiny*, p. 163
6   Rhodes James, R., *Churchill: A Study in Failure 1900–1939*, p. 57
7   *Hansard*, 3rd Series, Vol. 339, Cols. 69–70
8   *Hansard*, 5th Series, Vol. 34, Cols. 1465–1467
9   Roberts, *Churchill*, p. 121
10 *The Courier*, 10 October 1913
11 Ibid.
12 Ibid.
13 CHAR 21/22
14 Ibid.
15 Ibid.
16 CHAR 9/4
17 Ibid.

12. AN ACTIVIST VICTORIOUS

1   Hochschild, A., *King Leopold's Ghost*, p. 195
2   Ibid., p. 180
3   Ibid.
4   Ibid., p. 205
5   Ibid., p. 211
6   Ibid., p. 187
7   Morel F10/3
8   Ibid.
9   *The Courier*, 17 June 1913
10 Hochschild, *Leopold's Ghost*, p. 274

13. The Policeman, The Pilot and The Prohibitionist

1 *The Courier*, 28 December 1912

2 *The Scottish Prohibitionist*, 29 June 1912

3 *The Scottish Prohibitionist*, 13 July 1912

4 *The Scottish Prohibitionist*, 22 March 1913

5 *The Scottish Prohibitionist*, 15 February 1913

6 *The Scottish Prohibitionist*, 26 April 1913

7 Ibid.

8 *The Scottish Prohibitionist*, 10 May 1913

9 *The Scottish Prohibitionist*, 24 May 1913

10 *The Scottish Prohibitionist*, 14 June 1913

11 Hales-Dutton, B., *Pioneering Places of British Aviation*, p. 27

12 ES/16

13 *The Courier*, 30 June 1913

14 *The Advertiser*, 30 June 1913

15 ES/16

16 *The Scottish Prohibitionist*, 13 September 1913

17 *The Scottish Prohibitionist*, 27 September 1913

14. War

1 *The Courier*, 7 June 1915

2 Ibid.

3 Ibid.

4 Roberts, *Churchill*, p. 229

5 Gilbert, M., *Churchill: A Life*, p. 321

6 *The Courier*, 7 June 1915

7 Ibid.

8 Paterson, *A Seat for Life*, p. 156

9 Roberts, *Churchill*, p. 191

10 Ibid., p. 190

11 Ibid., p. 192

12 *The People's Journal*, 17 October 1914

13 *The Courier*, 12 September 1914

14 *The Courier*, 29 June 1915

15 Royle, T., *The Flowers of the Forest*, p. 195

16 *The Scottish Prohibitionist*, 12 June 1915

17 *The Scottish Prohibitionist*, 29 January 1917

18 Jenkins, *Churchill*, p. 277

19 Ibid., p. 286

15. On the Front Line

1   Dewar Gibb, A., *With Winston Churchill at the Front*, p. 59
2   Ibid., p. 61
3   Ibid., p. 61
4   Ibid., p. 67
5   Ibid., p. 68
6   Soames, *Speaking for Themselves*, p. 113
7   Ibid., pp. 162–163
8   Ibid., p. 118
9   Ibid., p. 116
10 Ibid., p. 120
11 Jenkins, *Churchill*, p. 294
12 Churchill, *Thoughts and Adventures*, p. 68
13 Dewar Gibb, *Winston at the Front*, p. 69
14 Soames, *Speaking for Themselves*, p. 129
15 Dewar Gibb, *Winston at the Front*, p. 109
16 Soames, *Speaking for Themselves*, p. 145
17 Dewar Gibb, *Winston at the Front*, p. 65
18 De Groot, G.J., *Liberal Crusader*, p. 49
19 Roberts, *Churchill*, p. 238
20 Dewar Gibb, *Winston at the Front*, p. 87
21 Ibid., p. 76
22 Soames, *Speaking for Themselves*, p. 159
23 Gilbert, *Churchill*, p. 347
24 Roberts, *Churchill*, p. 239
25 Dewar Gibb, *Winston at the Front*, p. 117
26 Ibid., p. 176
27 Ibid., p. 177
28 Gilbert, *Churchill*, p. 360
29 *The Courier*, 9 June 1916

16. The Home Front

1   *Dundee Evening Telegraph*, 31 August 1917
2   *Labour Leader*, 13 September 1917
3   DNB, Union of Democratic Control
4   DNB, Union of Democratic Control
5   Otte, T.G., *Statesman of Europe*, p. 543
6   *The Scottish Prohibitionist*, 4 August 1914
7   *The Scottish Prohibitionist*, 29 August 1914
8   Ibid.
9   *The Scottish Prohibitionist*, 25 March 1916
10 *The Scottish Prohibitionist*, 5 February 1916

11 Campbell, J., *F.E. Smith: First Earl of Birkenhead*, p. 407

12 Ibid., p. 420

13 *Evening Mail*, 5 September 1917

14 *Labour Leader*, 15 November 1917

15 Hochschild, *Leopold's Ghost*, p. 290–291

16 Soames, *Speaking for Themselves*, p. 195

17 *Dundee Evening Telegraph*, 8 March 1917

17. 'Shells versus Booze'

1 Paterson, *A Seat for Life*, p. 152

2 *Evening Telegraph*, 24 July 1917

3 DNB, Erskine

4 *Evening Telegraph*, 24 July 1917

5 *Hansard*, 5th Series, Vol. 77, Cols. 119–120

6 *Evening Telegraph*, 25 July 1917

7 *The Courier*, 25 July 1917

8 *Dundee People's Journal*, 28 July 1917

9 Ibid.

10 Paterson, *A Seat for Life*, p. 151

11 Ibid., p. 152

12 Ibid., p. 151

13 *The Courier*, 25 July 1917

14 Paterson, *A Seat for Life*, p. 152

15 *The Courier*, 27 July 1917

16 Ibid.

17 *The Courier*, 28 July 1917

18 Ibid.

19 Ibid.

20 *The Courier*, 31 July 1917

21 Paterson, *A Seat for Life*, p. 161

22 *The Courier*, 31 July 1917

23 Churchill, W.S., *The World Crisis 1911–1918*, III, Pt. 2, p. 541

24 *The Courier*, 23 November 1918

25 *The Courier*, 5 December 1918

26 Ibid.

27 *The Advertiser*, 5 December 1918

28 Gilbert, M., *Winston S. Churchill (Vol. IV): World in Torment 1916–1922*, p. 173

29 *The Courier*, 5 December 1918

30 *Evening Telegraph*, 28 November 1918

31 Jenkins, *Churchill*, p. 340

32 *The Courier*, 13 December 1918

33 Paterson, *A Seat for Life*, p. 178

18. WINNING THE PEACE

1 *The Scottish Prohibitionist*, 22 February 1919
2 Ibid.
3 Ibid.
4 Ibid.
5 *The Scottish Prohibitionist*, 1 March 1919
6 Ibid.
7 Ibid.
8 Paterson, *A Seat for Life*, p. 169
9 *Evening Telegraph*, 30 June 1919
10 Ibid.
11 *The Daily Herald*, 10 April 1920
12 Reinders, R.C., 'Radicalism on the Left: E.D. Morel and the "Black Horror on the Rhine"', p. 1
13 *The Daily Herald*, 10 April 1920
14 Reinders, 'E.D. Morel and the "Black Horror"', p. 8
15 *The Daily Herald*, 10 April 1920

19. REVOLUTION

1 *Sunday Post*, 26 January 1919
2 Ibid.
3 CAB 23-9
4 Ibid.
5 Ibid.
6 Ibid.
7 Ibid.
8 Ibid.
9 Ibid.
10 Ibid.
11 *Sunday Post*, 2 February 1919
12 CAB 23-9
13 Ibid.
14 *Sunday Post*, 2 February 1919
15 Barclay, G.J., 'Mythology and Reality In The Military Deployment to Glasgow in 1919', p. 41
16 Addison, *Churchill on the Home Front*, p. 204
17 Jenkins, *Churchill*, p. 350
18 Churchill, *World Crisis*, V, p. 263
19 Stafford, *Oblivion or Glory*, p. 216
20 Walker, *Juteopolis*, p. 440
21 Ibid., p. 441
22 Ibid.

23 Ibid., p. 442
24 *Evening Telegraph*, 10 December 1918

20. RESOLUTION

1   Stafford, *Oblivion or Glory*, p. 200
2   *The Press and Journal*, 3 September 1921
3   Ibid.
4   Roberts, *Churchill*, p. 277
5   Ibid.
6   *The Courier*, 18 October 1920
7   Soames, *Speaking for Themselves*, p. 232
8   Stafford, *Oblivion or Glory*, p. 201
9   Jenkins, *Churchill*, p. 361
10 CAB 23/27
11 Jenkins, *Churchill*, p. 366
12 CHAR 5/24
13 Ibid.
14 Ibid.
15 Ibid.
16 Ibid.
17 Ibid.
18 Ibid.
19 Ibid.
20 Vale, J.A. and Scadding, J.W., 'Winston Churchill: acute appendicitis in October 1922', p. 341

21. CLEMENTINE'S CAMPAIGN

1   *The Courier*, 10 November 1922
2   Jenkins, *Churchill*, p. 373
3   Vale and Scadding, 'Appendicitis', p. 342
4   Soames, *Speaking for Themselves*, p. 264
5   Paterson, *A Seat for Life*, p. 234
6   *The Courier*, 11 November 1922
7   *The Courier*, 9 November 1922
8   *The Courier*, 10 November 1922
9   Soames, *Speaking for Themselves*, p. 265
10 Ibid.
11 Jenkins, *Churchill*, p. 371
12 Ibid.
13 Gilbert, *Churchill (Vol. IV): World in Torment*, p. 875
14 Jenkins, *Churchill*, p. 372

15 Paterson, *A Seat for Life*, p. 238
16 Ibid.
17 *The Courier*, 10 November 1922
18 Paterson, *A Seat for Life*, p. 239
19 *The Courier*, 11 November 1922
20 Soames, *Speaking for Themselves*, p. 264
21 Ibid.
22 Ibid.

22. THE FINAL ROUND

1 Paterson, *A Seat for Life*, p. 244
2 Gilbert, *Churchill*, p. 457
3 *The Courier*, 13 November 1922
4 Ibid.
5 Paterson, *A Seat for Life*, p. 248
6 *The Courier*, 13 November 1922
7 Churchill, *Thoughts and Adventures*, p. 160
8 *The Courier*, 14 November 1922
9 Ibid.
10 Gilbert, *Churchill (Vol. IV): World in Torment*, p. 885
11 *The Courier*, 14 November 1922
12 Paterson, *A Seat for Life*, p. 267
13 Ibid., p. 264
14 Ibid., p. 270

23. LAST ORDERS

1 Churchill, *Thoughts and Adventures*, p. 154
2 Ibid.
3 Paterson, *A Seat for Life*, p. 276
4 Ibid.
5 *The Courier*, 16 November 1922
6 Paterson, *A Seat for Life*, p. 277
7 *The Courier*, 15 November 1922
8 Ibid.
9 Paterson, *A Seat for Life*, p. 274

24. CLOSING TIME

1 Jenkins, *Churchill*, p. 375
2 Wilson, T., *The Downfall of the Liberal Party 1914–1935*, p. 245

3 Churchill, *Thoughts and Adventures*, p. 161

4 *The Courier*, 17 November 1922

5 Ibid.

6 Churchill, *Thoughts and Adventures*, p. 161

7 For example, Cox, A., *Empire, Industry and Class*, p. 111

8 Gilbert, *Churchill (Vol. IV): World in Torment*, p. 890

9 Ibid.

10 *The Courier*, 17 November 1922

11 Ibid.

25. HANGOVER

1 *The Courier*, 8 October 1943

2 Ibid.

3 Ibid.

4 Torrance, D., *The Scottish Secretaries*, p. 157

5 CHAR 2/484A-B

6 Ibid.

7 Ibid.

8 Paterson, *A Seat for Life*, p. 292

9 CHAR 2/484A-B

10 Ibid.

11 CHAR 2/478

12 Morel F2/8

13 Ibid.

14 Morel F2/10

15 Morel F2/9

16 *The Courier*, 26 November 1923

17 Knox, W. (ed.), *Scottish Labour Leaders 1918–1939*, p. 243

18 Jenkins, *Churchill*, p. 376

19 *Evening Telegraph*, 12 October 1942

AFTERWORD TO THE PAPERBACK EDITION

1 *The Times*, 4 May 2008

2 Stewart, *Why Have the Scots Forsaken Churchill?*, p. 8

3 https://www.bbc.co.uk/news/uk-scotland-scotland-politics-47028246 (Retrieved on 22 November 2021)

4 EDM 1856, tabled 5 November 2002

5 *The Times*, 3 November 2002

6 Ibid.

7 Stewart, *Why Have the Scots Forsaken Churchill?*, p. 10

8 Cox, *Empire, Industry and Class*, p. 111

 9   Ibid., p. 223
10   Paterson, *Seat for Life*, p. 288
11   Barclay, 'A "Villain for All Seasons"', p. 14
12   Ibid.
13   Ibid., p. 17

Select Bibliography

The following represents a selection of the primary and secondary materials consulted for this work.

Archives and Records

The Churchill Archives, Churchill College, Cambridge
Edwin Scrymgeour Archive Collection, Dundee Local History Centre, Dundee
E.D. Morel Archive Collection, London School of Economics, London
The National Archives, London
British Newspaper Archive
Hansard

Articles, Pamphlets and Theses

Barclay, Gordon J., 'A "Villain for All Seasons": Churchill and Scottish Mythologies of Grievance', *Finest Hour: The Journal of Winston Churchill and His Times*, Third Quarter, No. 189, 2020, pp. 14–18

Barclay, Gordon J., '"Churchill Rolled The Tanks Into The Crowd": Mythology And Reality In The Military Deployment To Glasgow In 1919', *Scottish Affairs*, 28.1, 2019, pp. 32–62

Brown, Gordon, 'Foreword', *Finest Hour: The Journal of Winston Churchill and His Times*, Third Quarter, No. 189, 2020, pp. 6–7

Cesarani, David, 'The Anti-Jewish Career of Sir William Joynson-Hicks', *Journal of Contemporary History*, Vol. 24, No. 3, 1989, pp. 461–482

Kemp, John Douglas, 'Drink and the Labour Movement in Early Twentieth-Century Scotland with Particular Reference to Edwin Scrymgeour and the Scottish Prohibition Party', PhD Thesis, 2000, University of Dundee

Norrie, William, *The Life of James Scrymgeour*, William Norrie, Dundee, 1887

Reinders, Robert C., 'Racialism on the Left: E.D. Morel and the "Black Horror on the Rhine"', *International Review of Social History*, Vol. 13, Issue 1, 1968, pp. 1–28

Southgate, D.G., 'Edwin Scrymgeour', *Three Dundonians*, Dundee Abertay Historical Society, Publication No. 13, 1968, pp. 16–22

Stewart, Alastair, 'Why Have the Scots Forsaken Churchill?', *Finest Hour: The Journal of Winston Churchill and His Times*, Third Quarter, No. 189, 2020, pp. 8–13

Vale, J. Allister and Scadding, John W., 'Winston Churchill: acute appendicitis in October 1922', *Journal of the Royal Society of Medicine*, Vol. 112(8), 2019, pp. 341–348

Walker, Mary L. and Wilson, Mona (eds.), *Report on Housing and Industrial Conditions and Medical Inspection of School Children*, John Leng, 1905

Walker, William M., 'Dundee's Disenchantment with Churchill: A Comment upon the Downfall of the Liberal Party', *The Scottish Historical Review*, Vol. 49, No. 147, Part 1, 1970, pp. 85–108

Walker, William M., 'The Scottish Prohibition Party and the Millennium', *International Review of Social History*, Vol. 18, No. 3, 1973, pp. 353–379

Books

Adams, R.J.Q., *Bonar Law*, London: John Murray, 1999

Addison, Paul, *Churchill on the Home Front 1900–1955*, London: Pimlico, 1993

Apps, Peter, *Churchill in the Trenches*, Great Britain: Peter Apps, 2015

Bonham Carter, Violet, *Winston Churchill as I Knew Him*, London: Eyre & Spottiswoode and Collins, 1965

Brock, Michael and Brock, Eleanor (eds.), *H.H. Asquith Letters to Venetia Stanley*, Oxford: Oxford University Press, 1982

Buchan, John, *The History of the Royal Scots Fusiliers 1678–1918*, London: Naval & Military Press, 1925

Brooks, David, *The Age of Upheaval: Edwardian Politics, 1899–1914*, Manchester: Manchester University Press, 1995

Campbell, John, *F.E. Smith: First Earl of Birkenhead*, London: Pimlico, 1991

Campbell, John, *Haldane: The Forgotten Statesman Who Shaped Modern Britain*, London: C. Hurst & Co., 2020

Churchill, Randolph S., *Winston S. Churchill (Vol. I): Youth 1874–1900*, London: Heinemann, 1966

——*Winston S. Churchill (Vol. II): Young Statesman 1901–1914*, London: Heinemann, 1967

——*Companion Volume II, Part 2, 1907–1911*, London: Heinemann 1969

Churchill, Winston S., *Thoughts and Adventures*, London: Odhams, 1932

——*Liberalism and the Social Problem*, Rockville: Arc Manor, 2007

——*The World Crisis 1911–1918*, London: Penguin Classics, 2007

Cox, Anthony, *Empire, Industry and Class: The Imperial Nexus of Jute, 1840–1940*, Abingdon: Routledge, 2013

Dangerfield, George, *The Strange Death of Liberal England*, London: MacGibbon & Kee, 1935

De Groot, Gerald J., *Liberal Crusader: The Life of Sir Archibald Sinclair*, London: Hurst & Co., 1993

Dewar Gibb, Andrew, *With Winston Churchill at the Front: Winston in the Trenches 1916*, Barnsley: Frontline Books, 2016

Donaldson, Frances, *The Marconi Scandal*, London: Rupert-Hart Davis, 1962

Gallacher, William, *Revolt on the Clyde: The Classic Autobiography of Red Clydeside*, London: Lawrence and Wishart, 2017

Gilbert, Martin, *Churchill: A Life*, London: Pimlico, 2000

——*Winston S. Churchill (Vol. III): The Challenge of War 1914–1916*, Hillsdale: Hillsdale College Press, 2008

——*Winston S. Churchill (Vol. IV): World in Torment 1916–1922*, Hillsdale: Hillsdale College Press, 2008

Grigg, John, *Lloyd George: The People's Champion, 1902–1911*, London: Methuen, 1978

——*Lloyd George: From Peace to War, 1912–1916*, London: Methuen, 1985

——*The Young Lloyd George*, London: Methuen, 1990

Hales-Dutton, Bruce, *Pioneering Places of British Aviation: The Early Years of Powered Flight in the UK*, Philadelphia: Airworld, 2020

Hart, Peter, *Gallipoli*, London: Profile, 2013

Hattersley, Roy, *Campbell-Bannerman*, London: Haus, 2006

——*The Edwardians*, London: Abacus, 2006

——*David Lloyd George: The Great Outsider*, London: Abacus, 2012

Heffer, Simon, *The Age of Decadence*, London: Windmill Books, 2018

Hochschild, Adam, *King Leopold's Ghost: A Story of Greed, Terror and Heroism in Colonial Africa*, London: Picador Classic, 2019

Hutchison, I.G.C., *A Political History of Scotland 1832–1924*, Edinburgh: John Donald, 1986

Jenkins, Roy, *Asquith*, London: Fontana, 1967

——*Mr Balfour's Poodle: An account of the struggle between the House of Lords and the government of Mr Asquith*, London: Collins, 1968

——*Churchill*, London: Macmillan, 2002

Knox, William (ed.), *Scottish Labour Leaders 1918–1939: A Biographical Dictionary*, Edinburgh: Mainstream Publishing, 1984

Lawrence, Jon, *Electing Our Master: The Hustings in British Politics from Hogarth to Blair*, Oxford: Oxford University Press, 2009

Lee, Geoffrey, *The People's Budget: An Edwardian Tragedy*, London: Shepheard-Walwyn, 2008

Lloyd George, David, *War Memoirs of David Lloyd George*, Vol. 1, London: Odhams, 1933

——*War Memoirs of David Lloyd George*, Vol. 2, London: Odhams, 1938

Lough, David, *No More Champagne: Winston Churchill and His Money*, London: Head of Zeus, 2015

Miskell, Louise, Whatley, Christopher A., and Harris, Bob (eds.), *Victorian Dundee: Image and Realities*, East Linton: Tuckwell Press, 2000

Otte, T.G., *July Crisis: The World's Descent into War, Summer 1914*, Cambridge: Cambridge University Press, 2014

——*Statesman of Europe: A Life of Sir Edward Grey*, London: Allen Lane, 2020

Paterson, Tony, *Churchill: A Seat for Life*, Dundee: David Winter & Son, 1980

Purnell, Sonia, *First Lady: The Life and Wars of Clementine Churchill*, London: Aurum, 2016

Read, Simon, *Winston Churchill Reporting: Adventures of a Young War Correspondent*, New York: Da Capo Press, 2015

Rhodes James, Robert (ed.), *Churchill Speaks 1897–1963: Collected Speeches in Peace and War*, London: Chelsea House, 1980

——*Churchill: A Study in Failure 1900–1939*, London: Penguin, 1981

Roberts, Andrew, *Churchill: Walking with Destiny*, London: Allen Lane, 2018

Royle, Trevor, *The Flowers of the Forest: Scotland and the First World War*, Edinburgh: Birlinn, 2007

Shelden, Michael, *Young Titan: The Making of Winston Churchill*, London: Simon & Schuster, 2014

Small, Edward, *Mary Lily Walker 1853–1913: Forgotten Visionary of Dundee*, Dundee: Dundee University Press, 2013

Soames, Mary (ed.), *Speaking for Themselves: The Personal Letters of Winston and Clementine Churchill*, London: Black Swan, 1999

Stafford, David, *Oblivion or Glory: 1921 and the Making of Winston Churchill*, Newhaven: Yale University Press, 2019

Stewart, Bob, *Breaking the Fetters: The Memoirs of Bob Stewart*, London: Lawrence & Wishart, 1967

Thomson, Ben, *Scottish Home Rule: The Answer to Scotland's Constitutional Question*, Edinburgh: Birlinn, 2020

Torrance, David, *The Scottish Secretaries*, Edinburgh: Birlinn, 2006

——*A History of Scottish Liberals and Liberal Democrats*, Edinburgh: Edinburgh Universtity Press, 2022

Turner, John, *British Politics and the Great War: Coalition and Conflict 1915–1918*, New Haven: Yale University Press, 1992

Tomlinson, Jim and Whatley, Christopher A. (eds.), *Jute No More: Transforming Dundee*, Dundee: Dundee University Press, 2011

Walker, William M., *Juteopolis: Dundee Textile Workers 1885–1923*, Edinburgh: Scottish Academic Press, 1979

Wheatcroft, Geoffrey, *Churchill's Shadow: An Astonishing Life and a Dangerous Legacy*, London: Bodley Head, 2021

Wilson, Trevor, *The Downfall of the Liberal Party, 1914–1935*, London: Faber and Faber, 2011

Websites and Reference Books

The Churchill Project, Hillsdale College, USA: https://winstonchurchill.hillsdale.edu (Retrieved in December 2021)
Oxford Dictionary of National Biography

Index